Neglected or Misunderstood: Introducing Theodor Adorno

Neglected or Misunderstood: Introducing Theodor Adorno

Stuart Walton

Winchester, UK
Washington, USA

First published by Zero Books, 2017
Zero Books is an imprint of John Hunt Publishing Ltd., Laurel House, Station Approach,
Alresford, Hants, SO24 9JH, UK
office1@jhpbooks.net
www.johnhuntpublishing.com
www.zero-books.net

For distributor details and how to order please visit the 'Ordering' section on our website.

Text copyright: Stuart Walton 2016

ISBN: 978 1 78535 382 6
978 1 78535 383 3 (ebook)
Library of Congress Control Number: 2016961470

A CIP catalogue record for this book is available from the British Library.

Design: Stuart Davies

Printed and bound by CPI Group (UK) Ltd, Croydon, CR0 4YY, UK

We operate a distinctive and ethical publishing philosophy in all
areas of our business, from our global network of authors to
production and worldwide distribution.

CONTENTS

For Laurence Coupe

Preface and Acknowledgements

It has become customary to begin any study of the work of Theodor W. Adorno, especially one intended to function in some sense as an introductory guide, by pointing out that he would have strongly disapproved of it. More introductory guides were the last thing a damaged intellectual world needed. What it required instead was thinking that did not already take its own premises for granted, that pushed all its thoughts to a dialectical extreme, until, in his celebrated formulation, they no longer understood themselves as thoughts. Summarising, explicating, simplifying were the work of a dead academic tradition that critically failed to understand the profound need for critical thinking. In a world enmortgaged to the destruction of human experience, experience itself only lived in the gaps and fissures that remained in the consciousness of those who had not wholly surrendered, guilt-stricken survivors of the twentieth century's catastrophes as well as present-day *flâneurs* in the cultural metropolis.

The present work, then, sits uneasily alongside its companion volumes on other neglected and misunderstood contemporary theorists. For one thing, Adorno is hardly neglected. He is a set text, a modern master, a major thinker, whose theoretical innovations have achieved classic status, and whose body of theory is held to display obvious continuities with other modern and postmodern intellectual currents. This was admittedly not always so in the English-speaking world. When I arrived in Oxford in 1983 to begin studying for a doctorate on his work, I was warmly greeted at a sherry evening for new graduates by one of my college's senior Fellows with the cordial wish that my scholarly days would be fruitful, and would result in my finding somebody more interesting to write about than Adorno. In this latter, I conspicuously failed, with the result that, more than thirty years later, I have written the kind of introductory guide for which I can only hope he would have forgiven me.

On the second point, as to whether his work has been misunderstood, the answer seems resonantly obvious. In the view of much academic philosophy and cultural studies, Adorno is a truculent pessimist and stubborn elitist, the tyrannical father-figure who won't let you watch TV until you've done your homework, and the monothematically fastidious representative of a mandarin culture blown aside not so much by the monstrous evils of his own historical hour, as he himself thought, as by the democratising jamboree of popular distractions that pitched camp on its cleared ground, once principally cinema and television, now more the Internet and video-gaming. A familiar interpretation of his theory of the culture industry has it that he wanted us to use our leisure time not in consuming mindless entertainments, but in studying provocative and challenging artworks and books that would enable us, in the words of a short online video summary: 'to expand and develop ourselves... and to acquire the tools with which to change society'.[1] This makes him sound like a latter-day self-help merchant, a spiritual aerobics instructor for the masses, urging consumerism's slobs to get some mental exercise. Not only did Adorno argue that the links between autonomous artworks and the victims of a repressive social conformism had been broken, probably irreparably, but he particularly criticised the capitalist conception of leisure time as the continuation of laborious duty. The colonisation of consciousness by the culture industry was such that no straightforward nostrum for counteracting it was conceivable. Moreover, his social philosophy is not an injunctive or didactic programme, not a practical manifesto of any sort, but more a diagnostics of the post-traumatic soul, the report of an infinitely attentive insight, aware of its own material historical roots.

A theoretical apparatus can never be frozen outside the onrush of time, and made applicable to all ages and all societies. It too stands on the moving platform of history, itself a product of the society in which it arises. The critical theory of the Frankfurt School, among whose first generation Adorno played an outstanding role, was more conscious of its own historical situatedness than most. While it diagnosed the tendencies of a society careering towards barbarism, it simultaneously suffered the fate prescribed by those tendencies, being banished on political and racial grounds to a distant sunny exile, in a social milieu that would prove to be a preview of the future of Europe after the rain. The very least one can hope to achieve in a monograph of this nature, against the impulse to reduce what was once a living stream of thinking to a summary of key points, is to set it in motion once more, to apply its own technical procedures to the large subjects it addressed – what western philosophy knows as the largest subjects of all – and to wonder constructively what dialectical efficacy might still animate it in the already fifty-year-old world that has succeeded it.

Terry Eagleton wasn't at the sherry evening, but nor did he attempt to wean me off Adorno. His own critical appraisal of Frankfurt School thought made him an inspiring supervisor, as well as one who encouraged in my work the indispensable habit of self-reflection. His influence on this book may be historically distant enough, but remains present in the textures of its thinking.

I might have stumbled on through half a lifetime in the Anglophone intellectual habitus before I came upon some reference to Adorno in a compendium of modern cultural theory, instantly mistaking him for one of the gloomy uncles of the European philosophical family, had it not been for Laurence Coupe, who lent me his copy of *Prisms* when I was eighteen. Through long nights of wakeful study, I annotated the essays in it as the most rudimentary means of even partially understanding them. The essay on Kafka opened unsuspected new horizons of interpretation, while the demolition of jazz struck a minor-seventh chord in a young man whose own most recent musical commitment had been to a movement that wanted to demolish official youth music once and for all.

My sincere gratitude is due to both these intellectual mentors. I would also like to thank Douglas Lain for his editorial oversight of the book, the other early readers of the proposal, Christopher Derick Varn and Alfie Bown, and the book's copy-editor, Elizabeth Radley.

The rest I owe to my first and greatest teacher, Sheila Walton.

Stuart Walton
November 2016

Introduction: Nothing Innocuous Left

Survival itself has something nonsensical about it.
Minima Moralia

Wilhelmine Germany in the early years of the twentieth century was a nation in flux. Politically restive at home and reckless abroad, it had entered a state of constitutional transition after the resignation of the enfeebled Iron Chancellor, Otto von Bismarck, in 1890, early in the reign of Kaiser Wilhelm II. Wilhelm was not a man for the prudent background role his grandfather had taken as monarch, but actively intervened in the affairs of state from day to day, pulling the strings of a succession of puppet Chancellors as Germany was gradually transformed from its eastern flank by a seeping Prussian militarism. Countervailing currents within the national culture produced progressive developments in education and the arts. Liberal academies that emphasised the virtue of freethinking individualism opposed the militarised schooling to which the majority of boys were subjected, replacing sword-drill and morning musters with intellectual expansiveness and the spirit of questioning. An adventurous, socially dissident tendency in the arts propelled Germany to the leading edge of the European avant-garde, the provocative dramatic works of Frank Wedekind throwing a rope bridge between Ibsenite naturalism and the coming formal assaults of expressionism, while painters sought greater spiritual honesty through a hard-contoured representational style that gradually, via a series of fissiparous short-lived movements, turned either abstract or rigidly geometrical in the cubist manner. The Kaiser had issued a forlorn proclamation to the effect that it was only art if he recognised it as such, and prompted the regressive use of black-letter Gothic in printed documents that would persist into the National Socialist era. Meanwhile, the political boat was

5

rocking since the formation in the 1890s of the Social Democratic Party (SPD), candidly Marxist at its inception and destined improbably to become the largest electoral force in Germany as early as 1912, when it was kept out of power only by a succession of expedient conservative coalitions, in which Prussian military and Catholic ecclesiastical influences combined to thwart the impending advance of a discontented proletariat.

The Hessian city of Frankfurt on the river Main had been a lightning-conductor for the national constitutional upheavals of the previous century. After the liberal revolutions of 1848, it became the seat of the first democratically elected legislature in Germany, a body that met in St Paul's cathedral and was promptly liquidated for its pains the following year, when the Prussian monarch, Friedrich Wilhelm IV, despite being offered something resembling the role of constitutional sovereign by the legislators, announced that he would not accept what he viewed as 'a crown from out of the gutter'. A war of unification between Austrian and Prussian interests fought over seven weeks of 1866 led to the Prussification of the whole of Germany, a process in which Frankfurt with its liberal political culture and its voluble free press was forcibly incorporated into the new administrative province of Hesse-Nassau. It was at around this time that Bernhard Wiesengrund, a successful wine merchant and exporter, relocated his business from the small market town of Dettelbach near Würzburg into the city of Frankfurt. Established in 1822, the business was thriving sufficiently that a move to the trade fairs and well-heeled custom of a commercial entrepot made obvious sense, and eventually, in 1864, Bernhard and his wife Caroline moved up in the world to a four-storey house in the residential quarter of the old city, in an imposing grand terrace, Schöne Aussicht, on the north bank of the Main. The address already had a certain cultural cachet: Arthur Schopenhauer had lived at number 16 for the last twenty-seven years of his life, having died only four years before the Wiesengrunds moved into

number 7, next door to the painter Friedrich Delkeskamp, while
Felix Mendelssohn, a summer guest in 1836 of the Schelble
musical family who lived at number 15, wrote of the enviable
prospect between trees along the river, with its plethora of boats
and barges and its pretty shores opposite. Indeed, the street name
means 'beautiful outlook', a German cognate to the French *belle
vue*. On Bernhard's death in 1871, the business was inherited by
his son David Theodor, who maintained it until he handed over
the reins to his second son Oskar Alexander, the elder brother
having met an untimely death at seventeen in 1886. Oskar took
over a flourishing export business, with overseas customers in
Britain and the United States, eventually opening a second outlet
in Leipzig.

The Schöne Aussicht house doubled perfectly as home and
business premises, having a large internal courtyard and vaulted
cellars. It was built in the neoclassical idiom with narrow but tall
shuttered windows and external cornicing between the storeys,
and number 7 boasted a small balcony on the first floor. Oskar's
wife, Maria Calvelli-Adorno della Piana, daughter of a fencing
master, hailed from a family of Corsican nobility who had been
on intimate terms with the Bonapartes, ever since an ancestor had
been personally promoted in the French army by Napoleon
himself. The Calvelli-Adornos had music flowing through their
veins. Maria was an accomplished coloratura soprano who began
attracting the notice of the local press in her early teens. Her
sister Agathe and brother Louis were singers too, and Agathe was
also a pianist, and the whole family gave frequent public recitals
under the aegis of their mother Elisabeth. It was in the midst of
Frankfurt's dynamic musical milieu that Oskar Wiesengrund, an
ardent concert-goer and patron of the opera, met the Calvelli-
Adornos. His courtship of Maria raised eyebrows in his own
assimilated Jewish family. Not only was she a devout Roman
Catholic, her family had seen better days, and she was also five
years older than him. Nonetheless, the relationship prospered,

and they were eventually married in 1898, a few months after the death of Maria's mother. The couple had to travel to London to do so, in the register office at St Pancras, because the bride was still a French citizen, and therefore not legally eligible for a German marriage licence.

Maria's sister Agathe moved into Schöne Aussicht with her after the wedding, and would live with her and Oskar until her death in 1935. She was in every respect a member of the immediate family, a second mother rather than aunt to the Wiesengrunds' sole heir. Maria having miscarried an initial pregnancy in 1900, the son that was born to them three years later would be an only child. Theodor Ludwig was born at home shortly before dawn on Friday 11 September 1903, and although his grandfather David doubtless saw in the healthy infant an eventual successor to the wine business, the two mothers set him on a rather different course, superintending a musical education that effectively began with one or the other of them intoning the Brahms *Lullaby* to him in the cradle. Theodor was baptised into the Roman Catholic faith at the cathedral church of St Bartholomew's a month later. His father is designated on the birth certificate as a 'merchant and Israelite'.

The city in which Theodor, who would be known to family and friends as Teddie throughout his life, grew up was an elegant but socially stratified environment. In its poorer districts, east European Jews, refugees from the Russian and Polish pogroms, were clustered in tenement houses, while in the affluent Westend, fashionable villas housed family firms in the financial and legal sectors, the Palmengarten boasted tropical flora and a chandeliered ballroom, and the whole area was newly enclosed by a circular thoroughfare, the Alleenring, as though to segregate it from the hubbub of the commercial city. Horse-drawn carriages still rumbled across the Alte Brücke over the Main, their wooden wheels interspersed with the clattering of trams, sternly overlooked by a nineteenth-century figure of the Holy Roman

Emperor Charlemagne with his forked beard and drawn sword. Rows of imposing neoclassical buildings lined the quayside, the red sandstone tower of the cathedral, rebuilt in fanciful Gothic after a fire in the 1860s, rising behind them. In 1914, not long after Germany declared war on Russia amid the rapidly erupting hostilities that led to the Great War, Adorno's family moved south of the river to 19 Seeheimerstrasse in the village suburb of Oberrad.

Adorno attended the Kaiser-Wilhelm-Gymnasium grammar school from 1913 until he was seventeen. He was by and large a model pupil and excelled in everything except mathematics and physical jerks. His handwriting style, which was considered atrocious, let him down, although it looks remarkably legible in his teens, compared to the cramped cursive italic of his later years. For all that his well-behaved diligence kept him out of trouble, he took a sharply critical view of the pedagogical relationship, as is apparent from a presumptuously orotund item he wrote for the school magazine in his final year. 'From the outset,' it declares, 'there is a disharmony of the soul between teacher and pupil'.[1] It was his first published piece of work. During his school years, through a friend of his parents, he met a Jewish civil engineer, the future novelist and theoretician Siegfried Kracauer, who was fourteen years his senior, and with whom he struck up a close intellectual – and probably eventually sexual – friendship. At Kracauer's instigation, on Saturday afternoons, they jointly read and interpreted the first of Immanuel Kant's three principal philosophical works, the *Critique of Pure Reason*, and in later life, Adorno would declare that these sessions taught him more about how to understand the play of forces at work beneath the surface of a text than he ever learned from academic teachers. Contemporary works that exercised profound influences on him were Georg Lukács' austerely idealistic *Theory of the Novel* (1916) and the messianic historical work *Spirit of Utopia* (1918) by Ernst Bloch, both thinkers who would shortly go on to espouse the Marxist analysis of social history. While he spent the early part of the war poring over a *Pocket Guide to the World's Navies* and buying model warships at the school shop, imagining himself growing up to be a naval commander, by the time of the German defeat and Versailles, Adorno had been drawn to the mood of revolutionary upheaval that was abroad in the German cities.

The same air of pensive apprehension, even allowing for the fact that it was not the custom to smile for professional photographers a century ago, imbues all portraits of Adorno from his childhood on. At seven, in the regulation small boy's maritime garb of reefer jacket and ribboned cap, and at fourteen, standing behind a chair-back with his left hand draped limply around the neck of Wolf, the German shepherd dog, he looks possessed by the same nameless trepidation, his basin-cut high fringe accentuating the large suspicious eyes. Pictured on holiday with his mother and aunt a year after the latter photograph, standing on the steps of a garden pavilion at the Post Hotel in the Bavarian spa town of Amorbach, he has evidently undergone, at fifteen, the transition to a careworn adulthood, complete with small professorial moustache, his hair now side-parted, his hands clasped before him as though waiting, in premonitory fashion, for a class of students to simmer down and start paying attention.

In 1921, Adorno began his undergraduate study at what would later become the Johann Wolfgang Goethe University in Frankfurt, reading philosophy, psychology and sociology. The university had only been founded in 1914 through private bequests by the city's liberal citizenry, and took a progressive approach to higher education, rapidly gaining a reputation for itself as a seedbed of Marxist and Jewish scholarship, although during the economic crisis that followed the Versailles settlement in Germany, its sources of funding had begun to dwindle, resulting in courses being cut. Adorno attended for seven semesters in all, and as well as studying the sociological work of

Max Weber, an important early influence, he also joined a seminar in epistemology, and went to hear lectures in the art history and music departments. Having obtained his doctorate in the summer of 1924 *summa cum laude*, he began work on a thesis for his *Habilitation*, the postdoctoral qualification that functioned in the German academic system as the licence to teach. The thesis, to be written under the supervision of his philosophy tutor, Hans Cornelius, was entitled *The Concept of the Unconscious in the Transcendental Doctrine of the Soul*. When Cornelius read the completed manuscript in 1927, he was dismayed at its apparently wilful obscurity and verbose self-indulgence and, having indicated that he would surely fail it, prompted its voluntary withdrawal. The truth was that Adorno, like many young scholars at his age, was torn by a mass of conflicting influences. Not only Weber's rationalistic sociology, but the monumental *History and Class Consciousness* (1923), the seminal work that inaugurated Lukács' Marxist maturity, had exercised powerful countervailing impulses to the Husserlian phenomenology and Kantian transcendentalism that were the ostensible focal points of the thesis. In the psychology seminar, Adorno had met an older student, who was also Cornelius' assistant, Max Horkheimer, with whom he would establish a lifelong amity, and who was at this juncture more vigorously leftist in his political orientation than he would ever be again.

In 1923, probably in a café in the Westend of Frankfurt (Adorno's memory in later life would not quite supply the precise date), he had met Walter Benjamin, another failed *Habilitation* candidate, whose *Origin of German Tragic Drama* had provoked much the same nonplussed bafflement as Adorno's work would. Benjamin, whose tragically curtailed career would leave one of the most mercurial but haunting legacies in all of contemporary philosophy, made an instant impression on Adorno. In a series of personal recollections devoted to Benjamin's memory published in 1964, Adorno would write that 'whatever Benjamin said sounded as if it emerged from a mystery. Not that he was an esoteric thinker in a catastrophic sense, but it was as if insights that fly in the face of ordinary common sense have some particular evidence in their favour that completely dissipates the suspicion of arcane knowledge, let alone bluff'. Benjamin was only eleven years older than Adorno, but could already have been a wizened sage to the younger man. No other method of thinking than his exerted a more profoundly liberating fascination on the twenty-year-old Adorno: 'It was as if this philosophy had revealed to me for the first time what philosophy would have to be if it were to fulfil its own promise'.[2] Benjamin's thought appeared to do nothing less than suture back together the twin realms of the phenomenal and noumenal, what was present to concrete experience and what lay beyond its boundaries, whose separation had been ratified in the philosophical tradition ever since Kant. Benjamin was what a mystic would look like if he had not abandoned materialism, and with his own passage into – and creative transformation of – the Marxist tradition, he became one of its most idiosyncratic interpreters, next to Adorno himself.

The other great inspiration at this time would prove the means to escape the conundrum that Adorno saw between trying to get ahead in the world of academic philosophy, with its interminable compromises, and the sort of alternative bohemianism that led one too close for comfort to what he would later deride as 'the world of arts-and-crafts, crackpot religion and half-educated sectarianism'.[3] On 11 June 1924, at a festival in Frankfurt under the auspices of the Allgemeiner Deutscher Musikverein [Associated German Music Society], Adorno had been present at the premiere of Alban Berg's *Three Fragments from Wozzeck*, op 7, a foretaste of the opera that would receive its first complete staging the following year in Berlin. Adorno knew the conductor of the Frankfurt performance, Hermann Scherchen, and asked him for an introduction to the composer. Within the first few minutes of their conversation, Berg offered to take Adorno on as a composition pupil in his home city of Vienna, straight after his graduation in July. In the event, it was only in the new year of 1925 that Adorno was able to move to the Austrian capital, where he immersed himself in its music scene. Not only did he become a composer in the atonal method of the group known as the Second Vienna School, working in the advanced idiom of Berg and his colleagues Arnold Schönberg and Anton Webern, but he became a prolific music journalist, a contributor to journals such as the *Musikblätter des Anbruch* [Daybreak Music Journal] and *Pult und Taktstock* [Desk and Clock]. His reviews and monographs were densely allusive, opaque even, too much so for the inclination of Berg, who wanted the new music to be understood by as wide an audience as possible, but Adorno's youthful intellectual precocity was already in full spate, and what is now cheerfully known as 'dumbing down' was entirely antithetical to his nature.

Prior to Adorno's departure for Vienna, a development that was to have a career-long significance in his work took place. In summer 1924, on the Viktoriaallee in Frankfurt, in a new building designed by the modernist architect Franz Röckle, the Institute for Social Research was founded. Established by an endowment from the private business interests of the Weil family, the foundation was intended to become a centre for leftist intellectuals of all stripes, from SPD to communist. Its original name, the Institute for Marxism, had been rethought in favour of something more apparently neutral in its focus, so as not to arouse aversion in the already turbulent ferment of the Weimar Republic. Its early luminaries included the Polish economist Henryk Grossman, a labour movement agitator and organiser who had served in the European war, the literary academic Leo Löwenthal, the social scientist Friedrich Pollock, Carl Grünberg, a professor of political economy, the philosopher Herbert Marcuse, and the scion of the benefactor's family, Felix Weil, who would become the Institute's director. Fraternal relations were established with the Marx-Engels Institute in Moscow, which was to have resulted in a critical edition of the works of the Marxist founders, but the collaboration quickly withered as Stalinist orthodoxy began to exert its grip in the Soviet Union in the early 1930s. Adorno was instinctively drawn to the Institute's work, and by the time he returned to Frankfurt later in the 1920s, he made several unsuccessful attempts to contribute to its journal, the *Zeitschrift für Sozialforschung* [Journal for Social Research], none of which got past the editorial board. Variances of opinion emerged about the direction in which the Institute ought to steer, and when Max Horkheimer, newly appointed to the chair in social philosophy at the University, became its director early in 1931, a new social sciences emphasis was introduced. Horkheimer considered that traditional philosophy was in decline, and that a new critical theory that attempted to weld together Marxian sociology and Freudian psychology was the most fruitful way forward.

Adorno differed. On his return, he had completed his second, and successful, application for the *Habilitation*, with a complex, densely woven analysis of the works of Søren Kierkegaard that would eventually be published in 1933 as his first book, *Kierkegaard: Construction of the Aesthetic*. His supervisors, Horkheimer and the theologian Paul Tillich, found the text both suggestively original and dynamically novel in its methodology, the former detecting in it 'a mind with the power to advance philosophy at certain points'.[4] Now rewarded with the post of *Privatdozent*, or private lecturer within the state higher education system, Adorno intended to do precisely that. In May 1931, he delivered his inaugural lecture in the philosophy faculty at the University, 'The Actuality of Philosophy', in which he argued that, rather than simply abandoning the western speculative tradition, a critical theory suited to the times might look to the ways in which, in Hegelian fashion, a social dialectic could be seen to emerge from within philosophy itself. Pressed to the exigency of revealing its own internal contradictions by what he called a 'logic of disintegration', a procedure that would become known as immanent critique, idealist thinking could be made to illuminate its origins in the movements of history, and thereby be transformed into a properly revolutionary materialist dialectics. Adorno spoke in favour of a dialectics of the smallest unintentional elements of social phenomena, and against the totalising systems of phenomenology, the logical categories of the post-Kantians, and Heideggerian ontology. He argued that, instead of surrendering to the determinative principles of the mathematical natural sciences, philosophy should raise its own experimental, interpretive procedures to the status of a critical method, so that the puzzles to which philosophy has always claimed to seek the solutions could be illuminated in the historically changing constellations in which they move. In a formulation that would have resonance for the entirety of his subsequent thinking, towards the end of the address, Adorno stated:

> I am not afraid of the reproach of unfruitful negativity... If philosophical interpretation can in fact only prosper dialectically, then the first dialectical point of attack is given by a philosophy that cultivates precisely those problems whose removal appears more pressingly necessary than the addition of a new answer to so many old ones. Only an essentially undialectical philosophy, one that aims at ahistorical truth, could maintain that the old problems could simply be removed by forgetting them and starting afresh from the beginning.[5]

The task that Wittgenstein's analytic logic, no less than Heidegger's ontology, had set themselves was hereby swept aside as a false trail, to make way for what philosophy could more profitably do, which was to analyse the minutest cells of the empirical to determine the movements of concrete history. 'For the mind is indeed not capable of producing or grasping the totality of the real, but it may be possible to penetrate the detail, to explode in miniature the mass of merely existing reality.'[6]

While Adorno's philosophical style continued to be met with courteous puzzlement on the editorial board of the *Zeitschrift*, its editors did intend to publish writings in aesthetics, and recognised that in him they at least had an unmatched musicologist. Accordingly, the first essay of his printed in the journal was his 1932 contribution 'On the Social Situation of Music', which took a historical-materialist approach to the position of music in contemporary capitalist society. Music no longer constituted a spontaneous expression of the spirit, as in the idealist conception, but had instead become a commodity like virtually everything else, and was as subject to the abstract exchange principle as were consumer goods in the market. But while the Institute's contributors addressed themselves to the larger historico-political question of why a full-scale proletarian revolution had not come about in Germany, the twentieth century's single most atrocious historical convulsion was about to engulf the country. With tasteless irony, Adorno's study of Kierkegaard was published on 27 February 1933, the day that Adolf Hitler declared a national emergency, suspending the freedom of the press and becoming dictator. Unexpectedly, the book was not banned, most likely, as Adorno would sardonically comment years later, because the censors didn't understand it. Within six months, however, his teaching permit had been revoked by the authorities, barely two years into his academic career. The Institute of Social Research became a proscribed organisation, and its members' publications were banned.

While most of the Frankfurt thinkers fled Nazi Germany as reflexively as at the firing of a starting-gun, Adorno, now prudently using his mother's Aryan name, lingered on, seemingly half-believing that the regime would prove to be short-lived, as the entrepreneurial class that thought it had cleverly used the Nazi Party for its own ends, and could then discard its rough-necked blockheads when their interests had been secured, would duly evict it from office. As the fateful year of 1933 wore on, there were no such signs. The Institute was briefly re-established in Swiss exile in Geneva, before it moved en masse to the United States, and became an affiliate body of Columbia University in New York. After a year of indecision, Adorno himself acceded to the inevitable, and applied for a scholarship at Oxford University. He was admitted to Merton College in 1934 to write a doctorate on Edmund Husserl's phenomenology, and while he was dismayed to discover that he would not be permitted to teach, only pursue his research in cloistered isolation like a medieval scholar, as he put it, England proved a safe haven. His father's younger brother Bernhard (now known as Bernard Wingfield) had a business and family in London, and in any case, Adorno was not quite living the isolated life. He was eventually joined in the UK by his fiancée, Gretel Karplus, with whom he had been in a relationship since the previous decade.

Gretel, who was a year older than Adorno, came from a family of Viennese industrialists, friends and business associates of Adorno's father's wine company. They had a leather-processing works in Berlin, and lived in bourgeois comfort on the Prinzenallee, a little to the north of the great urban park of the Tiergarten. Gretel met Teddie during one of the frequent exchanges of visits between their families. He developed a deep emotional attachment to her, while she found his quixotic intelligence and his self-confidence instantaneously fascinating. Furthermore, she moved in the most exciting intellectual circles in Berlin, and already knew Walter Benjamin, Ernst Bloch and Bertolt Brecht. She and Adorno became engaged soon after, but it was only when he had been living in Britain for three years, on 8 September 1937, three days before his thirty-fourth birthday, that they married, in the register office at Paddington. He thus became the third generation of his family to marry in the UK.

With hair-raising insouciance, given the political situation, Adorno continued to return to Germany at the end of every Oxford term to visit his family. In 1935, the beloved Aunt Agathe, his 'second mother', died, leaving Adorno feeling that a significant part of a past that would never be restored had been lost to him. He returned for the funeral, and grew increasingly concerned at the likely treatment of his parents if they remained behind. Meanwhile he had achieved a certain paradoxical state of acclimatisation in England, but Gretel wasn't keen. The food and the rain depressed her, and Adorno began to consider seriously the prospect of joining his erstwhile colleagues in the United States. In 1938, he was invited to New York, after an intervention by Horkheimer, to join the Institute in exile, working on an affiliated research venture called the Princeton Radio Research Project, run by an exiled Viennese sociologist, Paul Lazarsfeld. The Project's brief was to analyse the broadcasting of music on the radio, and needed an appropriately trained music consultant. After the paperwork was completed, Adorno and Gretel paid a farewell visit to Benjamin, now holed up in isolated indigence in Paris, and then departed on 16 February on the SS *Champlain*, an opulent passenger ship of the French Line, for New York.

The radio project did not go particularly well. From the outset, Adorno quibbled with the methodological premises on which the listener research was to be conducted, and wilfully refused to grasp the protocol that the Project's sponsorship money had been invested with the aim of finding out how best to improve radio's connection with the masses. Adorno considered that the radio programmes, especially the educational strands dedicated to popularising classical music, were themselves an instrument of the obfuscation of their consumers, and with Lazarsfeld growing increasingly impatient at the long, rigorously critical theoretical papers Adorno was submitting, now collected in the compendious volume *Current of Music: Elements of a Radio Theory* (2006), his involvement in the project was duly terminated in 1941.

A further move was on the cards, this time by train to join the rest of the German expatriate intellectual community living in California, in what had become known as Weimar-by-the-Sea. Here, in the coastal neighbourhood of Pacific Palisades, on the west side of Los Angeles, amid the palm trees and the ocean breezes, lived a diaspora that included Thomas Mann, Bertolt Brecht, Arnold Schönberg, Lion Feuchtwanger, Max Reinhardt, Hanns Eisler, Lotte Lenja and Fritz Lang. The empty chair at the table was for Walter Benjamin, whose death by morphine overdose on the Spanish border in 1940, following an epic flight on foot from southern France over the Pyrenees, ahead of the advancing Nazi invasion, threw the darkest shadow of the European evil over the lives of the California exiles. Teddie and Gretel eventually settled in a two-bedroomed house with a little garden on South Kenter Avenue in the Brentwood Heights district, not far from Sunset Boulevard and the epicentre of the Hollywood film industry. Far from remaining aloof from the surrounding milieu, the Adornos became enthusiastic socialites and partygoers, consorting with a mix of deracinated artists and philosophers, as well as luminaries of the cinema. At one notable occasion, Adorno hammered out passages of Mozart and Wagner operas on the piano while Charlie Chaplin improvised mimed enactments of them. Adorno also met Greta Garbo, newly and abruptly embarked on a disdainful retirement from the films, and the two of them regularly took tea together, engaging in an absorbing converse that history's otherwise ubiquitous video cameras agonisingly missed.

It was during the early 1940s that Adorno and Horkheimer together began working on the drafts that would eventually be published in private in 1944 as *Philosophical Fragments*, and then, through an independent Amsterdam publishing house, Querido, in 1947, under the title *Dialectic of Enlightenment*. In view of the utter disaster that had drowned European civilisation under a tide of irrational barbarism, the authors set out to answer the question as to what had gone wrong with the enlightenment project, which was after all supposed to have liberated humankind from the tyranny of mythic unreason. For its rewriting of western history as a reversion to myth under the sign of instrumental rationality, and its enduringly provocative analysis of the degradation of the humanist ideals of art into an enormous apparatus of mendacity given the name of the 'culture industry', in the very midst of which the writers were currently languishing, the book would attain in the post-war world the status of a classic text of critical theory, lambasted in conservative quarters, all but disowned by subsequent generations of the Frankfurt School, but for all that an indispensable, unignorable force-field of courageous thought. We shall look at it in detail in chapter 2.

Despite the condition of exile, these West Coast years were by no means an unmitigated torment. Adorno's biographer Stefan Müller-Doohm entitles his chapter on the California period 'Happiness in Misfortune', which is by no means wide of the mark. Adorno had managed to secure his parents a safe passage out of Hitler's Germany, and they were now domiciled in New York, where they would spend the brief remainder of their years. He collaborated with Thomas Mann as music consultant on the composition of the novelist's *Doctor Faustus* (1947), a restaging of Goethe's great tragedy in the world of the contemporary avant-garde, and he co-wrote a treatise, published in the same year, on *Composing for the Films* with Hanns Eisler, who had begun as an uncompromising Marxist-Leninist colleague of Brecht and become an Oscar-nominated composer of Hollywood film scores, before returning to Europe after the war to write a national anthem for the fledgling German Democratic Republic.

When Adorno himself gingerly returned to the old continent in 1949, it was in time to greet the publication of his first full-length solo work of musical analysis, *The Philosophy of New Music*, a pugilistic comparison of the respective oeuvres of Schönberg and Igor Stravinsky, the former celebrated for abolishing the tonal system of western music in an age for which it was no longer fitted, though chided for the rigidity into which his music had fallen with the twelve-tone system, the latter eviscerated for his reactionary restoration of anachronising classical ideals. Schönberg declared the book the most appalling thing that had ever been written about him, a verdict that did not prevent Adorno subsequently writing a lengthy heartfelt obituary of the composer on his death in 1951. Also in Adorno's luggage on the return journey from the US was the manuscript of a set of reflections, written throughout the 1940s, on the nature of contemporary society and cultural consciousness, *Minima Moralia: Reflections from Damaged Life* (1951), one of the century's most remarkable and protean personal testimonies.

Although certain of the returnees, such as Eisler, Brecht and Ernst Bloch chose to settle in the GDR, at the westernmost fringe of the Soviet bloc, most stayed in the west. Adorno and his colleagues in the Institute for Social Research returned to Frankfurt, where they found themselves enjoined by the authorities of the Federal Republic to assist in the painstaking task of cultural and political reconstruction that was underway in the wake of the Nuremberg trials. The Institute was refounded in new premises in 1951 under the directorship of Friedrich Pollock, who remained at the helm until 1959, when the leading role would pass to Adorno himself.

As the 1950s progressed, Adorno became a public figure in Germany. He gave talks and interviews on radio, and wrote for the national newspapers as well as for academic journals. The sociological fieldwork that he and a team of researchers had conducted in the US after the war, to try to establish whether it was possible to identify and cure incipient fascist traits in ordinary citizens, with the aim of ensuring that the horror symbolised by Auschwitz could never break upon humanity again, was published under the title *The Authoritarian Personality* (1950). The authors detected likely susceptibilities to fascist propaganda not only in the most obvious character-types, such as anti-Semites and xenophobes, but also in people who were just unthinkingly conformist in their attitudes, people at the bottom end of the economic scale, who believed that the odds were stacked against them and that some sort of politically incoherent revenge on society was their prerogative. Controversially, Adorno saw no functional difference between the operations of totalitarian propaganda and the swathes of confected dishonesty in which the culture industry wrapped its clients. Society was becoming a total machine, and even where it did not construct bonfires of books in the streets, or transport people to industrialised death camps to be efficiently liquidated, it strove to account for every last waking moment of consciousness of its members. What made things all the more bitter was that a culture of forgetting was very soon in operation in West Germany, in which a cloak was thrown over the Nazi past as some of the former regime's functionaries were restored to positions of public authority, and even so-called high culture took on a conciliatory restorationist tone, all as if nothing adverse had happened. This was what led Adorno to probably his best-known dictum, expressed in the opening item in an essay collection *Prisms* (1955): 'To write poetry after Auschwitz is barbaric'.[7] To this day, few know that he eventually recanted it.

The reconstitution of the Institute for Social Research in its Frankfurt home prompted a period of feverish productivity from all its members, but none more so than from Adorno. There appeared to be no theme in philosophy, aesthetics or sociology to which he was not prepared to address himself. Essays in music, including monographs on Wagner and Mahler, and literary criticism were among his published output, while his lecture courses at Frankfurt University extended from a philosophical approach to the works of Beethoven up to the most ethereally abstract matter of Kant and Hegel. In the autumn of 1958, having seen a production of *Endgame* on the Vienna stage earlier in the year, Adorno flew to Paris, where he had asked his publisher, Peter Suhrkamp, if he would arrange an introduction for him to its author, Samuel Beckett. The two of them met in the five-star surroundings of the Hotel Lutétia, and went on into the night, their conversation becoming so mutually absorbing that it continued on to the Montparnasse brasserie La Coupole, and then further still to a late dinner at Aux Iles Marquises, Beckett's favourite restaurant, on the rue de la Gaité. For all that he would privately declare himself bemused by the earnest intensity of Adorno's interest in his work, Beckett found the professor from Frankfurt hard to ignore, while Adorno felt that he had identified in the Irish writer the true heir of the modernist legacy of Proust and Kafka, a writer whose work steadfastly refused any accommodation with the miserable condition of the world around it. Adorno wrote a long essay on *Endgame,* which appeared in the second volume of his *Notes to Literature* (1961), and at a *Festspiel* for Beckett held under Suhrkamp's auspices at a concert hall in February 1961, he read an extract from it with more than his usual degree of fierce concentration and impeccable diction, concluding the reading with a virtuoso's bow on the podium. Adorno's admiration for Beckett remained undimmed over his remaining decade, and he had intended to make him the dedicatee of his last great work, the not-quite-finished *Aesthetic Theory* (1970).

The 1960s were to prove a nemesis for Adorno, both politically and personally. In the early part of the decade, his publishing and teaching activities continued unabated. There were more literary and musicological essays, including an *Introduction to the Sociology of Music* (1962), and a slender volume entitled *The Jargon of Authenticity* (1964), which attempted a concise disembowelment of Heidegger's ontology and the intellectual fashion, existentialism, that it had generated. Adorno considered this nothing but an empty subjectivism, reduced to trying to wring semantic profundity from its own impoverished stock of linguistic counters, while it raised the nullity of existence to a *sine qua non*. The intellectually myopic read such tendencies in Beckett. This work had originally been an integral part of what was to become the *Negative Dialectics* (1966), but Adorno published it separately once it seemed to have outgrown its context. The work from which it parted company was to be one of the century's most innovative, boldly confrontational works of abstract philosophy, and broke Adorno's lifelong antipathy to writing large books. He referred to the finished product as his 'fat child'. It opens by acknowledging the dogged survival of philosophy in the era that should have put an end to it by changing the world according to the Marxist prescription, and continues through deconstructions of Kant's ethical work, the *Critique of Practical Reason*, and Hegel's philosophy of history, to arrive at a series of meditations on the fate of metaphysical experience in a world that has put its faith, to both right and left, in concrete materialism. Work on it was intellectually exhausting, and Adorno declared in conversation, after the book went to press, that from now on he would write only on aesthetic themes.

In 1967, the Federal Republic hosted a state visit by the Shah of Iran, a national leader widely reviled on the radical left for his repressive and corrupt regime. Large-scale, frequently turbulent demonstrations were mounted against it, and at one of them, a German student, Benno Ohnesorg, was shot dead by police. Adorno was horrified that such a measure could be countenanced in a nation that had officially forsworn the shooting of civilians, and expressed his solidarity with the student opposition. Gradually, however, over the next two years, the unrest turned irreconcilably against all authority, whether murderous or benign. The principal leftist student movement, the Sozialistischer Deutscher Studentenbund (SDS) [German Socialist Student Union], staged protests against the university authorities, and taunted members of the first Frankfurt School generation with the accusation of aloof acquiescence in the system. They wanted to see professors of political science on the streets, not still standing bow-tied in the lecture-halls sermonising about Marx and Hegel. During a particularly rowdy sit-in at the premises of the Institute of Social Research in 1968, where students were in occupation, Adorno committed what many on the left still regard as his cardinal sin, calling the police to evacuate the building. In California, Herbert Marcuse was sufficiently enthused by the news from Europe to consider the student unrest, which came to a head in the street confrontations in Paris in May 1968, to be the herald of a broader social upheaval that might threaten the global capitalist order. Adorno now strongly disagreed, detecting traits of left fascism in incidents such as the victimisation of a student who had failed to attend a demonstration, and had had his room smashed up in a reprisal of revolutionary justice. When an attempt was made on the life of the student leader Rudi Dutschke, he supported the wave of angry protest. He supported the students' blockade on deliveries to the campus of right-wing newspapers, and in the spring of 1968, he wrote to the general secretary of the metalworkers' union, urging the trade union movement to call a general strike against a state succumbing to the techniques of demented repression. While he went to heroic lengths to meet the student leaders, however, liaising with them and acceding to at least some of their demands, he denounced the idiotic brutality of many of their actions, their singular lack of theoretical basis, and the determination to find victims among their own kind.

The SDS claimed its biggest victim of all on 22 April 1969. In what was to have been the opening lecture of a course entitled 'Introduction to Dialectical Thinking', Adorno had planned to encourage interventions and questions from the student body as a departure from the traditional one-way lecture format. Scarcely had he begun speaking than a pair of tall leather-jacketed activists from the militant wing of the SDS strode to the podium, and demanded that Adorno perform an act of expiatory self-criticism for having resorted to calling the police the previous year. When he demurred, they wrote a piece of doggerel on the blackboard behind him that read, 'If Adorno is left in peace, capitalism will never cease'. Amid the banging of desks, and chants of 'Down with the informer!', one section of the students tried to quieten the rest, and Adorno announced that he would wait for five minutes while the students decided among themselves whether they wished him to give the lecture. The vote was never taken. Instead, three women students approached the podium and performed an erotic assault on the professor, exposing their breasts to him and showering him with rose and tulip petals, while attempting to caress him. In a state of humiliated agitation, Adorno fled the lecture-hall, shielding himself from the sight of the activists with his briefcase. Members of a dissident sociological group then handed out printed flyers announcing that Adorno was dead. The protest became known in the annals of student japery as the *Busenaktion* [bosom action]. It had officially served to show that, not only was Adorno the handmaiden of capitalist hegemony, but was also a desiccated old stiff.

Although he continued to try to give lectures for the remainder of the academic year, he was profoundly disheartened by the turn events had taken. While a steady descant of disapproving correspondence from across the Atlantic continued to come from Marcuse, a leftist theoretician who had continued working for the US secret service fully five years after the end of the war, Adorno wrote to the chancellor of Frankfurt University, asking for better protection for academic staff in the forthcoming year if they were to continue to perform their contractual duties.

In July 1969, Adorno and Gretel went on holiday to the Swiss resort of Zermatt. It was there, a fortnight after their arrival, in the little tourist town of Visp in the Valais, that Adorno suffered what appeared to be a second heart murmur that day. He went into the local St Maria hospital for an examination, and was admitted for tests and observation. When Gretel returned the next day, 6 August, with a clutch of books to keep him occupied, she was told he had suffered a sudden traumatic coronary thrombosis less than an hour earlier, and had died instantaneously, a month short of sixty-six. He was laid to rest one week later in the family tomb at the Central Cemetery in Frankfurt. His funeral, at which there were no religious obsequies, was broadcast on the Hessen state radio, with contributions from the minister of state and various of Adorno's intellectual colleagues. Ernst Bloch, now a frail but mentally undiminished eighty-four, was there. Marcuse had flown over from the US, evidently desolate with a sense of bereavement, and broke the silence that followed the ceremony by declaring that nobody was capable of speaking on behalf of Adorno. Nonetheless, Horkheimer did, describing him as a productive and anticonformist titan, 'one of the greatest minds of this age of transition.'[8]

In the centre of Frankfurt, a monumental artwork was unveiled in 2003, to mark the centenary of Adorno's birth. Standing in the middle of the square named after him, it is a cubic vitrine of reinforced glass, 2.5 metres wide across each face. Inside is a baize-topped writing-desk and chair. On top of the desk, next to a lamp with a domed shade, are some papers, a copy of *Negative Dialektik*, and a metronome. For its blank inhuman pomposity as much as anything, the monument is regularly pelted with stones and other missiles by roistering malcontents, to see whether its glass walls will break or crack. They do not. The monument is impervious to the jeering of the masses, not least because it is uninhabited by any trace of the human, least of all of one who reviled all monuments.

Elsewhere in the city, on the Senckenberganlage just outside the present headquarters of the Institute for Social Research, is a pedestrian crossing, regulated by a traffic signal. The signal is affectionately known as the *Adorno-Ampel* [Adorno Light], in acknowledgement of the fact that, in 1962, following an incident in which a pedestrian was run over and killed while trying to cross the road here, Adorno had written to the city authorities to request that a traffic light be installed for safety purposes. The light was eventually put up in 1987.

These are the physical memorials to Theodor Adorno. The rest is his work.

One

Society and the Individual

Within repressive society the individual's emancipation not only benefits but damages him. Freedom from society robs him of the strength for freedom. For however real he may be in his relations to others, he is, considered absolutely, a mere abstraction.
Minima Moralia

In February 2014, targeted advertising and the communications systems that enable it achieved another significant advance in their capabilities, when it was announced that a pair of satellite television companies in the United States had joined forces to offer to clients a newly developed package called Addressable TV.[1] For the first time, advertisers would be able to tailor their messages to specific consumers through TV commercials that target individual viewers. While the TV in one home might be encouraging its undecided viewers to vote for a particular candidate in the forthcoming general election, their neighbours would be receiving an ad urging them to switch their shortly expiring home insurance to another company. Data about the economic circumstances and likely consumer preferences of each household, derived from the information gleaned about their customers' identities known by the broadcast companies, would be made available to advertisers so that they need not waste their resources by beaming commercials to those who have no interest in them. The system works on exactly the same principle as the targeted advertising facilitated by retailers' loyalty cards, or by the spyware that captures the browsing history of Internet subscribers. Advertisers are accorded the right to know as much as is practically, and more or less legally, available about their potential customers, whose interests they affect to serve by assuring them that they will target them with only such advertisements as they are interested in seeing. When social media websites that allow users to reject particular ads then ask them what it was that they didn't like about them, the options never include the right to say that they don't like advertising. Anybody objecting that they don't wish advertising to be aimed at them at all, at whatever degree of personal specificity, is viewed by the industry as a recalcitrant dissident who must be brought to heel, and by broadband providers and media companies as a foolish puritan who wilfully refuses to appreciate that the services he is enjoying must be bought not just by his subscription, but also by his dutiful attention to the commercial propaganda of the companies' own clients. Those who do not wish to comply can invest in an online ad-blocker, or press the Mute button on the remote control every time the TV ad-breaks begin, but the onus, which may well be a financial one in itself, has shifted to the intended recipient of advertising to try to escape it, where once it fell on the advertiser to solicit his attention. A powerful distillate of contemporary experience might be the Internet user being interrupted while trying to read the news by being made to look at targeted ads for ad-blockers.

To the Adorno who wrote, with Max Horkheimer, in *Dialectic of Enlightenment* (1947) that in late capitalist consumer culture, 'something is provided for everyone so that none may escape', nothing about targeted advertising would have seemed unfamiliar. What it is predicated on is the shameless mendacity that its potential recipients are individuals. The emphases of this circumstance have undoubtedly shifted in the seventy years since Adorno and Horkheimer wrote. If it seemed the case in the 1940s that a one-size-fits-all approach conformed the culture industry's clients into one amorphous mass, training them to react in the same ways to the emotional and ideological stimuli of mass entertainments, such as popular music radio stations and the productions of Hollywood, the present practice is very much for constituting them as a collective of individuals, each with his or her own respective tastes, inclinations and interests, which are courteously acknowledged by the system so that it might speak more personally to each of them, but for the greater concealed purpose of bringing them into line with other participants in the consumer economy. A pretence to a belief in the preciousness of individuality was only a belated accrual on the balance-sheet of capitalist economic relations, which had otherwise relegated it to the status of a sundry item, except where it served the self-image of entrepreneurialism. If business ventures themselves were allegedly always started by far-seeing innovators with the imaginative energy and resources to get them off the ground, their potential clients were an indistinguishable mass, amalgamated into the sum-totals on the asset side. What people's individual preferences might be were once their own affair, as long as one of their preferences turned out to be for the entrepreneur's wares. Now capitalism in its globalised phase is keen to know everything it can about them, partly because gigantic corporate entities have so many different products and services they might sell them, but also because flattering them that they are individuals is thought to be the best way of bringing them into the commercial fold. The concept of individuality, excoriated as a personal tenet in the form of bourgeois individualism in the era of revolutionary collective subjects, endured as a stance of libertarian defiance on the western flank of the Cold War divide, since the demise of which it has become transformed from a hardened pig-headedness into a gentler insistence on universal mutual respect, but is no less ideology for that. Indeed, inasmuch as its assumptions largely pass unnoticed, it is arguably more ideological than ever, because a society that would crumble to bits if individuals were allowed the full measure of their constitutional gains hardly has the interests of individuals at heart. It was the insight of Marx that economic relations at the nascent monopolistic stage of capitalist development had taken on the lineaments of primitive anthropology, one that subordinated consciousness to revered fetish-objects invested with mystical significance, a mechanism that members of the Frankfurt School would argue in the following century had extended from the economic relations of production to the overall structure of society itself and the cultural forms it has historically generated. To understand this thought-process, it is necessary to turn back to the opening chapter of the *Dialectic of Enlightenment*, on 'The Concept of Enlightenment', to see how the most formidable critique of western civilisation mounted in the twentieth century, and perhaps in the entire Marxist tradition, came to view the fate of the individual in mass society.

The narrative structure within which Adorno and Horkheimer frame their argument about the progress of enlightenment is a circular one, in which human history has coiled back on itself like the narrative of *Finnegans Wake*. This is not to say that a techno-logical society has literally regressed to prehistoric conditions, but that the context into which consciousness has been led by the progress of rationality bears elements of the thought-forms of the age of primal fear. The circularity of this process lies in the fact that mythological thinking, by which the terrors of the natural world were attributed to gods, contained within itself the seeds of the enlightenment towards which it strove, which then, as enlightenment became the total context of the quest for scientific knowledge and understanding in the eighteenth century, began to revert to the monolithic nature of myth in the form of the unquestioned and changeless objectivity that science took as its ideal. As the authors succinctly put it: 'Just as the myths already realise enlightenment, so enlightenment with every step becomes more deeply engulfed in mythology'.[2] What this movement contradicts is the official notion that enlightenment, as one of its consequences, produces a progressive liberation of the individual human spirit, which is now freed from its incarceration in antique superstition and set at liberty in a society that has the interests of each at heart. The project of enlightenment is dominion over all, the idea that everything will fall to the disposal of learning and therefore of control. Science realises the edict of God in the Judaic creation myth, that all things that live will be subject to the executive power of a humankind made in his image. The power that knowledge also always is becomes the structuring principle not just of learning, but of relations between the thinking intelligence and the whole objective world that it submits to itself, and ultimately of society itself. 'The awakening of the self is paid for by the acknowledgement of power as the principle of all relations'.[3] Sovereignty over the objective constitutes everything there is as an undifferentiated mass, in that every element is equally susceptible to rational inquiry, which respects the distinctions between phenomena only in order that, by subsuming them to the force of reason, they may be homogenised. The raw material of the myths were the occurrences of the natural world, of what was experienced as sheer contingency in human affairs, subjected to a categorising and ordering principle, in which narrative form they prepared the compartmentalisation of knowledge into which the universities would eventually organise it. Mythology was humankind's way of telling itself what it needed to know, but instead of liberating thought from the entanglement of blind conceptual domination, enlightenment only enmeshed it further in real domination by making the mastery of nature simultaneously the principle of social organisation. In this sense, the Frankfurt School turned Hegel's notion of human history as an incremental progress in the consciousness of freedom against itself, so that the purely abstract freedom that Hegel saw in the Greek city-states reverts to worldwide domination, rather than developing towards the concrete freedom that he thought had been imperfectly realised in his own time.

Nowhere is the perpetuation of heteronomy over the

individual to be more starkly seen than in capitalist exchange relations, the economic form *par excellence* of the European Enlightenment. The formal equivalence of all under the exchange principle, which abolishes the social hierarchies of feudalism, in a market in which all alike may theoretically become consumers to the limit of their economic resources, is the motor of a social process by which, concomitantly, the raw material of each consumer's individuality is shaped into an isomorphism with all others. The democratisation of the market, which will sell its goods to anybody without regard to their station in life, simultaneously abolishes distinctions of character among its customers, whose innate talents and potentials become in turn so many commodities to be sold on the market. The progress of homogenisation, spiritually as much as economically, requires that there be initially some heterogeneous material that must be conformed. If everything was already the same anyway, there would be no principle of equality. Equality is the banner behind which exchange society already marched long before the storming of the Bastille, albeit not egalitarianism in political representation, but in the availability of all for exploitation. The degree to which enlightenment aligned itself with social actuality, in Adorno and Horkheimer's argument, was the precise degree to which it acknowledged that a residue of individuality nonetheless remains. Individuality is an affront to a society conceived on the model of a collectivity, and inasmuch as individual properties never quite disappear, even in the bourgeois age, the enlightenment process sides with the social impulse in functionally suppressing them. Instead of the anarchy of a mass of self-determining individuals, what enlightenment results in, through the abstraction to which it conforms the objects of knowledge, finds its social counterpart in the malleable horde into which its economic structures have moulded society.

There is a fundamental lacuna for Adorno and Horkheimer between the ideology of equality's fairness and the primal injustice of treating everybody in the same way. The universality of the law of equivalence is after all derived from the subordination of brute nature, which no longer operates on human beings with unmitigated and inscrutable force, but is now mediated through the perceptions of consciousness, and thereby comes to inform both the conceptualising labour of enlightenment and the structures and operations of justice in bourgeois society. What is gained by no longer seeing the world as an amorphous, heterogeneous, fathomless chaos is paid for by surrendering to the principle of universal equivalence. Humans were once only at the mercy of the elements as much as were the animals, but the transition to civilisation, in constituting natural forces as a single power, entailed their coming to worship the elements as no mere animal ever could, so granting them an alienating power over themselves. It is this which reduces individuals to equivalents, the status that liberalism then erects as a fetish. By subjecting the primordial forces to the law of equivalence, civilisation prepared the way for equivalence itself to become a fetish, a process that can be seen as much in legal proceedings as it can in economic relations. 'The blindfold over Justitia's eyes,' the authors write, referring to traditional allegorical representations of Justice as being blind to the claims of one vested interest over another, 'does not only mean that there should be no assault upon justice, but that justice does not originate in freedom'.[4] In the medieval era, the principle of equality before the law intended only that all should be answerable to an objective body of statute regardless of caste, instead of the mass being subjected to the executive whim of the privileged, but succeeded instead in making the law a monolithic authority, before which, ever since, all must exhibit due obeisance or be ground down, but which nonetheless accommodates the ruses of the privileged to evade it, even where it might still fulfil its own concept by putting unearned privilege on trial.

The proposition that individuality exists only to reaffirm the principle of equivalence is one of the fundamental dialectical paradoxes on which the thinking of Adorno and Horkheimer's text rests. Equivalence is less a static state, or an abstract principle, than a social process. It is the subsuming of particular attributes in the mass that makes the mass manipulable, and which constitutes it as a homogeneous mass in the first place. Political movements, from the French Revolution on, that have taken equality as a goal to be achieved, a state of affairs to be brought about and realised through the application of policy, which has turned out to be no better than ideologically assuming equality to be a present fact, reached their culmination in the totalitarianisms of the mid-twentieth century. 'That all men are alike is exactly what society would like to hear,' Adorno argues in *Minima Moralia* (1951). 'It considers actual or imagined differences as stigmas indicating that not enough has yet been done; that something has still been left outside its machinery, not quite determined by its totality'.[5] Nothing prepares each individual for the equalisation process as concretely as the bullying he or she will undergo at some point in school, when the power of the mass is expressed in its derisive refusal to tolerate differences of character, physical demeanour or academic ability. If the victim is to achieve peace, it must always be on the oppressors' own terms, which are as non-negotiable for him as they once were for the oppressors themselves. The radical critique of multiculturalism mounted in the present day has its moment of truth in the sense that the multicultural society is predicated on an assimilationist elision of differences between cultures, which issues in everybody being expected to salute the flag of the dominant culture, for all that the untruth of the critique consists in its advancement of a static relativism, in which the dialectic of better and worse attributes between cultures is hushed to the respectful silence of the mausoleum. The better state, for Adorno, would be 'one in which people could be different without fear'.[6] Inasmuch as equivalence must annihilate traces of individuality wherever it finds them, even while claiming in the voice of the advertisers to be honouring them, it could be said to rely on a certain measure of recalcitrant individualism as its fuel, on much the same principle as in a reactionary predicative logic, the exception is always held to prove the rule, rather than standing for what it ought honourably to be, the means by which the power of the rule is subverted.

Just as the first philosophical categories represented the domination of the tribe over its individual members, by subordinating all experience other than the most trivial to the generalising tendency, so the whole logical order of conceptuality represents the hierarchy of which social reality is composed, including the division of labour. There is an unbreakable continuity between society and domination. Society needs the division of labour for its self-preservation, and it needs its members to subjugate themselves to its functions, rather than merely constituting it in their aggregation. The whole that society becomes assumes a minatory predominance over its constituent elements, becomes literally more than the sum of its parts, an institution in itself. For Adorno and Horkheimer, this process has its roots in the primeval transition from the state in which every member of a group each had his or her individual part to play in influencing nature, whether by hunting or gathering or performing tasks that were less subject to the dictates of natural existence, to a state in which ritual became the established way of appeasing and petitioning nature, its unvarying recurrence subsuming its participants into the one directed purpose, in which their variant activities were solidified as the division of labour, as between male and female, young and old. Although nature was as capricious in response to the appeal of fetishised ritual as it had been before it produced beings capable of formulating ritual, the self-sameness of the ritual cast nature itself into the status of an overpowering immutable force. The institutionalised dread produced by that conception was then translated into the imitative dread by which social elites overpowered the rest. Everything that exists is subject to predation, which relationship is reflected in raw social hierarchy, in the investigative labour of science, in the structure of deductive logic with its given-thats and therefores. If social universality assumes not the solidary form that Emile Durkheim optimistically read into it, to the individual members of any social group, the domination to which they are subject takes on the form of universality. 'What is done to all by the few, always occurs as the subjection of individuals by the many: social repression always exhibits the masks of repression by a collective'.[7] At the most brutally instrumental level, the bullied child experiences the terror meted out to him as a reflection of the views of the majority, with whom he in some way fails to conform, but whose correctness is not undermined by its resort to intimidation. Intimidation is inscribed in its innermost core, and is at its most virulent precisely where it detects antibodies within its own system. 'It is this unity of the collectivity and domination,' the authors write, 'which is expressed in thought forms'.[8] The hierarchy of philosophical categories reflects the social hierarchies that gave rise to them in all eras, from the Athenian marketplace to the high tables of Oxford. In the commands that elites issue to the lower orders, to their slaves and children and wives, language itself accommodates the principle of domination, whereupon it has no particular further need for the abstract ideas, a process in which Adorno and Horkheimer accuse institutionalised science of colluding. By the time of the Renaissance, what matters henceforth is concrete findings, the labour of classification that reproduces the division of labour, and which consigns what resists classification to the insignificant peripheries. All that is left of the irrational in the face of the eighteenth-century ideal of enlightenment is the 'abstract fear' instilled in human beings by the collectivity from which enlightenment itself arose.

If the anthropological thrust of the argument in *Dialectic of*

Enlightenment appears to conventional critique as unremittingly bleak, it is to be borne in mind that any account of human development that would do justice to the universality of domination to which humanity has been subject must account for the failure not just of culture to prevent Auschwitz in the most celebrated paradigm, but of enlightenment to abolish fear. The opening words of the first chapter establish the gigantic context: 'In the most general sense of progressive thought, the Enlightenment has always aimed at liberating men from fear and establishing their sovereignty. Yet the fully enlightened earth radiates disaster triumphant'.[9] While enlightenment tried to drive out the power of myth, it only succeeded in reverting to myth through the fetishisation of instrumental reason. Every time one of the public secularists, who have earned a substantial stipend in recent years by restating what everybody has already had dinned into them by triumphant rationality, comments that enlightenment has freed us from having to believe in the old superstitions, they unwittingly reconfirm the status of enlightenment itself as a self-authorising superstition. An Internet group called 'I fucking love science' is replete with examples of the breakthroughs achieved in explanatory physics, as well as the invention of gadgetry, to which role public trust in the benevolence of science has always assigned the lab-coated boffin, but has missed the overt continuity with the worship of any idol displayed by such ideological commitments. Some people fucking love science; others fucking love Justin Bieber. There may even be some overlap. In the context of instrumental rationality, the only moments that the individual finds to elide the domination of collectivity inevitably appear to it as spasmodic interjections of the irrational, which is why the antidote to science is so often sought in the unverifiable claims of the supernatural, in bespoke amalgams of obscurantist spiritual belief, in the infantility of fantasy-worlds, in the use of intoxicants. The last case is a particularly fertile border-zone between approved consciousness with its hierarchy of priorities and a putative beyond, where obligation is dissolved not through willed resistance but through strategic self-incapacitation. Adorno and Horkheimer argue that intoxication performs the anthropological function of relieving the individual of the pressure of maintaining the psychic structural integrity of the self. What it costs each individual to learn the construction of a socialised self in childhood results in an instinctual predilection for intoxicated states, precisely as a means of momentarily losing the self, as regular relief from the grim determination to sustain the rational ego. This produces another aspect, albeit an officially disavowed and viciously circumscribed one, of the circadian rhythm, in which the euphoria of self-suspension is atoned for by a subsequent deathlike sleep, virtually the only technique remaining to the mass of humanity for mediating between the precincts of the preservation and destruction of the self – not the self-injurious indulgence to which all moralism, including the moralism of government health injunctions, have reduced it, but, however paradoxically, 'an attempt of the self to survive itself'.[10] If civilisation at every historical stage offered the individual nothing but servitude and toil, in furtherance of its own continued evolution, the abrogation of its edict could only be experienced as his or her severance from prevailing conditions, which too readily presents itself as nothing other than annihilation. Intoxication, particularly with narcotic rather than stimulating agents, rehearses the transition to a liminal zone where the self, having been surrendered, is returned more or less safely to itself each time. The escape is not into non-existence after all, but something that momentarily resembles happiness, which otherwise 'shines forth perpetually' over the stony road of subjugation and labour, 'but only as illusive appearance, as devitalised beauty'.[11]

The question arises as to what becomes, in the politically progressive tradition, of solidarity as a strategy, if collectives are always a context of terror and blind domination over their members. Solidarity as the directly realised collectivity of individuals has never existed at any social stage, *pace* Durkheim; what there has been instead is more like enforced collectivisation. If the same century at whose outset sociology expressed the hope that socialisation created genuine organic communities is also replete with examples of the successful overthrow and disso-lution of obsolete forms of authoritarianism, it is also equally replete with the forms of authoritarianism that were erected in their place. A reactionary historiographical trope often points to the terror generated by Jacobinism, Bolshevism, Maoism and other such manifestations as having its roots in the state struc-tures that these insurrectionary forces toppled, its supposedly radical variant represented by those who once tried to justify the bureaucratic tyranny of the Soviet state by pointing out that the Russian people had never really known anything else. And yet, viewed from another angle, the same argument could be reframed by emphasising that terrible conditions require a terrible demeanour in those who would seek to make them right. 'We must be terrible,' said Saint-Just, 'so that the people do not have to be' – a hopeless early wager on Freud's displacement mechanism. Nothing about the Frankfurt School critique of collectivism recommended the relapse into solipsism that existentialism preferred, in which Hell is simply the ghastliness of other people, like unsalubrious neighbours moving in next door, as opposed to the overarching abstract structure that creates Hell, and then subjects its members to infernal relations among themselves. Meanwhile, political praxis conceived on the model of abstract solidarity generates only one burst of pseudo-activity after another. The occupation of public spaces, which, during the days of the *soixante-huitards*, at least still retained a strategic objective, to prevent something appalling from happening, is reduced to a contentless outer lineament, the mood of the London Occupy movement, whose comedy-masked anti-capitalist participants proudly told the capitalist press they had no concrete political objectives at all. The declaration of Margaret Thatcher that there was no such thing as society, only individual men and women and their families, while it intended to absolve the state from its obligations in the welfare of its clients, involuntarily expressed what would be the condition of utopia, in which individuals were not yoked under the confining apparatus of the mass, but emerged only as the most shameless articulation of ideology, the hope that declaring something not to exist will effectively remove all consciousness of it, while it goes on very much existing, and shaping the beliefs and practices of those who have been persuaded no longer to believe in it. Under the abstract functional edifice of society, individuals regress to the level of Marx's *Gattungswesen*, species-beings, 'exactly like one another through isolation in the forcibly united collectivity',[12] the very condition that the liberation of the self through enlightenment was optimistically intended to transcend. The progress of human history in Hegel's conception, which is a progress in the slowly dawning realisation of freedom, and for which the reasoning self was the agent, loops back on itself into tyrannical unfreedom, because reason has not been the prerogative of the self, but instead been the counterpart and the implement of instrumental domination.

Buried at the heart of the administered society, as both its guilty secret and its motor force, is the prevalent antagonism between the principles of individuality and universality. The tendency of history by which, in the Hegelian theory, progress to freedom is becoming ever more manifest assumes that all will eventually submit, more or less willingly, to its principle, subjectively assuming it for themselves in their innermost beings. Hegel took the universal tendency to be identical with that innermost nature, an expression of it through the externalisation of human interests in the social process, but failed to see the simultaneously antagonistic effect of such a tendency, which requires individuals to submit to the collectivity as the manifest form of universality. A democratically organised state allegedly guarantees the right to individuality, but only on condition that that individuality is made forfeit to the requirements of the state, becoming as functionally nugatory as every single individual vote is in the bourgeois parliamentary system. 'Make your voice heard,' urges the voter registration campaign, in the full knowledge that merely raising his voice is the be-all and end-all of the registered voter. There is no guarantee anybody will attend to what the voice would like, even where it can be heard at all above the industrial clatter of the party machines. 'Expressed in the individuals themselves,' Adorno writes in *Negative Dialectics* (1966), 'is the fact that the whole, the individuals included, maintains itself only through antagonism'.[13] Moments when the individual sacrifices something of his own better instinct, to conform himself to the dictates of the universal, are interpreted by Hegel as meaning that the individual has reconciled himself to an objective historical process that is bigger than him, in the interest of the greater good, or through the primal urge to self-preservation as it may be, but what is falsely presented as reconciliation is, in the negative dialectical view, only greater entanglement in heteronomous force. 'The universal makes sure that the particular under its domination is not better than itself'.[14]

No society, least of all a fundamentally democratic one, can allow its individual members to become subjectively convinced of the objective hopelessness of their status. They themselves, after all, are supposedly coterminous with society. What is needed is for each individual to be able to persuade himself that his own individuality is primary to him: what he wishes is what matters most of all. It is his primal substance as an individual and, rather as Adam Smith contended that the pursuit of individual interest guarantees the economic health of the social whole, so societies that conceive themselves as free need their clients to be constantly thrown back on the basic self-preservation instinct, in order for the whole machinery to function. By this process, in reducing people to their own individual interests, it efficiently occludes their perception of the objectivity of the whole. Economic efficiency becomes nothing other than the sum total of the mass of individual interests, however much they may conflict with each other, or even prove occasionally inimical to social order. Precisely because the system reproduces the individual in a state of isolation, she can no longer see that her isolation is in itself a functional attribute of a system that forcibly unites all in their isolation. Isolation is the deindividualising of individuality, which ought to define itself against prevailing tendencies, not in oppressive accord with them. What the individual takes as her inalienable tastes and preferences have been 'predigested and supplied'[15] for her by the universal, which nonetheless hides its authorship of them, the better to keep a firm grip on her strings. Meanwhile, celebrity culture, which in Hegel's day meant victorious military commanders and bullishly dominant statesmen, but is more likely now to mean talent-show winners and the billionaire philanthropists of Silicon Valley, keeps throwing up examples of visionary individuality resulting in spectacular success, on the ideological principle that, because certain lucky types have realised the delusive dreams that everybody else is presumed to cherish, so everybody else must theoretically have an equal chance of doing the same. The relation between the individual and society has become an invariant, so that society may perpetuate itself not in the interests of the individuals, but at their expense, even while taking individuality to be its founding principle, the *principium individuationis*. As noted earlier, the category of the individual is borrowed in its late form from bourgeois exchange relations, as one of the contracting parties to all commercial transactions, in which he is limitlessly free to engage. In this way did its ubiquity become the universal principle of individualistic society, the inescapable law that all, in being subjected to their own personal self-interest, are united in a common social purpose. Precisely because it is universal is universality held to be in the right, and thus does it grant itself the privilege of not being a concept in the sense that individuality is.

Notwithstanding the monolithic nature of social universality, Adorno allows that there may be a moment of hope in that its towering edifice is still susceptible of letting chinks of light show through. What universality leaves to the individual is his own private dispositions, which may be the worst part of him, 'the evil instincts of a man imprisoned in his ego', or may equally be the critical residue that 'will not sacrifice itself to false identity'. Functionalised in virtually every aspect of his social persona, he is nonetheless still something more than the sum of those functions, and that something more is by definition what is antithetical to the power of social totality, and renders him incapable, even where he most wants to conform, of being an entirely efficient representative of the totality. 'Only as exempt from the general practice is the individual capable of the thoughts that would be required for a practice leading to change'.[16] To the Hegel of the *Philosophy of History*, what unites human beings, the moment of universality that emerges from, perhaps in despite of, their individuation is that they are all capable of knowing and thinking, whatever their temporary intentions and particular interests may be. What this turns into, however, is a 'contempt for individuality', which dialectical materialism took over from the spokesman of idealist dialectics, in which the contingency of the particular as against the necessity of the universal is transcended through the forced participation of the particular in the universal. Against the totalising menace of the universal and its rage for consensus, the individual who is able to trust both to his own experience and the consistency of his own critical perceptions is also capable of seeing the ideological untruth of the social totality: 'for the mind to perceive and to name that side of it is the first condition of resistance and a modest beginning of practice'.[17]

The tentative nature of Adorno's conclusion flies in the face of at least two centuries of oppositional political practice, which has been predicated since the call to arms in July 1789 on the premise of collective insurrection. Only a hostility to present conditions that emerges from the power of numbers and of common purpose stands a chance, in orthodox revolutionary thinking, of overthrowing the existing power structures. Freelance individual efforts are doomed to the status of lonely eccentricity, while small units of resistance are only ever likely to result in momentary outrages that confirm the status quo in its normative correctness. What happens to solidarity if all are living under what Adorno calls the spell, 'the subjective form of the world spirit, the internal reinforcement of its primacy over the external process of life'? In the subjective assumption of this primacy, people have come to believe that what there is in them that might run counter to the prevailing spell is only the residue of 'opaqueness and irrationality' that conformity has not quite eliminated.[18] It should be borne in mind crucially, though, that Adorno is not prescribing political strategy for an ideal state of consciousness, but pointing out that this is all that is available under present conditions, in which one of the aspects of universal consensus that nearly everybody has internalised is that revolutions don't work and only end in tyranny, a predilection that has its rational moment in the irresistible evidence that so many of them have. A freely associated collective of individuals might be a dynamic historical force, but where collectivism is directly commanded, as it was in the Soviet satellites and still is in the half of Korea officially styled a democratic people's republic, in requiring subordination of each individual only produces the antagonism that it must then ruthlessly suppress as a deviant tendency. The irony is that more or less everybody already accepts that they belong to the society they constitute, without that society, whatever its official political system, needing to lash them together in compulsion. 'The idea that a union of free men would constantly require them to flock together belongs to the conceptual circle of parades, of marching, flag-waving, and leaders' orations'.[19]

What drives the ruthless homogenisation of individuals in mass society, according to Adorno, is the distorted principle of equality. Egalitarianism has been the social programme of an emancipatory politics ever since it was raised to the middle term of the motto of the French Revolution, where it took its place between liberation and brotherhood, ideally enabling the latter to promote the former. Conceived against the pyramidal hierarchy of absolutist feudal rule, *égalité* was the guarantee that birth would count for nothing in the new dispensation, that nobody would be artificially privileged on the basis of blood-lineage and property-holding. As we have seen, it derived its conceptual energy from the sphere of commerce, in which a militant bourgeoisie carved out for itself the right to trade on equal terms in an open marketplace, and thereby stamped the political ideal of fair treatment with the character of the freedom of all to be exploited. There is nothing unambiguously self-recommending about the idea of equality, which can just as much inform the equitable distribution of misery as it can the removal of social handicaps to self-development. Indeed, the reified social forms of late capitalism, and the ideological apparatus of the culture industry, have arguably achieved a far more pervasive equalisation of individual value than more officially libertarian political systems have managed. The fundamental predicate of equality is fungibility, that very interchangeability written into the economic exchange process, which cares nothing for the personality traits and foibles of the consumer other than that they be moulded to fit what the racket is offering them. Anybody who appears to want something more or something different is either radically selfish or else a congenital malcontent, a diagnosis they willingly accept on the occasions when they come across anything for which they do after all, despite themselves, profess an unfathomable fondness. If there is only mute incomprehension at what the advertisers appear to presume of him, there is for all that a reassuring sense of togetherness in discovering that somebody else has the same guilty predilection for some piece of shameless trash as he himself does. Indeed, it becomes something they share, and so the incomprehension ceases to be apparent: 'What has been achieved is a false reconciliation. What should be close at hand, the "consciousness of suffering," becomes unbearably alien. The most alien thing of all, however, the process that hammers the machinery into men's consciousness and has ceased to contain anything that is human, invades them body and soul and appears to be the nearest and dearest thing of all'.[20] We shall return to the culture industry in more searching detail in chapter 4.

In the sociopolitical arena, equality is no more benevolent than it is in cultural terms. In aphorism 66 of *Minima Moralia*, 'Mélange', Adorno describes the political ideal of equality as a 'boomerang'. While it sounds like a lofty enough aspiration, often enunciated with the best of intentions, it has a habit of rebounding on its exponents. At the most fundamental level, everybody's senses of sight and hearing can tell them that people are not the same as each other. They belong to different sexes and ethnic groups and speak different languages. To Adorno, there is no particular distinction between assuming equality as a fact in an ideological manner – everybody starts out with an equal chance of becoming president of the United States – and positing it as the goal of a reformed society. 'Abstract utopia is all too compatible with the most insidious tendencies of society. That all men are alike is exactly what society would like to hear'.[21] There is a particularly complex dialectical nicety to Adorno's argument at this point. Referring to the principle on which the Nazi concentration camps were first founded, at least until Auschwitz refined their purpose to nothing other than mass extermination, he says that the function of imprisonment is to make the imprisoned into the image of their jailers, not simply according to the cynical wisdom that insists that everybody is equally guilty, the bourgeois version of original sin, but in the sense that the difference that the inmates personify, for which they were rounded up and incarcerated in the first place, is what is punishable. If the stalags and gulags have any re-educative effect at all – and increasingly, they were as pointless to those who ran them as they were to their victims – it is to turn them, in a secularised version of the theological *metanoia*, into members of the dominant side. Not much can be done in this context about ethnic differences, other than at the level of a lethal idealism. Adorno goes on: 'The racial difference is raised to an absolute so that it can be abolished absolutely, if only in the sense that nothing that is different survives'.[22] Where the individual was permitted physically to survive, just about, what he was expected to survive was himself, the incriminating remnant of his own individuality. Propounding the equality of all men, even as a utopian goal, is thus to collude with the levelling action of a society that resists heterogeneity in all its forms. Where equality does exist, Adorno suggests, is in the interests of those who dominate the arms industry or Hollywood, and which a politics concerned with liberation ought to fix in its sights, rather than raising the exchangeability of their clients and victims to an ideal. Even in Dr King's most celebrated oration, which is generally misconceived as a call to abstract egalitarianism, what properly distinguishes people is not skin colour but the deepest intentions that constitute their characters, and by which the nefarious at all levels can be distinguished from the blameless. In a rare excursion of his own into racial politics, Adorno asserts that to contend that black people are the same as whites in the American society of the mid-1940s is only to perpetuate the injustices already done to the former, who can hardly, under the pressure of society as it is, conform to the cultural aptitudes expected of white people, 'to satisfy which would in any case be a doubtful achievement'.[23] No abstract egalitarianism has yet come to light that does not harbour somewhere within itself a distaste for one or other social group, ethnic or otherwise. A British hit single of the 1960s insisted that only when the world was remade as a gigantic melting-pot, in which all differences would be dissolved into a universal cultural beige, would harmony break out. To Adorno, who didn't quite live to hear it, it could only have been an apologia for a totally administered society that, far from being a utopian dream, was already here: 'The melting-pot was introduced by unbridled industrial capitalism. The thought of being cast into it conjures up martyrdom, not democracy'.[24]

As Adorno will insist time and again, no category in thought or experience can be appealed to for what it claims to be in itself, but only through what it has become within the historical process. This is what informs his, to many commentators, notorious diagnosis of the sickness into which the principle of solidarity has fallen. At their most honourable, the forms of practical solidarity that animated the workers' movements of the late nineteenth and early twentieth centuries realised the ideal of fraternity by recovering it from its ideological status as an airy abstraction. A progressive organisation such as a trade union or party represented a cell of opposition to prevailing forces, a cell in which individual members might lay aside their own personal concerns for the greater good of social advancement, which became a palpable potential under the influence of such unity. The normative principle of self-preservation, by which each of the members of bourgeois society secured his or her own interests, was suspended, and the gains achieved by such action are not to be slighted. Indeed, there are even today sporadic examples of collective belonging producing advances not just in material conditions, but in social consciousness too. In solidarity, individuals learned more about the way of the world than an impotent isolated cynicism, despite the rectitude of its refusal, could teach anybody other than the cynic himself. The readiness to sacrifice themselves for each other, modelled progressively on the camaraderie of successful military units, is what binds solidary groups and helps win campaigns. In Adorno's account in *Minima Moralia,* such success brings out the best in groups acting concertedly, when they do so 'without being possessed by an abstract idea, but also without individual hope'.[25] In other words, solidarity depends on having concretely realisable aims, as well as the elision of immediately personal concerns. With the solidi-fication of the Party into an institution of the state in eastern Europe, solidarity sickened into a compulsion, its members ventriloquising what they thought the state power wished them to say. Its campaigns were no longer oppositional, as they were in the pre-revolutionary phase, but instead became versions of the exhortatory imperatives of those membership organisations in bourgeois society dedicated to improving morale, the workers' soviet recast as the Band of Hope. The element of compulsion, designed to enforce collective discipline, only revived the principle of bitter self-interest, in which everyone used the estab-lished system for what he could get out of it, via bribery or the currying of favour. Not for nothing are anti-corruption drives a permanent feature of societies that should have consigned nepotism to the dustbin of history at their inception. The one attempt within post-revolutionary state politics to reintroduce genuine dynamic solidarity as a motor force in society, namely the Chinese Cultural Revolution, succeeded only in uniting people through manipulative suggestion against imagined scape-goats, whether they were the despised cultural artefacts of the feudal centuries or the next-door neighbours, both of which were smashed with the same fervour. These too were 'possessed by an abstract idea', the destructive superseding of the old by a fatal idea of the new as good in itself, whereas what breathed life into real solidarity was the making concrete of an abstract idea, not in terms of its incidental by-products but in ways that exemplified it in living experience. The Leninist postulate that while people have freely fought to the death to bring about and defend communism, nobody in history ever willingly died for capitalism, had its truth content in the fact that such fighting was itself one of the concrete realisations of liberty, much as it would come to be systematically falsified when the sacrifices became a matter of administrative prescription by the state.

If the forms of collectivity that have replaced solidarity have chilled human relations to the bone, all that remains, as Adorno melancholically admits, is a kind of individual aloofness that is quite as cold as the enforced associations it sees all around it. Class relations in bourgeois society are perpetuated by the demeanour of condescension towards the joiners-in, but neither is the falsely modest avowal that one is after all the same as the rest any better. 'To adapt to the weakness of the oppressed is to affirm... the precondition of power, and to develop in oneself the coarseness, insensibility and violence needed to exert domination. If, in the latest phase, the condescending gesture has been dropped and only the adaptation remains visible, this perfect screening of power only allows the class-relationship it denies to triumph more implacably'.[26] The state of fastidious withdrawal is a social condition facilitated by the very milieu from which it withdraws, which allows a certain measure of temperamental dignity to the maverick, even while his detachment as such functions as the reinforcement of normativity. Everybody loves a character, the more so for their apparent willingness to take upon themselves an hour or two in the public pillory. An abiding cultural cliché insists that the British will forgive anything of an eccentric, even supercilious coldness, but such tolerance is less because of its heart-warming evidence of individualism than because such individuals appear to reassure the others of their place in the sanctuary of conformity. Where he is not simply mentally ill, the refusenik in society may have a greater insight into social objectivity than do its willing participants, but his status is as much guaranteed by it as theirs is. 'His own distance from business at large is a luxury which only that business confers. This is why the very movement of withdrawal bears features of what it negates. It is forced to develop a coldness indistinguishable from that of the bourgeois'.[27] Saying nothing about prevailing conditions may be no less incriminating than obstinately excoriating them: 'In the case of taciturn people, it is too often impossible to tell whether – as they would like one to believe – the depth of their inwardness shudders at the sight of anything profane, or whether their coldness has as little to say to anything as anything has to say to it'.[28] Nevertheless, it is only at the level of the individual that insight into the calamity of the totally administered society is made manifest. Capitalist exchange relations have annihilated the particularity of the individual, rather than brought about, in accordance with their own ideology, a reconciliation of individual and collective interests, and because the victory has been granted to the force of a post-individual collectivism that fancies itself the realisation of the ends – and end – of history, whatever social truth remains now resides in the consciousness of the damaged individual. 'In the period of his decay, the individual's experience of himself and what he encounters contributes once more to knowledge.' This thought drives the procedural engine of the *Minima Moralia*, with its retailing of personal occurrences, its anecdotes and confessions, to stage a critique of modern experience from a profoundly dissident, unreconciled standpoint. 'In face of the totalitarian unison with which the eradication of difference is proclaimed as a purpose in itself, even part of the social force of liberation may have temporarily withdrawn to the individual sphere. If critical theory lingers there, it is not only with a bad conscience'.[29]

In mass society, Adorno argues, individuality only acquires ontological meaning through the individual's defining himself institutionally. Interest groups, guilds, unions, freemasonries, sports clubs, societies for the promotion of virtues or the suppression of vices, in forming their members into an amalgam of like-minded souls, reproduce the enforced collectivity of the rationalised social totality. Society takes on in its own interests the bloated egoism of which it offers to relieve the individual. 'Powerless in an overwhelming society, the individual experiences himself only as socially mediated. The institutions made by people are thus additionally fetishised: since subjects have known themselves only as exponents of institutions, these have acquired the aspect of something divinely ordained... You become once again in consciousness what you are in your being in any case. Compared to the illusion of the self-sufficient personality existing independently in the commodity society, such consciousness is truth'.[30] It is only that this negative truth, in being translated into the terms of positive self-identification, becomes a lie. 'What do you do?' is the polite question that so often opens the converse of people introducing themselves to each other at a social occasion, the sociality of which is thereby a little diminished by the need to sort its participants by occupation. When the other replies that she works in finance, or the health service, or even where the response is that she is trying, whatever she does for a living, to write a novel, these subjectively assumed identities help trap her in amber, because these instantiations of the division of labour have become the reifying categories of socialisation. The division of labour, far from creating individuals by its specialisations, has only perpetuated the total social context of homogeneity to which the various functions are consecrated. Even the 'social misfit' – the graffiti artist, the eco-warrior, the inveterate negationist who views even buying insurance policies as a compromise with the prevailing racket – has his role to play. As a direct result of the identification of individuals with their social roles, the discontinuity between what they feel inside and what they are on the outside manifests itself in alienated interpersonal relations, even where such relations ought to be free of material interests, such as in love. The dignity of a relationship is that it forms a third element between two people, one amenable to the outward forms of obligation and established practice. It is this that helps them last, precisely because the alliance itself is stronger than the vagaries and vicissitudes of individual psychology, for all that it is the latter that brought the lovers together in the first place. 'That, however, does not abolish what goes on in each individual: not only moods, inclinations and aversions, but above all reactions to the other's behaviour. And the inner history stakes its claim more forcefully the less the inner and outer are distinguishable by probing... In the realm of utility every relationship worthy of human beings takes on an aspect of luxury. No one can really afford it, and resentment at this breaks through in critical situations'.[31] The truest moments in relationships are therefore those in which all the vulnerability of fear, suspicion, visceral hurt, sharpens to an internal point, but these are precisely also the moments that threaten their objective existence, in which one party accuses the other of being too demanding or neurotically mistrustful. And so in order to survive, relationships are briskly cleansed of just those aspects, now classified as dysfunctional, in which they manifest their greatest spontaneity, and exhibit the genuine freedom invested in them at the outset. Thus has rationalisation, according to Adorno, even been granted the power to write the rules of romantic attachment. 'The cleansing of human beings of the murk and impotence of affects is in direct proportion to the advance of dehumanisation'.[32]

The gravest charge laid against Adorno's critique of the fate of the individual under modern social conditions is that of undialectical simplification. Referring to the abiding example of the work of Schönberg in Adorno's aesthetic writings as the exemplum of a 'lonely subjectivity' holding out against the power of unflagging social control, Nigel Gibson raises the provocative claim that '[t]here is something almost existentialist in Adorno's privileging individual virtuosity as the authentic expression of freedom. In this binary of individual versus social, he dismisses the social individual'.[33] In this stance, Gibson finds him guilty of eliding Marx's conception of the self-production of humanity through uncoerced social labour, and only seeing instead the kind that is subjected to the principle of abstraction in capitalist exchange relations: 'in Manichean fashion Adorno equates the social with totalitarianism'. Referring to the passage on solidarity from the *Minima Moralia*, Gibson accuses Adorno of erecting a static binary opposition between 'the "identity" of totality and the social on one side, and anti-totality and the individual/monadic on the other', but this hopelessly misses the mutually informing relation between the two that animates Adorno's thinking on the social individual throughout. It isn't that Schönberg represents through his cultural production a heroic outpost of individuality amid a sea of ominously swirling social coercion; it is rather that the effect of social coercion is that it has reduced the unreconciled individual, where he remains at all still conscious of his individuality, to precisely such a tragically isolated state. The methodological procedure of negative dialectics is, in one sense, more or less as Gibson characterises it, that of monadic analysis, although he wrongly also caricatures it in scientivistic terms as 'experimental dissection', which could scarcely be further from the truth, but what this procedure illuminates is the dialectic of universal and particular, in which traces of the universal imprint themselves in the particular down to its atomic particles. Assuming that the particular is distinct from the universal, set over against it as its polar opposite, is to reproduce exactly the static conception of dialectics that results from its deformation by the exchange principle. 'Adorno's Manichean opposition of the "authentic" individual versus the social,' Gibson charges, 'leads him to dismiss all human social productivity, decontextualising alienated labour from its capitalistic context.' Quite apart from the fact that Adorno scarcely 'dismisses' social productivity, as opposed to subjecting it to sustained critical scrutiny, it is moreover specifically in the context of capitalist alienation that social productivity is criticised. Referring to the contention in the *Minima Moralia* dedication to the effect that only by opposing production itself under current conditions might human beings bring about another type of production that would be worthier of them, Gibson insists that this thought represents an abdication of the critical faculty in the face of alienated labour by a 'humanism' placed within scare quotes, thereby abstracting the humanistic principle from human life. Adorno is not an advocate of 'humanism' in the eighteenth-century sense. The German word towards which Gibson is gesturing is *Humanität*, simultaneously 'humanity' and 'humaneness', and it is precisely that quality and none other that offers a coruscating critique of what has happened to labouring individuals under capitalist social and economic relations. In what sense Gibson feels such humaneness has been 'abstracted' from human life in Adorno's argument is none too clear, but in any case the 'one-dimensional, decorporealised human being' whom he claims to find expressed in Adorno's thinking is itself a flimsy caricature. Part of the problem, as so often, lies in an unquestioning and profoundly dehistoricised reading of Marx, in whose work a distinction between labour as a conscious, purposeful activity and abstract labour under capitalism is indeed drawn. If only social conditions had been frozen in 1844 when the analysis was made, it could be upheld as a historical invariant. In fact, the economic process analysed in *Capital* twenty years later gives a more reliable guide to the direction in which capitalist economics would tend, that is, to an increasingly greater monopoly of social relations and the consciousness produced by them. The transformation of even purposeful labour into alienated labour was already suspected by Georg Lukács in *History and Class Consciousness* (1923), notwithstanding the revision made in his introduction to the 1967 edition, when, chafing under the restraints of the Hungarian party state, he acknowledged that he had muddled the respective concepts of alienation in Hegel and Marx, and come to conceive all labour as coercive and alienating. The products of labour become alienating to their producers as soon as they enter the marketplace as commodities, but in the century and a half that has passed since the theory of the fetishism of commodities, the alienation of labour through its externalisation has arguably taken on more the form of Hegel's notion of alienation through sheer externality, against the non-specificity of which the Marxist theory was conceived. Alienation has put down ever deeper roots in the social individual, as exchange relations have been progressively magnified on a global scale. Indeed, it could hardly be otherwise, since even if the forms of capitalist exchange have altered substantially since Marx's time, their underlying process of abstraction has altered not a jot. The history of labour as a category of human consciousness is the history of conceptual struggles between the notion of objectified, coercive activity, the commodification of labour power, and the concrete purposiveness of labour for use value, which last capitalism has proved itself supremely adept at assimilating. The relations of production, which should once have produced the revolt of labourers who represented the human element in them, have instead been subjected to pervasive rationalisation, such that labour itself is no longer the dual category that Marx perceived in it, a point that Gibson himself half-acknowledges when he gives, as one example among many that one could adduce of the logic of capital, '[t]he decline of leisure time and increasing overtime in the US over the past twenty years'.[34] Not even the occasional localised struggles against the hegemonisation of time by people's working lives can do anything to subdivide their labour into productive and alienated varieties, to say nothing of the tendency by which even 'leisure time' itself has now been infected by the impress of labour. As Horkheimer was to put it in a text written shortly after his joint work with Adorno on the *Dialectic of Enlightenment*, '[a] philosophy that makes labour an end in itself leads eventually to resentment of all labour'.[35]

What is left of the individual following his integration into the social totality is his psychology, which is to say whatever imperfect way he finds of dealing with his own defeat as an individual. The *Dialectic of Enlightenment* traces the origins of individuality to the conflict in antiquity between the Greek mythological hero and his tribe, notably in the trajectory of Odysseus in the Homeric epic. Standing against the accumulated and concerted cultural authority of the race, which admits of no challenge, the hero tests his own will against it and is always defeated. Only in such cultural conditions, however, the urban milieu of the city-states, was the hero able to emerge in the first place. He emerges not from the orgiastic dances of tribes on the ungovernable hillsides and in the mountain regions, but from within the securely ordered precincts of the Greek polis. The individual is a city-dweller; he presupposes urban civilisation. By the time of the European enlightenment, he has become synonymous with the reasoning faculty, the author of his own moral decisions and the investor in his own financially secured future. In the analysis of Adorno and Horkheimer, however, it is at this precise moment, the historical hour of reason's consummation, that it begins to reverse into irrationality, taking the individual with it along its backward course to myth. One of the essential elements of individuality is the antagonism between its own principle and the circumambience of socioeconomic conditions, that very antagonism being largely constitutive of the individual. The *Bildungsroman*, or novel of formation, of the enlightenment tradition shows its heroes, conceived in the dawning age of industrialism but defining their own destinies in despite of what is expected of them, pursuing a precarious but self-revealing path through life. The crisis of the individual that has happened under late capitalism derives from his being pressured irresistibly to conform to social forces, which are now as ready to smash him to ruins as the hierarchical orders of antiquity were. His first imperative is now self-preservation, and in circumstances where every individual looks after himself or herself first and foremost, all traces of individuality are suppressed. These are precisely the traits that now make it harder for them to survive, and so they must learn to live without them, other than at the most vestigial level of private preferences, temperamental quixotry and erotic quirks.

If Hamlet is traditionally held to be the model of the first modern individual, his trial of himself against his enmeshment in the murk of fate, represented by his own family, is prefigured by the judicial trial of Socrates, the earliest great enactment of the conflict between the individual and society, which the individual must lose. Simply doing what is required without self-reflection is no longer enough; the actions of a man must be refracted through the prism of his own spirit, which presents his own self-validating truth to him. His own consciousness of the objective existent world becomes transcendent over the existent world itself, with the result that, already in ancient times, in currents such as Stoicism and Epicureanism, philosophy takes on the task of compensating subjectivity for its entanglement in a community that it now relegates to secondary status. Every species of idealism that privileges the noumenal realm over the phenomenal, the ideal over the real, was prepared in the Hellenistic elevation of the individual spirit, but exactly by surrendering the material of reality to what cannot be shaped by individual will, only speculatively reflected upon by it, the individual submits himself to the tyranny of the collective, what Adorno will repeatedly call 'the merely existent'. The emancipation of the individual in modern times is wrongly looked for in his emancipation from society, whereas what would truly liberate him would be the restitution of society from its present state of atomisation.

Writing in the 1940s, Adorno delineates the fate of the modern individual in the role played by dissident émigré intellectuals in wartime exile in the United States, among whom he naturally numbered himself. Members of the Institute for Social Research based in New York, and then in California, during the intellectual diaspora of the Nazi period were heralded as 'colourful person-alities' in the American cultural milieu. Even their tempera-mental truculence became a kind of *commedia dell'arte* role: 'Their eager, uninhibited impulsiveness, their sudden fancies, their "originality", even if it be only a peculiar odiousness, even their garbled language, turn human qualities to account as a clown's costume'.[36] The parodic persona willingly assumed adapts their radical otherness to prevailing conditions in the intellectual market, where irascible dissidence turns out to be as saleable a commodity as bumbling naïveté, the assimilation and tolerance of which becomes an indicator of the broad-minded nobility of the host nation. 'Those who put their individuality on sale adopt voluntarily, as their own judges, the verdict pronounced on them by society. Thereby they justify objectively the injustice done to them'.[37] The individual endures as a piece of superseded history, a relic from the era of the rampant entrepreneur, now frozen into a character type and preserved for museum-like posterity. 'In the midst of standardised, organised human units the individual persists... But he is in reality no more than the mere function of his own uniqueness, an exhibition piece'.[38] There is a gaping chasm between the role assigned him in society and the lack of autonomy that economic conditions permit him, in which the very individuality predicated of him as an actor in the exchange mechanism is undermined by the total functional context of that mechanism itself. 'Since he no longer has an independent economic existence, his character begins to contradict his objective social role'.[39] The same point is put by Horkheimer in his chapter on the decline of the individual in *Eclipse of Reason*

(1947):

> [T]he individual subject of reason tends to become a shrunken
> ego, captive of an evanescent present, forgetting the use of the
> intellectual functions by which he was once able to transcend
> his actual position in reality. These functions are now taken
> over by the great economic and social forces of the era…
> Individuality loses its economic basis.[40]

It is what Adorno describes as 'the absolute predominance of the
economy' that inhibits any possibility of seeing the crisis of
modern individuality purely in social-psychological terms. A
psychoanalytical response to today's internalised repression is
fatally undermined not only by the fact that psychoanalysis takes
as its task the reconciliation of damaged individuals to a faulty
world, but that the very index of social-psychological health is
anyway taken to be internal adjustment to the heteronomous
norms prescribed by society. 'The regular guy, the popular girl,
have to repress not only their desires and insights, but even the
symptoms that in bourgeois times resulted from repression'.[41]
This is only achieved at the cost of a great psychic mutilation, the
evidence for which is available in the predominant phenome-
nality of supposedly healthy integration. The insight of early
psychoanalysis, that guilty secrets often lay buried precisely
where they were most affably denied, the demeanour of denial
and displacement activities, proves true in contemporary society,
where the most sordid purposes are glossed over with an air of
cheery resignation, and 'the inferno in which were forged the
deformations' of brainless sunny-naturedness and quiescent
acceptance of what will happen anyway remains untapped now
by psychoanalytical investigation. If adaptation to existing
circumstances is a psychic survival mechanism – one that
perhaps, Adorno speculates, even pre-exists the emergence of the
neuroses from instinctual repression – it appears to have come

about as a means of fooling the self into thinking that, by means of its accepting external conditions equably for what they are, the conflict within them has already thereby been resolved, rather than having been penetrated by the daylight of genuine knowledge. 'It is what it is,' people say, when they are confronted with a set of circumstances or polemical proposition to which they have no adequate response, but whose overwhelming imperative over them they wish to cheat of its predominance by pretending to the bogus profundity of an insight into it, albeit one that is nothing better than an unblushing tautology. The placid demeanour demanded of job applicants in their interviews and once appointed, in the work situations that require them to be 'calm under pressure', is required as a means of demon- strating that they will take anything thrown at them without making trouble. These deformations are physiognomically visible in the deathless radiance that serial adjusters display: 'The very people who burst with proofs of exuberant vitality could easily be taken for prepared corpses, from whom the news of their not-quite-successful decease has been withheld for reasons of population policy'.[42] Society as a whole has taken on the sickness once isolated in troubled individuals, and abolished the idea of sickness precisely by universalising it into a parodic idea of health. In what modern ethical philosophy has come to read as one of his more notorious diagnoses, Adorno claims that even the way technology and contemporary design require their users to operate their products has assisted in the production of a new anthropological type of humankind. Car doors that have to be slammed, doorknobs that have to be wrenched around, window panels that have to be shoved upwards or sideways, rather than opened outwards as casement windows once were, all require a gestural violence that suits the repressed pathology of the century of Auschwitz: 'The movements machines demand of their users already have the violent, hard-hitting, unresting jerkiness of fascist maltreatment'.[43] In a complex extrapolation of this thought, Adorno goes on to say when the human encounter with objects is reduced to the simple effect of their functionality, when all that is left is simply to use them long enough only to operate them, the complexity of experience in the potential range of its interactions with the objective world becomes a bedraggled parody of itself. Only an experience that 'is not consumed by the moment of action' would be truly worthy of the name of experience. In the twenty-first century, the violent jerkiness has become the button-pushing, keyboard-tapping repetitiveness with which virtually all operational and communicative functions are carried out, the violent shoving having been replaced by the extension of bureaucratised anonymity to the private home as much as to the workplace. The evidence is written all over social media, the messages in which are tapped out by people who think, much as they read, where they do the latter at all, only with their fingertips.

It is important to see the differences between this analysis and a standard humanist account that looks for the roots of the malformation of the individual in a social pressure that beguiles each one with the thought that they could be somebody else. This is a diagnosis put forward by Zygmunt Bauman. People are encouraged to see their pre-given selves as inadequate, and instead opt for one of the alternative identities offered them by the culture industry. 'What is really new,' he argues, 'is the twin dream of escaping from one's own self and acquiring a made-to-order self; and a conviction that making such a dream a reality is within reach'.[44] Even if what Bauman really intended was the complementary sartorial metaphor of an off-the-peg identity, the error is to constitute the individual as having a pre-given self specific to himself, from which social pressure has coaxed him to release his grip. If there is a pre-given self, it is the self precisely given by society, and the swindle would consist in the individual's transition from one socially prescribed persona to another, in which he imagines he is engaged in an act of creative self-fashioning, not from some allegedly true authentic self to a socially conformed one. In any case, the freedom of the individual, as it was delineated in the plot vicissitudes of the *Bildungsroman*, is that he found out by degrees who he was in relation to the world at large, by a mixture of accommodation and resistance to its norms, whereas what Bauman's individual ought to be content with is the self he was given, instead of trying on different ones in society's fashion-store. The point is, among other nuances, an implied critique of celebrity culture, which culture stands in itself as a gigantic indictment of the misery of everyday existence, from which it promises the hopeful an escape, while concealing its own share of complicity in the misery, but about the fact that everyday existence is miserable, for an abundance of socioeconomic reasons, it is quite right. A humanism that counsels reconciliation to the pre-given is inhumane, and its condemnation of the utopian impulse as delusive allies it powerfully with all conservatism, which likes nothing better than to hear that people don't really believe in an ideal world. The offer of the dream becoming reality currently available is correctly skewered as a tasteless imitation of utopia, but that does not mean that hoping for a transformation of the existing state of things is reprehensible. Indeed, if everybody were to take the view derided by Bauman – in other words, if his critique was of individualism itself rather than individual aspiration – society might have survived its totalitarian delusional phase and become truly the context for a realisation of its members' interests.

What Adorno's theory of the social construction of the individual emphasises is that the process is twofold. It is brought to bear both externally, as an undialectical humanism would acknowledge, in the circumscriptions and privations that everyday duties exert on the individual, but also internally too, so that what people think they want is nothing other and nothing more than what society wants them to want. The result is a tantalisingly bifurcated relation to reality characterised by the general condition of unfreedom. What people are in their inner nature is determined by social coercion. Whether they consider themselves to be formally free or unfree in the political sense is not in itself a primary determination, for all that it produces an acuteness of suffering in circumstances of extreme repression. These thoughts are among the most controversial in Adorno's critique of the concept of freedom in Kantian ethics. 'For the ego,' he writes, 'makes even the insight into its dependence difficult to gain for the subjective consciousness'.[45] It is precisely because people constitute themselves as individuals in the ideological sense that they succumb all the more readily to social heteronomy, which needs the myth of the subject's autarchy to perpetuate itself. 'The principle of individualisation, the law of particularity to which the universal reason in the individuals is tied, tends to insulate them from the encompassing contexts and thereby strengthens their flattering confidence in the subject's autarchy.' By convincing themselves they are autonomous individuals, whether as citizens of western consumer society or of authoritarian regimes hell-bent on repressing their individuality, it is individuality itself, raised to the status of a historical invariant, that gives the lie to the conception of their formal freedom. 'Under the name of freedom, their totality is contrasted with the totality of whatever restricts individuality.' In other words, individuality is seen as a precious immutable essence that is under threat and must be protected, something of which is gestured towards in pop philosophy's favoured platitude of 'what it means to be human', as though what it means to be human might never have changed since mudbrick dwellings began to accumulate in the river basins of the Near East. Freedom cannot be guaranteed through an appeal to the individuality principle because that principle is 'by no means the metaphysically ultimate and unalterable'. The paradox thus arises, acutely so during the libertarian social revolutions of the 1960s, that the insistence on individuality against a society that requires conformism of its members, if they are to survive at all, is an even more precise calibrator of objective unfreedom than is conformity itself. Defining oneself as ruggedly autonomous in the midst of ovine acquiescence requires the very acquiescence that it wants to stand out from; if there were no general herd instinct, there would be no herd to wander away from, and individuality would shrivel to nothing. The double nature of this paradox consists in the fact that the individual at once feels himself suffocated by a society from which he needs at all costs to demarcate himself, while at the same time the very fact that he feels its essence is alien to him is in itself the indication of his alienation from it, which is no more a defiant act of choice than was the pilloried miscreant's putting his head in the stocks, and yet that ideology of freely choosing is just what bourgeois liberalism celebrates in its own deluded conception of individualism. As Adorno puts it, '[t]he individual's independence, inappropriately stressed by liberal ideology, does not prevail; nor is there any denying his extremely real separation from society, which that ideology misinterprets'.[46]

There are historical moments, Adorno allows, in which individuals have opposed their own particular interests to those of society, as distinct from those moments when a whole class or sector of society has done so. In the former case, where a gross injustice has been highlighted, for example, the question of whether society permits individuals to be truly free has been put directly to it, and carries with it the challenge as to whether society as a whole is therefore free or not. The problem with these discrete moments is that, even where the injustice is ameliorated, but especially when it isn't, the effect is only to reassure the social totality that it is the only court of appeal. 'Temporarily, the individual looms above the blind social context, but in his windowless isolation he only helps so much more to reproduce that context'.[47] Naively opposing itself to the social context, the individual ego overlooks its own conditioning by it, in defiance of the otherwise correct insight in Hegel's *Phenomenology of Spirit* (1807) that it is only when it perceives itself in its own otherness that the subject comes to know itself. Freedom and unfreedom are tightly entwined with each other, in that freedom can only authentically arise from a three-dimensional perception of its own conditioning by unfreedom. In conditions of the domination of nature, and the hierarchical domination of people in social stratification, the archetypal image of freedom comes to be the ruler, the entrepreneur, the manipulator of capital reserves and labour power, one who is not contractually or financially dependent on those beneath him, and this is what sets in stone the idea that individual freedom would be the outcome of a tussle for supremacy. In Kant's conception, argued in the *Groundwork of the Metaphysics of Morals* (1785), freedom divorced from causality is what induces even the most nefarious elements in society to award themselves the credit of a feeling of enhanced self-satisfaction by acting benevolently and altruistically. Freedom is coupled with the idea of moral worth, of self-exaltation, but with freedom comes the responsibility to act morally, which life amid the acquisitive bourgeois society of the mercantilist age systemically undermines. 'Through an apologia for its perverted form,' Adorno claims, 'society encourages the individuals to hypostatise their individuality and thus their freedom'.[48] Where psychological conditions such as obsessive-compulsive disorder or cyclical paranoia have set in, they are the objective indicators of the fact that the subject's sense of its own freedom has failed it, and its inner nature is as much subject to general irrational coercion as is the consecration of its physical potential to alienated labour. Acting not autonomously but reactively is what undermines the ego's conception of itself as a free individual, despite the delusion that the repetitive behaviour in neurotic compulsions is the way the ego convinces itself that it is taking control. 'And yet,' Adorno adds, 'what would be equally free is that which is not tamed by the I as the principle of any determination'.[49] If the individual consciousness could be liberated from needing to feel it was exercising its rule, like a royal prerogative, over externality, it might stand a chance of being itself less subject to the external in which it is so helplessly entangled, whether neurotically or not. 'People are unfree because they are beholden to externality, and this externality in turn consists also of people themselves'.[50] Liberation would not consist simply in reversing the arrangement so that externality was beholden to the individual, but in a release from the relation of subjection either way, as long as it is not predicated on the fallacy of freedom from the external altogether. 'Detached from the object,' says Adorno, 'autonomy is fictitious'.[51]

The narrative outlined over the twenty-year period from the *Dialectic of Enlightenment* to the *Negative Dialectics*, which tells of the progress of domination from the mastery of natural forces to the mastery of the weaker elements of society to the final sway of heteronomy over the inner natures of individuals, is criticised by some commentators for its insufficient complexity, and for its inadequate attention to the historically changing relations between inner and outer nature, between nature and human history. These are criticisms levelled notably by Joel Whitebook (in *Perversion and Utopia*, 1995) and by JM Bernstein (*Adorno: Disenchantment and Ethics*, 2001). In the standard Freudian model, human history is a process of the victory of the instinct for self-preservation over the pleasure principle, and the renunciation of libidinal impulses within the structure of the superego is just what is constitutive of social development as a whole, according to Freud's late text, *Civilisation and Its Discontents* (1930). Adorno's writings show a complicated relationship with psychoanalytic theory, sometimes appearing to accept its fundamental tenets, especially with regard to analysis of the neuroses, as unquestionably given. A large part of the critical uproar generated by his

Philosophy of New Music (1949) focused on the psychoanalytic treatment in its second half of the works of Stravinsky. Nonetheless, he retained an incisive historicising critique of the putative invariance of Freudian categories, particularly that of the ego, and he uses the key Freudian concept of narcissism to fashion a central plank of his critique of present-day society. Far from maintaining an unbridgeable gap between self-preservation and the libido, Adorno suggests that the former has become imprisoned within the latter in the context of reified society, so that people actively wish, as a matter of narcissistic identification, for what is going to be done to them anyway, despite the fact that what is done to them is the very means by which desire itself is cauterised. Alastair Morgan summarises the point thus: 'The problem is not so much the feeling of helplessness in the face of an all-powerful society, because the ego as ego can articulate and express this feeling, but the narcissistic ego falls in love with its own situation of helplessness, such that it doesn't recognise the situation for what it is, it cannot "experience or confront [this] helplessness"'.[52] It is through this process that reification becomes deeply rooted within social subjectivity, which is a considerably more complex postulate than the one-dimensional account of instinctual repression that Whitebook sees in Adorno's theory. Furthermore, there is no rigid differentiation for Adorno between nature and history, inasmuch as history hitherto has for him been only the extension of natural history that Marx saw in it. Until it can be freed somehow from the buried imperative of self-preservation, it cannot earn the status of a properly human history. He recuperates this notion from Hegelian Marxism in his lecture series on 'History and Freedom' (1964–5), where the story of human development is metaphorised as a giant roused from slumber, which then storms forth into the world and tramples over everything in its path. 'Human history proper can only begin,' as Fabian Freyenhagen encapsulates it, 'once we really have emancipated ourselves from the dominant influence exerted by the drive for self-preservation – once the giant awakes [again] and "human beings become conscious of their own naturalness and call a halt to their own domination of nature, a domination by means of which nature's domination is perpetuated"'.[53]

The axial concept, much addressed in recent Adorno scholarship, is the question of redemption. In addressing what might begin to loosen the reified structures of experience within capitalist society at the level of the individual, Adorno mobilises a concept from theology, one that had already been put to secular use by Benjamin in the idea of the irruption of messianic time into what the latter calls the 'empty homogeneous time' of history. Messianic time is what will arrest the churn of historical time, which ceaselessly washes over humankind as its collective victim. In the era of direct political praxis, the task of revolutionary activity is precisely to stop time in its tracks, not accelerate it, the fundamentally misconceived notion, given the name of accelerationism by a recent critic, Benjamin Noys,[54] that if only capitalism's inherent tendencies were to be speeded up, they would implode under their own contradictions and leave a charred but liberated residue behind that could then be called a post-capitalist society. In Adorno's thinking, notably in the famous final aphorism of the *Minima Moralia*, redemption serves something of the same function that it does in Benjamin, but with the proviso in the era that has intervened after the great revolutionary struggles appear to have failed, that redemption takes on the character of the hypothetical, but nonetheless realisable, postulate that it has in apocalyptic eschatology. 'The only philosophy that can be responsibly practised in face of despair is the attempt to contemplate all things as they would present themselves from the standpoint of redemption. Knowledge has no light but that shed on the world by redemption: all else is reconstruction, mere technique'.[55] The theologian Jacob Taubes argues that, by making redemption emphatically a hypothesis, it is in effect an aestheticisation of the idea, both in the sense that

Adorno literally forces the notion of redemption to migrate to the sphere of aesthetics, and also in the sense that, as a hypothesis, it reduces redemption itself to the status of indifference, a mere paradigm function similar to the programmatic content of parables, thought experiments or moral fables. After giving the aphorism in full, Taubes hears only the echo of the final clause as a predicative judgment: 'the question of the reality or unreality of redemption itself,' Adorno suggests, 'hardly matters'.[56] For Taubes, this is 'an aestheticisation of the problem', which becomes 'a *comme si*, an as-if. It hardly matters whether it's real'.[57] What Adorno has argued, however, is that the standpoint of redemption places thought itself in an all but untenable aporia. It must simultaneously take up a position a hair's breadth beyond damaged life in a reified society if it is not to surrender itself to the force of the existent, and thereby simply propagate every 'distortion and indigence' of the present world, and yet accept that there is no such position, because any such knowledge 'must be first wrested from what is, if it is to hold good'. How does a critical, self-reflexive thought, immersing itself in current reality, produce a mirror-image obverse of the current faulty world without being infected by the very conditions in which it is immersed, and which it wishes to criticise? 'The more passionately thought denies its conditionality for the sake of the unconditional, the more unconsciously, and so calamitously, it is delivered up to the world. Even its own impossibility it must at last comprehend for the sake of the possible'.[58] It is in comparison with the non-negotiable contradiction inherent in that dilemma that what concrete form redemption might take, if indeed there is one, 'hardly matters'. This is less a judgment on the operativity of the theological concept than it is on its status as set against the task with which thought must perforce confound itself. This is not, as in Taubes' purblind reading, a refusal of redemption *per se*, otherwise it would not form the central balancing fulcrum of this aphorism. That there has to be a redemptive thought in faulty reality is not in question for Adorno; it is only that its application to the lineaments of the fallen world entangles critical consciousness in a further set of practical difficulties from which nothing in either faulty reality or redemption itself can extricate it. In orthodox Judeo-Christian theology, one would argue that the redemption promised by the divine must be held before the gaze of a suffering humanity as the eventual fulfilment of the messianic, but at the same time, nothing in present reality reflects it, and nor should it be or could it be concretely figured, precisely because it would then partake hopelessly of the very reality that needed redemption, and from which it was offering the escape-route. A true dialectical thought needs to guard vigilantly against what, in the previous aphorism, Adorno calls an 'apologetic, restorative element' in thinking, by which it might fatally try to reconcile human beings to the present degraded state of affairs, producing the effect of a profane theodicy in which people 'accommodate themselves to the given constellation and do what is asked of them'.[59] Contra Taubes, Adorno is not claiming that redemption is not possible, only that establishing whether it actually exists or not is less important than presuming it does, because nothing else can save us.

Alastair Morgan is correct in his notation of Adorno's notion of redemption as 'a constructed experience, not an adopted posture'.[60] The same would be true of an orthodox theological apprehension of the redemptive impulse, where it ought to fulfil the function of an openness to the conception of a changed state of things, in which the threadbare present would be recuperated, as against the exposition of a policy, to which degraded forms of evangelical Christianity have reduced it. The best chance of achieving a transformed view of the present is the immersion in objectivity that *Negative Dialectics* calls for, not in the sense of a surrender to what there is as it is, but in the sense of conceiving the critical objects of thought immanently, illuminating the ways in which the object has historically appeared within the subject, the task succinctly stated in the Preface to that work as 'us[ing] the strength of the subject to break through the fallacy of constitutive subjectivity',[61] as the latter is conceived in Kantian transcendental idealism. Experience awaits redemption by a thought that would reflect the fallibility of such experience in its own substance. 'Life does not live,' according the Ferdinand Kürnberger epigraph that appears at the head of Part One of the *Minima Moralia*, but it does follow what Adorno characterises as 'a wavering, deviating line' which, under current conditions, may well plot the contours of a transformed existence, however improbable of fulfilment it currently appears, precisely by its falling short of it. There is always the consciousness of something missing, which is the guilty conscience of unrealised thought. Adorno's analogy is with the school lessons that one decided to miss for the sake of luxuriously staying in bed, which nonetheless imprinted on the truant the awareness that he would never make up the ground he had thereby lost. 'Thought waits to be woken one day by the memory of what has been missed,' Adorno writes, 'and to be transformed into teaching',[62] into enlightened instruction on how to build the better world imprisoned in thought.

Two

History, Philosophy, Politics

Universal history must be construed and denied. After the catastrophes that have happened, and in view of the catastrophes to come, it would be cynical to say that a plan for a better world is manifested in history and unites it.
Negative Dialectics

The historical epoch bounded by Hegel's late philosophical history lectures and the valetudinarian epic of Spengler represents the high-water mark of programmatic historiography. In conceiving history as having a theme, which the events and personages that form its fabric exist to extrapolate, to realise in concrete form, the nineteenth century sought as no other before it to subject the vicissitudes of human affairs to schematic exposition. To the late Romantic generation and those who came after, the philosophy of history served the same function as early modern theodicy did in the works of Leibniz. Where once the combined fates of the human and the natural worlds justified the ways of God to humanity, philosophy of history after Hegel fulfilled the office of a narrative progress towards humankind's own enlightenment, its liberation to reason and freedom from the ancient bondages of primordial terror, tyrannical authority, institutionalised slavery and the dictates of the ecclesium. Marx and Engels urged industrial society on towards its metamorphosis in the self-production of proletarian consciousness, a collective self-unshackling of dynamic social forces. Nietzsche diagnosed a fatal etiolation at the heart of the most advanced European cultures, precisely by dint of their subsumption of generative will under the principle of the collective, the herd instinct, prophesying that only a rumbustious, bleakly heroic individualism could undo its fetters – for the heroic individual, that is. Spengler then arrived, like the priest at the deathbed of western culture, to ratify the moribund state of the patient by pronouncing the extreme unction. Suddenly, in the aftermath of the Great War and the failure of revolution in the heart of Europe, the intellectual fashion had turned from narratives of victorious liberation to accounts of decline and fall. The destination of western history, the Faustian grasp at an infinitude of scientific knowledge and artistic possibility, turned out to be a *terminus ad quem* at which its passengers had been deposited homeless, the arc of human development evaporating above it as it thinned in its extension across the firmament. Twenty years after Spengler, in the *Dialectic of Enlightenment,* as we saw in chapter 1, Adorno and Horkheimer resituated the roots of modern alienation in the triumph of instrumental reason, through the enthronement of abstract rationality over subjective experience, a phenomenon instantiated above all in the apparatus of mass deception represented by the culture industry of capitalist modernity.

In contrast to the foregoing *Weltalter* (*Ages of the World*) of Friedrich Schelling, Hegel looks for the motor forces of history not in obscure theosophical reclamations of its divine beginning, but in the objective development of human societies. There is, to be sure, a divine component in Hegel's history, but it is the benevolence of a God overseeing his people's progression towards self-realisation, not the mysterious and unknowable demiurge of Schelling's systematic fancy. Hegel's account of historical development is highly schematic but it is not, in Schelling's sense, a pure system. It does not conform to invariable and predictable pathways, but it does display an overall tendency towards the concretion of freedom, however halting and circuitous the progress towards it may be. The often-excised Introduction to the *Philosophy of History*, published posthumously in 1837, sets out a framework for the interpretation of history that is founded on the three principal types of geographical environment: arid elevated highlands with their extensive steppes and plains, where nomadic peoples live; the river plains where the first great centres of settled civilisation arose; and the coastal regions that have immediate access to seas and oceans. To these correspond their respective sociocultural formations. On the barren steppes of central Asia, in the Near Eastern deserts and the rarefied altitudes of the South American plateaux are static subsistence cultures, which at best do no more than send out emissaries of themselves to a wider world of which they know practically nothing. On the irrigated valley plains, nascent civilisation came to being with its restricted sense of spiritual independence and its profoundly hierarchical agrarian societies, such as those of China, India, Babylon and Egypt. Finally, civilisation achieves its most spectacular advances when, arriving at the coastal edges, it sees not merely the attenuation of the land but the boundless world of possibility opened by transit across the waters, for navigation, commerce and conquest. The great maritime thoroughfare of the Mediterranean orients the efflorescence of western culture through the Athenian, Roman and Renaissance periods, a wave of acculturation that sweeps from Europe's southern heartlands into the centre and north – France, Germany and Britain – and then north-eastwards into the Slavonic culture areas. On to these geographically contiguous and temporally successive sectors can be roughly mapped the progress of the World Spirit, via reason, towards the consciousness of freedom. In the most primitive societies, such as those of oriental despotism and the savagery of the sub-Saharan interior of Africa, freedom is available only to the *one*, the ruler, the tyrant, the tribal leader, to whom all must pay obeisance, from blood-tribute and sacrifice to unquestioning ritual subservience. In the Greek and Roman worlds, *some* are free, the citizens of democratic, aristocratic or military polities who have some claim to be heard in forums and public assemblies, tribunals, courts of law, while the rest are born to or sold into slavery. At the highest and most recent level, in the constitutional monarchies of the Germanic and Anglo-Saxon worlds, in the home of unfettered general will, *all* are free, equal before the law, their subjective liberty realised objectively in the institutional form of the state. In Shakespearean mode, Hegel compares the separate stages of historical development to the ages of human beings. Central Asian nomadism would be the uncomprehending childhood of human history, the Greek period its idealistic adolescence, the Roman era its mature adulthood, in its acceptance of the rigour of hard labour and legal duty, and the culminating Germanic phase its transition to old age, in which the experience and self-understanding of the spirit are of more moment than the enfeeblement suffered by physical nature. 'Freedom has found the means of realising its concept and its truth,' says Hegel. 'This is the goal of world history.'[1]

Whatever the evident simplicity of this account, it is vital to note that these phases are not simply the nodes of a seamless linear progress, like stations along a railway route, but are the sites of often violent and convulsive transformations. In coming into its own, spirit negates itself in its previous form. Something of it must perish in order for the progressive moment in it to proceed, and in this it bears all the hallmarks of the dialectical process made flesh. It is the capacity for contradiction inherent in its opposite poles that produces the continuous evolution of conceptual thinking, a procedure in which sudden advances encounter, and are often checked by, the resistance of retrenchment, before retrenchment itself gives way to further opposition. Linking the dialectical process and historical development in Hegel's work, Adorno puts it thus:

The Hegelian concept of the dialectic acquires its specific character, and distinguishes itself from shallow versions in vitalist philosophy... through its movement in and through the extremes: development as discontinuity. But it too arises from the experience of an antagonistic society; it does not originate in some mere conceptual schema. The history of an unreconciled epoch cannot be a history of harmonious development: it is only ideology, denying its antagonistic character, that makes it harmonious. Contradictions, which are its true and only ontology, are at the same time the formal law of a history that advances only through contradiction and with unspeakable suffering. Hegel referred to history as a 'slaughterbench'...[2]

And yet Adorno's later critique of the Hegelian conception of history, outlined in his 1964–65 lecture course at Frankfurt on the topic of 'History and Freedom', turns on the suggestion that Hegel subverts his own dialectics of the mutual realisation of the universal and the particular by theorising the movements of history on the basis of what ultimately transpires in it, thus privileging the universal and falling into the trap of writing history from the standpoint of the victors. Whatever there was of particularity in the outcome of historical events is subsumed by an exclusive focus on outcomes rather than processes. That said, this tendency does at least have the virtue of qualifying Hegel as a realist, in that he is fundamentally aware of the preponderance of the universal in present conditions.

As regards the progress of reason in history, the self-realisation of which is for Hegel the motive force of historical development, Adorno takes a darker view. If reason has liberated itself from the specificity of each individual's impulse to self-preservation, it has only been in order to give itself over to the countervailing interests of the collective, as indeed is mirrored in the evolution of philosophy. As Adorno puts it in the lecture-course:

[T]he idea of species-reason, that is, the form of reason that comes to prevail universally, already contains, by virtue of its universality, an element restricting the individual; and in certain circumstances this element can develop in such a way as to turn into an injustice on the part of the universal towards the particular, and hence in turn to the predominance of particularity. Thus, on the one side, reason can liberate itself from the particularity of obdurate particular interest but, on the other side, fail to free itself from the no less obdurate particular interest of the totality.[3]

The spirit of the subjective consciousness is at once the product of the emergence of the individual with the rise of the bourgeoisie, and at the same time is subjugated by the overarching victorious World Spirit. In this, and not only this, Hegel's thought reveals its origins in Kant, where individual critical voices raised in this or that concrete ethical situation must ultimately always give ground to the categorical imperative. On the other hand, one of the unavoidable moments of truth in Hegel's conception, according to Adorno, is that even though individuals are crushed by the principle of totality in the momentum of history, it is agonisingly only through conceiving itself as a totality that humankind has managed to survive, right down to the era of the European dictatorships. What can be rescued from the apparent structural determinations of Hegelian history is the emergence of the idea that underpins all universal history. There may be a multitude of factual inaccuracies in Hegel's account of the progressive self-realisation of freedom through the stages of history, traced as we saw in the notion of freedom of the One in oriental despotism, of Some in classical antiquity and then of All – at least potentially – in the modern Germanic constitution, and yet there is a core of formal truth to it in its outline of the subjective progress of freedom. In oriental societies, it may well have been, Adorno suggests, that the only way to endure the impress of autocracy really was to externalise one's own suffering, which renders to autocracy the measure of its power, into the homogeneous totality that oriental philosophy made of its societies. The fate of the individual, as we saw in the preceding chapter, is the elided element in universal history. In Athens and Rome, the development of a sense of individuality was only permitted to a relatively small segment who constituted the slave-owning class, and was therefore scarcely more than an incidental adjunct to these societies. In the conception of individuality precisely as distinct from the social whole, it can only ever be a stunted growth, something reserved for private citizens, in the privative context of which it inevitably withers. This is as true in the bourgeois era as it was in the time of Epicurus. 'Within repressive society,' Adorno argues in *Minima Moralia*, 'the individual's emancipation not only benefits but damages him. Freedom from society robs him of the strength for freedom. For however real he may be in his relations to others, he is, considered absolutely, a mere abstraction.'[4] Christianity, with its conception of the individual soul earning and awaiting its salvation, is what helped the concept of individuality to saturate the consciousness of the whole of late Roman society and undermine its elitism. That in turn was then replaced in the early modern era by the individual as the constitutive element of the economic exchange principle in bourgeois society, which has led directly to the grave crisis of the individual in the present age. If universal history fell into disrepute in the early years of the twentieth century under the impact of positivism and its insistence on the brute heterogeneous facts of the various matters, historiography forfeited its capacity for taking the long view, as is evidenced by the present fashion for micro-histories of all kinds. And then again, historical materialism would be failing in its duty if it did not point out that an ontological universal history can so easily subside into ideology where it dismisses the discontinuities of which ontic history is woven. Adorno points out in the section on the Hegelian philosophy of history in *Negative Dialectics* that Hegel himself had conceived universal history as being unified precisely by reason of its contradictions.

The way was already prepared in Hegel's late lectures for a materialism that would come to insist that concept and reality are not axiomatically bound together under conditions of domination. Nonetheless, the two are not mutually exclusive. To throw out what appears as the murky bathwater of historical metaphysics is also to lose the baby of history's material essence:

> [D]iscontinuity and universal history must be conceived together. To strike out the latter as a relic of metaphysical superstition would spiritually consolidate pure factuality as the only thing to be known and therefore to be accepted; it would do this exactly in the manner in which sovereignty, aligning facts in the order of the total march of One Spirit, used to confirm them as the utterances of that spirit.[5]

If nothing at all can be predicated of the contingencies of history as between one era and the next, or for that matter between antiquity and the convulsions of yesterday, human beings are after all surrendered to historical fate, which appears as anything but contingent in the era when the final discontinuity, that which separates all individuals from the overall social context they are told they constitute, reigns supreme.

The happy periods in history, which history itself appears to have overlooked, are the 'blank pages' in Hegel's account, because the antithesis to what prevails in them is absent. There is no struggle between opposing principles and therefore no development. Not only does reason only proceed through the self-overcoming of each historical epoch, but it does so also by refusing, or leaving behind, those periods and cultures that do nothing other than reflect a state of nature. Just as organic processes do nothing other than repeat the same eternal cycles, each attainment of maturity only the teleologically determined expression of what was already implicit at the first germination of the seed, so human societies would atrophy and stagnate if they developed only along securely predictable lines. This is the non-deterministic element in what is often wrongly seen as a deterministic philosophy of history. The progressive development of the World Spirit is a progress by means of determinate negation, in which spirit produces itself through the successive interruptions and mediations of consciousness. Paul Nadal puts this point as follows: 'The principle of development in the world of spirit contains within itself a fundamental hindrance, which consciousness must overcome in order to move from potentiality to actuality, that is, to actualise its concept in development, and in so doing move into a higher form.'[6] For Adorno, it is exactly the idea of the historical process realising itself over people's heads that constitutes the reversal of freedom into unfreedom. The essence of freedom must be a certain spontaneity, the exercise of will in the midst of heteronomy, and yet in the conditions of externalised reason, in which freedom has allegedly objectified itself in the form of the constitutional state, freedom has attained the status of what Hegel had consigned to the garbage – 'bare desire, volition in its crude and savage form'. Freedom persists as a foreign body in conditions of the utmost conformity, but it has become one of the elements that instrumental reason, which has willed not only the state and its laws, but also a form of human collectivity germane to them in the shape of bourgeois society, is impelled to annihilate. Whatever does not exhibit an essential continuity with the existent, from Webern's orchestral pieces to the recalcitrant individual, has become the enemy of a reason grown to dimensions that Hegel could scarcely have guessed at. The consciousness of freedom itself, to which all history has theoretically tended from the hominin's first preference of one particular reproductive mate over another, has produced in modern times the consciousness that freedom itself is one of the stages of society to be determinately negated, swept aside by an immanent tendency within the very society that produced it. To be sure, had he been living at

this hour, Hegel might have prophesied that the totally administered world of the present day was only another wrong turning,
doomed to be superseded by the next transformation in the
consciousness of freedom. A time in which the progress of
freedom is cloaked in the habiliments of its merciless elimination,
not by overt repression as in the despotic highlands, but by
inducing free peoples to internalise the acceptance of their own
unfreedom as the price of social self-preservation, is after all a
time in which the cunning of reason has assumed its most artful
form.

What lies beneath the doctrine of the triumphal advance of the
World Spirit is the submission of the weak in their defeat to the
more powerful. The outcome of historical events, whatever has
transpired and supervened in them, becomes the transcendent
form of the spirit. There is something of the dialectical interde-
pendence espoused in Hegel's method, as between the universal
and particular, in the relation of universal historical tendencies
and particular human interests, but the latter are the vehicles of
the former, which in some anthropomorphic sense uses them for
its own ends.

> This vast congeries of volitions, interests, and activities,
> constitute the instruments and means of the world spirit for
> attaining its goal, of elevating it to consciousness, and making
> it reality. And the goal is none other than finding itself,
> coming to itself, and contemplating itself as reality... [T]hose
> vibrancies of individuals and peoples, in that they seek and
> satisfy their own purposes, are, at the same time, the means
> and instruments of a higher and broader purpose of which
> they know nothing – which they realise unconsciously.[7]

It is the conception of this process, however, that ought to be
foreign to the dialectical procedure, which in the effect of
sublation, *Aufhebung*, maintains something of that which had

been overcome, rather than simply obliterating it in its supremacy. '[T]he fact that dialectically one moment needs the other, the moment contradictorily opposed to it,' Adorno writes, 'this fact, as Hegel knew well but liked to forget on occasion, reduces neither moment to a μή όv [non-being].'[8] Instead, the World Spirit becomes a being-in-itself, the manifestation of a transcendent universal principle that absorbs particularity but negates it as an abstract category at the same time.

When Marx applied this analysis to the economic structure of society in the *Foundations of the Critique of Political Economy*, the work known as the *Grundrisse*, abandoned in 1858, he gave the whole conception an all-important further dialectical twist. The principle of exchange value subsumes all products and activities within the overall context of the capitalist mode of production, a system in which all the parts become interdependent, both in the spheres of production and of consumption, until exchange value becomes the universal mediator of all relations and thereby a constant necessity. The chief effect of the system is to reproduce itself. In the conception of classical economics, typified by Adam Smith's invisible hand, the universal pursuit of private interests by both owners and their employees in the production system guarantees the successful promotion of the general interest, capitalism's version of the Holy Spirit moving in mysterious ways. Marx first scoffs at this argument by saying that the sum total of private interests is nothing but that, the entirety of private interests, not the general interest, and also points out that there is no particular reason to view the simultaneous pursuit of interests as mutually supportive as opposed to mutually obstructive, so that the overall result is negative rather than positive. The salient point, however, which Hegel proved unable to perceive, is that private interests themselves do not pre-exist economic relations but are themselves socially determined. There are no terms on which one can pursue one's interests, nor any means for realising them, other than those set down inescapably in the social relations of the economy, which therefore inevitably means that interests are always tied to the reproduction of the social structure. Capitalism in this sense is a gigantic tautology. Through its social and economic mechanisms, it generates in human beings the desire to reproduce those very mechanisms. According to Smith's idealist formulation, everybody starts out with a *tabula rasa*, on which anything at all that occurs to them might be realised, regardless of whether it sustains the capitalist machinery or not. Against that myth, Marx argues that not just the form and the means of the realisation of so-called private interests are determined by social conditions, but the very content of the desires themselves are socially conditioned. In this sense, they are not of course private interests, only the socially prescribed interests of private persons. If the World Spirit has being-in-itself, it is in this respect only. Individuals are subsumed under the conditions of economic production, rather than vice versa.

If Hegel knew perfectly well that the contemporary reality belied the idea of his philosophy of history that the state was the perfectly rational form of the World Spirit's ascent to self-realisation, the reconciliation between the two could only be achieved by contemplating the state as an idea in itself, an abstract category. Any fool, he thought, could find fault with the particular constitutional arrangements of a specific state, but what mattered was the objective universal form of the state. The thought is parent to the wish of every Panglossian social theodicy since, that reconciliation between society's antagonistic forces has essentially been achieved in the emergence of a political consensus to which all subscribe, a notion that both cheats the dispossessed and the exploited of their due, and indefinitely defers the possibility of an actual reconciliation, in deference to the mythical one that has already been brought about.

Freedom comes to its supreme manifestation in the state for Hegel, which thereby stands as a substantial unity in the

Aristotelian sense, in enormous preposterous defiance of the dialectical process. What is missing is any appreciation of the differentiated relation between the state as an institution and the society which is both its active process and its producer. Although society ought to be the mediating factor through which the state is refracted, in capitalist modernity the latter has taken on the character of an unmediated fact. In that sense, the notion of the 'absolute and motionless end in itself', to which Hegel accords the status of a substantial unity, is misapplied to society, when it properly belongs, as Marx saw, to the ideological form of the state. 'What induced the thesis is that the "motionlessness" he [Hegel] attributes to the general purpose might indeed be predicated of the institution, once it has hardened, but could not possibly be predicated of society, which is dynamic in essence. The dialectician confirms the state's prerogative to be above dialectics because – a matter he did not delude himself about – dialectics will drive men beyond bourgeois society.'[9]

Marx would rescue the dialectical process that Hegel thus attenuates in three explosive paragraphs of the famous 1859 Preface to the *Contribution to the Critique of Political Economy*. Here, there is no doubt about the programmatic nature of the economic development of society, in which 'men inevitably enter into definite relations' determined by the antagonism between the technical forces of the production process and the class relations in which that process takes place. The moment in vanished primordial times when an exchange of goods between individuals, or between two groups of individuals, departed from the principle of equitability and benefited one party to the transaction more than the other was the moment of the first emergence of social classes and the inevitability of antagonistic relations between them. The systematic enactment of unequal exchange enshrines exploitation as a universal social principle, and although the form of economic relations has passed through successive phases in human history, as between the tribal groups of the Palaeolithic periods, the slaveholding societies of ancient times, the feudal hierarchies of the medieval era and the modern bourgeois form, or capitalism, of the period in which Marx was writing – itself the evolution from the entrepreneurial forms of the early industrial revolution to the emergence of giant capitalist monopolies from the mid-nineteenth century on – the principle of antagonism is the historical constant. Antagonism is produced by exploited humanity's coming to consciousness of its own material circumstances; indeed, all social consciousness just is the expression of material circumstances, whatever political ideologies, religious mythology, artistic productions, philosophical systems or, *pace* Hegel, legal constitutions have to say about it. Such critical consciousness generates the means for the transformation of society at each stage, for all that these successive transformations may be long drawn out, spasmodic and soaked in blood. In perhaps the most famous formulation in the Preface, Marx states, 'Mankind thus inevitably sets itself only such tasks as it is able to solve'. The full problematic nature of society only comes to light when such means for its reparation, the solution, lies ready to hand. That solution itself, partly retroactively, partly from within the social dynamic, creates the understanding of the problem to which it offers the remedy. Antagonism, Marx stresses, is not the voluntaristic antagonism of individuals who have set out to criticise the existing system, whom the system might perfectly well be able to absorb, as it has absorbed malcontents, freethinkers and dissenters at all epochs, but has its objective being in 'the individuals' social conditions of existence'. Put simply, it finally becomes impossible to ignore the fact that you are living in dire penury when the resources for the amelioration of your condition, which resources your labour has after all helped create, are invested only in enriching the exploiting classes still further. The bourgeois form of the economy will prove to be, Marx predicts, the final stage still marked by antagonism, and will therefore be the final phase of prehistory, a term that does not just designate the primeval eras, but refers to all human history up to now, precisely because it has not yet freed itself from the structure of natural history, from blind nature itself. When it does, real human history, the history of human self-production, can begin. Those who have tried to argue over the years that Marxism, whatever else it is, is not a deterministic theory of historical development need to confront again the repeated indications of inevitability and invariability in Marx's Preface – 'men inevitably [*notwendige*] enter into definite relations', '[m]ankind thus inevitably [*immer*, always] sets itself only such tasks as it is able to solve' – from which virtually the entirety of historical materialism flows.[10]

In the lectures on 'History and Freedom', Adorno addresses the concept of historical progress, mistakenly suggesting as he does so that Marx himself barely uses the word 'progress'. Progress, where it aspires to more than the continuing techno-logical development of the means of production and denotes the forward-moving enhancement of human consciousness, is intimately bound to the mechanisms of exchange society. At the heart of the exchange principle, as Marx showed, is the lie of equivalence. If the transaction were truly equivalent, says Adorno, nothing would have changed. The fact that it is always asymmetrical is what accounts for the dynamism of the bourgeois economy, its principle of accumulation, expressed by Marx as the law of surplus value. Something, the lion's share as in the Aesopian fable, is always left over for the owners after the labour power of their employees has been bought and paid for on the open market. Genuine social progress could only come about in an exchange that was worthy of the name, entered into freely and fairly, and with neither side being cheated of their due. In the meantime, as Adorno puts it, '[e]xchange is the rational form of mythical eternal sameness', a parodic enactment of the cyclical processes of antique cosmology. '[T]he more the system expands, the more it hardens into what it has always been', thereby defying the principle of a true progress.[11] It is for this reason that Adorno demurs from the doctrine of inevitable progression in classical Marxism, which retained the same trust in the progress of the world spirit as the Hegelian idealism it aimed to supersede. The antagonism between the forces and relations of production in the bourgeois economy, and which should by now have produced the abolition of production for its own sake, at least in the advanced economies, continues unchecked because, as Adorno put it in an address to a congress of German sociologists in Frankfurt in 1968, under the title 'Late Capitalism or Industrial Society?', society is fully industrial in respect of the development of the forces and means of production, but still obstinately capitalist as regards their relations. Technological development, which could have liberated unfree labour power, has been hijacked to serve the ends of capitalist relations of production. Relations between human beings in the sphere of labour, in which Marx described them as mere literal appendages of the machine, have become metaphorically extensible to social relations as such, so that even the political and cultural super-structure of society is infected with the character of relations in the nineteenth-century workplace. 'Production takes place today, as then, for the sake of profit. And far exceeding what was foreseeable in Marx's day, human needs that were potentially functions of the production apparatus have now become such functions in fact, rather than the production apparatus becoming a function of human needs. People are now totally controlled.'[12] The use value of commodities has become completely divorced from any residual naturalness, as was already diagnosed by Marx, but the commodities have increasingly also even become detached from the ideology of their exchange value, where they have become nothing other than the acquisition of symbolic cultural capital, or what an earlier sociological term inadequately denoted as 'status symbols'. Meanwhile, as technological progress and widespread automation in the industrial sector have had the effect of diminishing the share of living labour that was supposed to generate surplus value, globalised capital has had to look to alternative sources in what was optimistically termed the information revolution, which it now prefers to give the exalted pseudo-academic designation of the 'knowledge economy', to find ways of supporting its continued expansion. In 2008, when the credit crisis created by sub-prime mortgage lending in the United States, which is to say lending to people who could barely afford to pay the interest on the loans, let alone pay down their capital value, spread virulently throughout the whole western economy, it was hopefully predicted by some on the left that the system might be about to come crashing down altogether. That capitalism was sustained by coercing its victims to finance its recovery was a belated manifestation of Hegel's cunning of reason. The fact that, beyond a marginal protest movement which failed to seize the public imagination because it only opposed the abstract ideological form of capital relations rather than their concrete reality, people acquiesced in the extorted bailout as though it were their duty exposed the degree to which their economically determined social roles have been incorporated into them down to their innermost impulses. A mass default on loan repayments might have finished the job the investment bankers themselves unwittingly started, but instead, willingly or otherwise, people were enjoined to pull together, under the fraudulent claim that everybody, all the way up to those who were sacrificing this year's bonuses, was doing his bit.

Economic relations produce social consciousness in the Marxist analysis, a diagnosis that nothing in the century and a half since has disproved, but what was always more speculative was that consciousness would become sufficiently critically self-conscious to see that the economic relations determining it needed to be overthrown. Two principal forces have conspired to block such awareness. One is the fact that, throughout the indus-trialised world at least, the standard of living of working people

has undoubtedly improved, along with better working conditions, shorter working hours and a more benevolent welfarism on
the part of even many large corporate employers. Workers have
been induced to think that the system cares ultimately about
them more than it did when it wrote off the crippling industrial
diseases it caused as natural wastage. The second, and
overwhelmingly more salient, point in the Frankfurt School
analysis is that consciousness has been co-opted to serve the
system's ends throughout the superstructural sectors of society.
Marx's dictum that theory becomes a real force once it grips the
masses is seen in perverted form today in the colonisation of
consciousness by the culture industry and its attendant
requirement for conformity. '[T]he consciousness of the masses,'
Adorno writes, 'has become identical with the system as it has
grown increasingly alienated from the rationality of the fixed,
identical self.'[13] What psychology terms ego-weakness has
produced a mass society whose very massiveness militates
against any expression of individualised dissent – not, in the
western world, through overt repression, but through the more
subtle means of recruiting people to the higher cause of serving a
social totality that has long become more than the sum of its
parts. The distinction between real and false social needs has
become all but invisible as socially useful labour in the bourgeois
sense denotes anything that produces a profit. Nowhere is this
more graphically demonstrated in the present day than on the
Internet, which in the ideology of leftish optimism is a democratic tool that might enable people to bypass the official structures, but which was commandeered from the outset by those
very structures, to the extent that what appear to be genuine
attempts at social connection are quickly exposed as having a
commercial motivation and thus as the continuation of business
by other means. Even where people turn to what are unironically
called social media as the antidote to the loneliness that actual
sociality produces, the contacts too frequently wither as it

becomes obvious to the more ruthless party that there isn't anything to be gained from them.

The posthumously published aphoristic essay, 'Reflections on Class Theory', originally written in 1942, during the period that he and Horkheimer were working on the early drafts of the *Dialectic of Enlightenment*, shows Adorno addressing the lineaments of Marxist economics and historical theory directly. He opens by referring to the famous statement from the *Communist Manifesto* that all history is the history of class struggles, and points out that the concept of class in the sense intended only emerged with the creation of the proletariat in bourgeois economics. Adorno upholds Marx's argument that the hierarchical class structure of society takes on the specious character of something naturally evolved, as though its laws – pre-eminently the laws of labour – have irresistible quasi-biological force. 'Natural law is historical injustice that has become obsolete,'[14] Adorno asserts, obsolete in the sense that under capitalist relations of production, it is no longer registered as injustice but rather as the static edifice of a social construction that is just the way things are. The contradiction implicit in this static conception, however, is that all ideas, from the Platonic variety onwards, emerge from the contemplation of present torment, from the realisation that things are not as they could be. Such is the dialectical motor of history. Dangers lie, however, in a shallow appropriation of the Marxist analysis, specifically with regard to the dialectical process. On the one hand, the dynamism of dialectics, its constant setting of states of affairs against each other, proves too readily assimilable to a capitalism that thrives on its own ceaseless self-revolutionising. The exploiting classes in capitalism like nothing better than the idea that constant mobility in the forces of production requires constant adaptability on the part of those engaged in it. Constant change conceals the true nature of the system. Then again, dialectics has a static side. The Hegelian dialectical process, Adorno argues, is not a developmental doctrine of history, for the reason that the new in dialectics does not wholly displace the old, but represents what has become of the old in present conditions. It is 'the old in distress, in its hour of need'. 'The system of history, the elevation of the temporal to the totality of meaning, abolishes time and reduces it to an abstract negation.'[15] Marx understood this point in all its implications, which is why he viewed the entirety of history to date as merely prehistory, ratifying Hegel's idealist understanding of historical processes as the self-understanding of prehistory, but it re-energises that understanding by defining the history of which Hegel gives such a meticulous outline as precisely prehistory. The point, however, is to change it. Human beings are simply the raw material in which the world spirit comes to consciousness of itself. They are history's victims, who must seize the moment of their self-identification as such in order to set real historical time in motion. The systematic unity of history in the Hegelian conception is supposed to give meaning to human suffering or, where that fails, write it off as incidental, and yet history itself is, as Adorno puts it, 'the epitome of suffering'. The ages of the world, however, do not simply succeed each other in heterogeneous progression, according to a constructive force that is drawing humanity towards the light of reason. 'Theory [i.e. Marxist theory] knows of no "constructive force" but only of one that lights up the contours of a burned-out prehistory with the glow of the latest disaster in order to perceive the parallel that exists between them.'[16] This is a lesson that has been both absorbed and forgotten by a present generation of so-called radical theorists who celebrate the potential for subversion in every fatuous new bit of technology, whether related to production or mere distraction, only because of its apparent newness. 'Only he who recognises that the new is the same old thing,' Adorno warns, 'will be of service to whatever is different.'[17]

Undeluded consciousness, as ever, would be the first prerequisite and the key to dismantling the present social system, which has become a machine for generating total illusion. In Adorno's unsparing analysis, the ruling ideology has attained a position in which it can cheerfully declare its own mendacity in emphasis of the utter impotence of those who still believe in it: hence postmodern irony and the widely noted culture of the simulacrum. With the disappearance from view of the workers as a class – not their disappearance as such, since exploitation reigns supreme in the allegedly classless society of globalisation, but the disappearance of their self-consciousness as a class – the struggle between classes has crumbled along with the self-belief of those who would have most to gain from it. Class struggle as an index of the historical real, as distinct from a tool of historiographical and sociological analysis, has dwindled to an idealistic chimera, barely more concrete than the liberal appeals for tolerance and humaneness regularly staged by those who feel that we all ought to learn to get on with each other. This has happened in the era that should have precipitated the objective conflict between capital and its servants. The tension between society's antipodes, however, has been stretched so wide and so fine, according to Adorno, that it has become invisible, like the exquisite fabric used to weave the Emperor's new suit, but class rule survives precisely where the objective perception of classes disappears. Where once social oppression divided the estates from each other in overt hostility, it has now so seamlessly absorbed the oppressed into its embrace that it has become omnipotent. Those who produce its wealth identify with the system as never before, to the extent that their self-consciousness as a potential agent of its undoing has evaporated. 'The immeasurable pressure of domination has so fragmented the masses that it has even dissi-pated the negative unity of being oppressed that forged them into a class in the nineteenth century.'[18] A state of oppression that doesn't feel like one might be thought a relative blessing, and is certainly what capitalism would adduce in its own justification as an element of progress, should it ever develop a taste for self-justification, but even the state of anaesthesia in which oppression is now carried on does nothing to mitigate the underlying suffering of all who must submit to it, any more than it alters the iron law of the extraction of surplus value.

As Adorno sees it, there is a contradiction in the relative conceptions in Marxist theory between the two principal contending classes. If the bourgeoisie is the unity it undoubtedly is, particularly in the light of its opposition to the interests of the class of workers, the latter are characterised in class terms as the aggregate of particular interests, which very interests had to be subsumed into a whole in order to construct the proletariat as a class. The working class is simultaneously a unity, in the sense that it is a subjective force of history, and a non-unity in terms of the whole field of its particular interests, which are disregarded by a unified bourgeoisie. Reduced to a class with a single historical aim, its economic emancipation, it loses that very quality – its heterogeneity – that it ought by rights to assert against a terroristic singularity. Bourgeois society in its liberal phase saw itself as respecting precisely the freedom of everyone to be himself, regretting the unpleasantness that not all had the evident self-possession to be such, even while it respected to the most fastidious degree the freedom of entrepreneurs to exploit the dispossessed. Now, Adorno declares in 1942, liberalism is over. A disavowed class rule of the most vicious stripe has taken its place, with the consequence that history is now less the history of class struggles than the victorious history of 'monopolies... gang wars and rackets'.[19] Notwithstanding the fate of the self-definition of classes in the turbulent years of the late nineteenth and early twentieth centuries, the successors of Marx, Adorno claims, chose to let class theory freeze as a 'pedagogic tactic' for recruiting working people to its colours, rather than continuing to develop it. It thereby helped to ratify the defeat of what should have been the proletarian revolutions in western Europe, especially in the years following the Treaty of Versailles, because it was still mortgaged to a conception of class consciousness that historical events were rapidly belying. Marxism became an abstraction, eventually a mere garnish to whatever unique and unpredicted events unfolded in its own history, as much as on the wider historical canvas. Everything that happened was made retroactively to fit a theory that was drained of its lifeblood, the organic understanding of all material social processes in the light of the changing forms of exploitation.

What might have sustained a class consciousness worthy of the name, at least with regard to political action, would have been a continuing critique of the fate of representational parliamentary democracy, the objective form of restricted liberal freedom. Where Marxism could have thrown bourgeois democracy to the lions after the gladiatorial clash of the Great War, it was superseded by the oligarchic form symbolised by vapid social-democratic parties acting as gadflies on the conservative establishment, a political structure in which privilege, as Adorno argues, was inscribed as an objective necessity of history. That alone accounts for the ossification of democracy, and not the handwringing liberal lament that, after all, people are not yet mature enough for it. Nothing about a critical theory that has hardened into ideology, the more so since it faced a monolithic social structure against which only hardness seemed to stand a chance of prevailing, troubles a class system that is always nimbly capable of outwitting it, just because it only offers one argument.

Marx and Engels pinned their hopes for the self-liberation of the losers in the capitalist racket on what would eventually become the intolerable exigency of their own condition, but if poverty is to drive the defeat of the system, the steady improvements in working conditions, the attenuation of the working day, rising wages during boom-times are all the enemies of revolutionary consciousness. Without quite elaborating the point,

Adorno scoffs at the notion of 'relative pauperisation' as a risible concept, both in the class essay and the 'Late Capitalism' lecture. The notion arose during the revisionist period of the Second International, when communism was watered into social-democratic constitutionalism, and the hope expressed was that the fact that they were still relatively poor compared to the proprietorial classes would carry more weight in workers' perceptions than the fact that they were relatively better off than they used to be. In any case, what capitalism thrives on is the permanent sense of crisis, the lurches in stock market values and the vicissitudes of speculation, which are conceived as quasi-natural processes capable of causing great disorder, like electrical storms and tsunamis, but essentially no more controllable than weather events. If nothing can control currency fluctuation, nothing concrete can be done to ameliorate the condition of its most luckless victims. Against the tides of crisis, a reserve army of industrial labour, periods of unemployment and even overpopulation in the metropolitan centres all help insure against social upheaval, rather than guaranteeing it. Today's definition is 'precarity', in which what keeps people quiescent is the idea that they are helplessly adrift on lumpy seas, so that anyone who has a job for the time being, or has been unexpectedly granted a few hours' work this week, under the terms of a contract that guarantees no such thing, will be so grateful that they are not among the forgotten that they will do nothing to upset the boat. In the meantime, poverty, relative or otherwise, is not only a material circumstance; it is the objective reflection of social and political impotence, against which piecemeal improvements in financial well-being are at all times thrown into relief. No revisionist reinterpretation of social relations can escape this. At its most virulent, the enforced powerlessness of the least well-off is what enables their recruitment into conflicts that are not truly theirs. Adorno puts the nexus of social and economic power relations in this way:

This impotence permits wars to be waged in all nations. Just as war confirms the *faux frais* [incidental expenses] of the power apparatus as profitable investment once the war is over, it also cashes in the credit of poverty that the dominant cliques cleverly managed to defer, although that same cleverness finds itself confronting an immovable barrier when it comes to poverty itself. Poverty can be eliminated only by the overthrow of the dominant cliques, and not by a process of manipulation, however disguised.[20]

In the Hegelian conception, the ruling classes, what Adorno here calls the 'cliques', are as subject to history's vicissitudes as are the rest, but this is to mistake the conscious will of those who control the mechanisms of power with an objective spirit realising itself through them without their being fully conscious of it. If history has an objective tendency, it is that the dominant class controls the social system in its own interests, and therefore determines the objective tendency. They *are* the objective tendency. Even when historical events appear to threaten their hold on power, they so often survive because power itself survives. The consciousness of freedom that Hegel saw realised in history is, for Adorno, not a general emancipation, but only the freedom of those in charge. 'History is progress in the consciousness of their own freedom passing right through historical objectivity, and this freedom is nothing but the flip side of the unfreedom of others.'[21] In primordial times, the influence that the powerful elements in a society had over the forces of nature, those forces that came to be designated as fate, was what granted them their power, in which freedom was objectively crystallised as the freedom to exercise power. Hegel's postulate of necessity being raised to freedom is therefore, for Adorno, the collusion between historical events and the cliques who oversee them. Freedom comes into its own not in the Prussian state, as Hegel had suggested in the 1820s, but in Hitler's posturing, which lays bare the complicity of freedom in the deterministic sense with command, coercion, brute self-assertion: 'the free man is the man who is in a position to take liberties.'[22] When Marx speaks in *The Eighteenth Brumaire of Louis Bonaparte* (1852) of history repeating itself, the farcical second iteration of historical events following the tragic prolusion, he intends to convict bourgeois history of precisely the self-serving tendency that Adorno translates into the era of the Nazi hegemony. Events themselves may indeed be a matter of mere contingency, but they are moulded, more or less traumatically, into the forms of pre-existing society in the era before the liberation of history. Thus Marx: 'Men make their own history, but they do not make it as they please; they do not make it under self-selected circumstances, but under circumstances existing already, given and transmitted from the past. The tradition of all dead generations weighs like a nightmare on the brains of the living.'[23] This thought, often adduced by conservative historians against the distorted turn that the liberation of the proletariat took in twentieth-century history, but intended originally as a succinct encapsulation of the objective trend of bourgeois prehistory, remains true down to the age of postmodernism.

In the present era, working people are more finely chiselled by labour processes that they ostensibly understand than they were by the dehumanising factory production from which they were alienated, the consciousness of which produced the proletariat in the first place. In classical Marxist theory, pauperisation and the reduction of working people to appendages of the machines they operated should eventually have guaranteed their irruption as the revolutionary subject of a transformed history, but what Marx and Engels did not envisage was a historical conjuncture in which people grew paradoxically contented with the economic disposition of society, partly because it ameliorated their conditions but largely because it succeeded in remaking them in its own image. The Adorno of the 1940s, already anticipating a postwar settlement in which capitalism would continue to reign unchecked, diagnoses the true wretchedness of the oppressed less in their economic plight than in their surrender of subjective autonomy to a system for the manufacture of conformity. In this condition, they suspect any articulation of the truth about social relations to be mere propaganda, leftist axe-grinding, bolshie troublemaking, even while imbibing undiluted the propaganda distilled by the culture industry, 'a propaganda culture that is fetishised and distorted into the madness of an unending reflection of themselves'.[24] It slips down so smoothly just because it appears to be a concentrate of real human experience, a sign that people's actual feelings are understood after all.

Despite the bleak cheerlessness of the bulk of its diagnosis, the class theory essay ends, conventionally enough, on a note of hope. This consists in Adorno's suggestion that reification, in reifying human beings, may have reached its limit. If the true relations of production have become concealed from people, because of the completeness of their alienation, the oppressed may well assume the official features of enlightened civilisation by taking it at its word and subjectively assuming their own freedom, seizing control of the forces of production from the grasp of the dominant power. If control has become total, then in a real sense there is no longer any point in control. 'The mimicking of the classless society by class society has been so successful,' Adorno argues, 'that, while the oppressed have all been co-opted, the futility of all oppression becomes manifest. The ancient myth proves to be quite feeble in its new omnipotence.' Contra Marx, then, oppression will not be broken by the resistance of the oppressed in agitation, but by oppression's self-destructive expenditure of itself once it has become universal, in social and cultural as well as economic forms. If the mythic advance of domination has been relentless, for that very reason 'its end today is not the end'.[25] Adorno would still sound this note of hope a quarter-century later, when he concludes the lecture to the German sociologists by saying that because the total social system has become independent, even of those theoretically in control of it, it has taken on the character of fate, and while it appears to be addressing people individually, it is no longer capable of doing any such thing, only of using them to address itself. 'Hence the overpowering order of things remains its own ideology and is thus virtually impotent. Impenetrable though its spell is, it is only a spell.'[26] This latter point represents a considerable advance on the position articulated in *Negative Dialectics*, published two years prior to this lecture, in which Adorno stated balefully that everything alive lives under a spell [*ein Bann*], something like the spell cast over consciousness by medieval sorcerers. If the metaphor has any traction, it must surely also connote a possible final breaking of the spell, just what Adorno appears to conceive at the end of the 1968 lecture.

Something of this relation of theory to the practical currents of history is hinted at in an often overlooked section of the 'Notes and Drafts' chapter at the end of the *Dialectic of Enlightenment*. Here, Adorno and Horkheimer meditate on the philosophy of history and its critique, particularly – in the section's final paragraph – with regard to Marxist historiography that is, cautiously enough in the contemporary circumstances of exile in North America, not explicitly named. The mistake in historical materialism, the authors claim, was to turn the content of history, the progressive ideas that might liberate humanity from its nightmare, into the form of history itself. This at least is what it inherited from Hegel, the idea that history has a theme, which it works to realise. When progressive ideas become conceptualised as the self-realisation of history itself, they lose what the authors unabashedly call their 'innocence': 'When the philosophy of history shifted the position of humane ideas as an active force into history itself, and caused the latter to end with the triumph of these forces, humane ideas were robbed of the innocence which is an integral part of their content.'[27] They draw an analogy with the Christian theodicy that says that, despite the prevalence of evil and universal suffering in the world, good is the stronger principle and will ultimately triumph. The teleology of this view, in all contexts, results in a propositional fetishisation, which then turns terroristic: 'It is idolised as the spirit of the world [Hegel] or as an immanent law [Marx and Engels]. In this way, however, history is transformed directly into its opposite, and the idea, which wanted to arrest the logical course of events, is distorted.'[28] The sense in which ideologies that lend themselves to being instruments of the organisation of society, whether they be the Church, abstract idealism or dialectical materialism, generate the blood-drenched outcomes that constitute the negative side of history, is the precise sense in which they can be held responsible for what is done in their name. In other words, even given the liberal piety that Christianity did not automatically need to result in the Inquisition, or the *Communist Manifesto* the Lubyanka, nor do they, as institutional forces in history get to absolve themselves of the crimes that institutionalism inevitably legitimises. The hope for better circumstances can only be rooted in respect for general suffering, even where such suffering is an unavoidable consequence of history's proceeding, as Marx candidly foresaw, by its bad side. These are the outcomes that reason, freedom, justice cannot avert in present conditions, and not to be figured as blessings in disguise, as the unrecognised continuation of human progress.

Inseparable from the critique of a philosophy of history in Adorno and Horkheimer is the antagonism between a transcendent and immanent interpretation of historical development. Adorno tirelessly insisted on the historical situatedness of all social and cultural development, all intellectual practices, throughout his career, but this fastidiousness has not been immune from challenge in recent thought. In a brief passage of a section on 'Dialectical historicity' in his *Absolute Recoil* (2014),

Zizek argues that, just as universal truths can be shown to be historically conditioned, and truths that can be applied to all history may paradoxically only emerge in particular historical conjunctions, so also, 'from Marx to Adorno, there is always a set of propositions that are presented as trans-historical universals'.[29] He goes on to cite Marx's 1859 Preface, as discussed earlier, and then claims that '[w]hen, in his *Negative Dialectics*, Adorno talks about the "priority of the objective" [i.e. the primacy of the object], when he asserts the non-identical, and so on, such statements are definitely meant to be taken as universal ontological principles whose truth is not limited to specific historical conditions'.[30] This, I believe, is a misreading. These postulates of Adorno's are further examples of universal truths emerging in a specific historical constellation, just as the truth about productive labour only finally emerged amid the reality of nineteenth-century capitalism. A society dominated by the exchange relation is one that reveals finally and fully that only a consciousness that accords the objective its primacy, and refuses to subsume it under the conceptual principles of identity thinking, is capable of advancing human interests. And nothing about that insight in the contemporary moment in which Adorno formulated it – the western Europe of the 1960s – militates against its being subjected to further elaboration in the light of whatever historical developments subsequently come to pass. The trans-historical nature of an ontological principle is not separable from the epoch in which it comes to consciousness, any more than the discovery of the descent of man, contained in concealed embryo in the theory of the origin of species, can be divorced from the last era of scientific lip service to the strictures of theological belief.

By the 1960s, Adorno had come to doubt that it was possible to produce a unified theory of a world careering towards the next catastrophe. The absurdity of the nuclear arms race, the assurance in the west that the post-war economy represented the best that could be achieved in the welfare of society, the calcification of Marxism in the east into a body of static dogma unashamedly described as an 'ideology' by its public exponents: these eventualities gave notice that a philosophy that attempted to conjure a prognostic vision of a better state of being out of these most unpromising raw materials was probably doomed from the outset. The idea that the world could be transformed from top to bottom, imminently, had congealed into a mythology that was hostile to the agility of thought. Since the era of Marx, society had successfully integrated all its elements into a total social process, and the condition of working people in particular was materially very different from what it had been when the first volume of *Capital* was published. 'Marx would have been the last person,' Adorno claims, 'to tear thought free from the real movement of history.'[31] The rustication of philosophy proclaimed by a political force whose task was to seize its moment turns out to have been premature, since the seizing of the moment turned into a historical fiasco, and no progress has been made on either side on the elimination of suffering, misery and fear in the generations since. 'After having missed its opportunity, philosophy must come to know, without any mitigation, why the world – which could be paradise here and now – can become hell itself tomorrow. Such knowledge would indeed truly be philosophy.'[32] In the present historical juncture, Adorno argues, the abolition of thought in favour of an allegedly progressive praxis will only serve to perpetuate existing conditions.

The paradox of the relation between theory and praxis is further explored in a late essay that closed the second volume of *Critical Models* (1969). Here, Adorno argues that the concept of praxis arose in ancient times from that of labour, and is marked by its character in all ages. It carries the baggage of unfreedom because it was once the marker of having to negate the pleasure principle in the interest of self-preservation, and has always been the task of those who are not privileged to be able to do nothing other than live the life that labour makes possible. Labour was conceptualised into praxis when it ceased to be about repro-ducing life itself, struggling to attain the means of subsistence, and became the means for reproducing the *conditions* of life, in all their stratification and inequity. The unity of theory and praxis was postulated in specific historical circumstances, but even where the chances are favourable, they do not and should not automatically become one. There is, by contrast, a progressive aspect to the separation of theory and praxis. Marx is of course right, Adorno concedes, to say that the privileged spiritual life is not a dispensation from material labour, for the reason that it relies on material labour for its existence, but that semblance is not purely and simply ideology. The liberation of thought from material activity is what would lead away from the predomi-nance of labour towards freedom, the goal being a society in which the life of the spirit ceased to be a privilege and became available to all. Does not the development of the technological forces of production appear to point in this direction? A purely contemplative life in the Aristotelian sense, Adorno says, is disreputable because it involves an antipathy to getting one's hands dirty, but could be the goal of a society in which bliss would consist in humanity's having escaped the infliction and suffering of violence in all forms of exploitation. As Adorno puts it, 'Aristotle's *Politics* is more humane than Plato's *Republic,* just as a quasi-bourgeois consciousness is more humane than a restorative one that, in order to impose itself upon a world already enlightened, prototypically becomes totalitarian. The goal of real praxis would be its own abolition'.[33] In any case, a reformist social-democratic praxis does nothing other than prolong the present injustices, and has always already been left behind anyway by the total knowledge of prevailing conditions available to theory. Not even in *Capital* is a direct transition mapped from theory, the 'critique' of the subtitle, to practical action, other than the notion that the proletariat, in the age when it was still visible as such, could be the source of its own emancipation, but the roadmap is conspicuously lacking. 'The theory of surplus value does not tell how one should start a revolution,'[34] Adorno states. A theory determined by praxis would involve nothing other than the surrender to the way things are, whereas a practice that simply followed the prescriptive instructions of theory would become arthritically doctrinal, and would in any event give the lie to theory itself. This is the only truth-moment in Spengler's scorn of Marxism as a rigidified economic theory with aspirations to bring about institutional change – that as soon as it collides with actual circumstances, it dissolves into farce. Nothing about this verdict would have troubled Marx himself, who never intended his body of theory to become a bluntly applied programmatic method, as distinct from a diagnostic tool for understanding the present course of society.

What most urgently needed to be understood, by the midpoint of the twentieth century, was that which most resisted understanding. Virtually nothing preoccupied the Frankfurt thinkers more over the quarter-century that followed the defeat of Nazi Germany than extrapolating the implications and consequences of the exorbitant criminality of fascism. Adorno famously calls the duty to preclude such events from ever happening again a new categorical imperative, imposed on humanity in its unfreedom by the catastrophe of Auschwitz and everything for which it stood. The suffering unleashed by fascism has diabolically reconnected morality to the physical material basis from which it ought never to have been severed in the first place. Indeed, it was precisely that severance that made Auschwitz possible. When the mind rules absolutely over the bodily realm, it results in the absolute evil of dismissing human suffering to the degree of being able to dispose insouciantly over it. This should, Adorno argues, burn away the last vestige of any idea that culture, the mind's supreme product, is the antidote to a suffering that it cannot prevent. It isn't merely that a cultural education does nothing to insure against people becoming torturers and murderers. What culture must also accept is that at its heart is untruth, and that the objective index of its mendacity is the autarchic status that was posited for it in Enlightenment thinking, by which it sought to overcome the fact that, by setting itself above everyday material life, it had set itself in opposition to it. Confronting the insolence of an ameliorative post-war culture, Adorno is at his most uncompromising: 'All post-Auschwitz culture, including its urgent critique, is garbage. In restoring itself after the things that happened without resistance in its own countryside, culture has turned entirely into the ideology that it had been potentially – had been ever since it presumed, in opposition to material existence, to inspire that existence with the light denied it by the separation of the mind from manual labour.'[35] Put otherwise, culture is founded on the diremption of the life of the spirit from that of manual labour, casting a shadow over the material life from which it has divorced itself, but to which it then offers to bring illumination by making a virtue of its separateness from material conditions. In this helplessly ideological state, it then proves powerless to influence what happens to material individuals, who become as formally replaceable, and thus wholly nullified in themselves, as they were in the extermination camps.

What has happened in the years since the defeat of fascism, says Adorno, is that metaphysics has merged with culture. The unspoken element in it, once the preserve of theology and its forms of hope, has been dissolved in the secular age into the affirmativeness of culture both elevated and commercial, which now presumes to speak for everything that cannot be encompassed by the rational administration of society, an administration that nonetheless includes the provision of culture itself. 'The aureole of culture, the principle that the mind is absolute, was the same that tirelessly violated what it was pretending to express.'[36] A repulsive current in early critical responses to the comfortless dramatic works of Beckett used to celebrate the dignity and durability to be observed in human beings who, with their legs sawn off, live in dustbins on half a biscuit a day. Somehow the human spirit endures, runs the ideological homily, even where people appear to have given up, 'as if the intent to address men, to adjust to them,' Adorno interjects, 'did not rob them of what is their due even if they believe the contrary'.[37] Metaphysical thoughts once trained their sights higher than offering the platitudes of consolation where real experience recoils from any such suggestion. Nonetheless, as the widespread utterance of cynical stoicism currently has it, that's where we are now.

After the initial triumph of fascism in Europe, the well-worn dictum that the first casualty of war is truth, which was true only to the extent that it overlooked the prior claim of peace itself, became resoundingly true in ways that were not foreseen. Not only were the earliest reports of atrocity not welcomed in the free press of the unoccupied countries, but such reports as there eventually were took on the character of fabrication, not just because their enormity so often defied belief, but also because they did not come with the imprimatur of full journalistic verification. The preformation of news by the organs of media power has created a nimbus of implausibility around even the most starkly horrifying news, which has only been concentrated to a state of complete obfuscation by the global media organisations of the present day. Adorno puts this argument in another of the reflections in *Minima Moralia* written as the second world war drew to a close: 'Every horror necessarily becomes, in the enlightened world, a horrific fairy-tale. For the untruth of truth has a core that finds an avid response in the unconscious.'[38] The virtue that fascism made of its destruction of democratic values, that it was openly and honestly espousing the refusal of so-called humane principles in the interest of national glory, finds its resonance in the obscene unconscious wish to see destruction prevail. 'So desperate have people become in civilisation... that they are forever ready to abandon their frail better qualities as soon as the world does their worse ones the obligation of confessing how evil it is.'[39] The legacy of Hitler is the confounding of truth and lies in the political arena to the extent that it has become all but impossible to distinguish them ontologically from one another, an outcome only ratified by the fact that truth can filter through the networks of communication only if it allies itself with power, so as not to be annihilated by it. At the same time, and not coincidentally, exponents of analytical logic in the philosophy departments were assiduously working to abolish the semantic distinction between truth and falsity, an operation willingly extended in French deconstruction, in which they appeared as another of the oppressive binaries of philosophical tradition.

By contrast, the truth moment in Parisian existentialism lay in its adumbration of the sense of unearthly detachment in which modern experience frequently marooned the helpless subject. In the 'Meditations on Metaphysics' that form the closing section of *Negative Dialectics*, Adorno puts it this way: 'Thinkers and artists have not infrequently described a sense of being not quite there, of not playing along, a feeling as if they were not themselves at all, but a kind of spectator.'[40] Although such a detached stance can appear cold and indifferent, its rescuing aspect is its attitude of resistance to a cold immediacy, the impulse that encourages everybody to join in and play their part. It is the same response that enables people to maintain a sense of equanimity in the face of the inevitability of death, a fact that fascinated Schopenhauer. In its distance from the way things are, it wants to assert that they could still be otherwise, even though such objectivity is bought at the regularly recurring cost of lapsing into the very chilliness that made bureaucratic participation in the crimes of fascism possible. Here is the modern dilemma encapsulated. How can wounded experience, the 'damaged life' indicated in the subtitle of *Minima*

Moralia, be accorded its due without reversing into precisely the frozen stoicism that does the victims of the damage a further injustice? 'People, of course, are spellbound without exception, and none of them is capable of love, which is why everyone feels loved too little. But the spectator's posture simultaneously expresses doubt that this could be all – when the individual, so relevant to himself in his delusion, still has nothing but that poor and emotionally animal-like ephemerality.'[41] For all Hegel's assurance that reason was gradually realising itself in history, with a force that would eventually induce humankind as a whole to accept history as its own self-realisation, what the events of the twentieth century bequeathed to it is the sense that history has backed human consciousness into a corner, a fragment of unconquered territory from which it can only look out helplessly, like one of those polar bears clinging to the last of the diminishing Arctic ice-floes. The progress of reason has become pure ideology, the voice of hopeless comfort amid the carnage. 'In a historical phase in which the view of reality as the fulfilment of reason amounts to bloody farce,' Adorno writes, 'Hegel's theory – in spite of the wealth of genuine insight that it unlocked – is reduced to a meagre form of consolation. If his conception carried out a fortunate mediation of history with truth, the truth of the philosophy itself is not to be isolated from the misfortune of history.'[42]

The relation of Adorno's thought to practical politics, or – as many have argued – the lack of such a relation, has been central to much of the left critique of him in the years since his death. He is charged by many with having subsided into an abstentionist state of resignation in the face of insuperable social forces, of giving up on the operative tenets of Marxism, both as an economic theory and as a philosophy of history, of selling the pass by sacrificing an efficacious oppositional politics to the adamantine diagnostics that produced the theories of the culture industry, of identity-thinking, of the mysterious spell under which all delusively labour, and even of colluding with the forces of darkness by calling the police to deal with a student sit-in. In contrast, another of the Institute's members, Herbert Marcuse, who repeatedly berated Adorno for his lack of insight into the revolutionary potential of the student uprisings, came to be seen as a more reliable ally in the anticapitalist struggle. Today, Adorno makes an appearance on cultural studies courses as the elitist spokesman of a vanished Eurocentric high culture put to flight by postcolonial artistic practices, somebody whose patrician grousing about the insufferable simple-mindedness of jazz and commercial movies can be swiftly dismissed as we progress to less hierarchical, more inclusive modes of cultural analysis, just as his apparently entrenched political immobility has been superseded by postmodern forms of participatory anticapitalist resistance.

Notwithstanding the fits of conservative hysterics in the West German press, which held Frankfurt critical theory indirectly responsible for the violent activities of the Red Army Faction, most derogatory comment on Adorno from the left has focused on his supposed retreat from Marxist positions. A recent contribution in this area, Robert Lanning's *In the Hotel Abyss* (2014), contains much that is characteristic of this body of opinion, beginning with its title, a reference worn shiny with overuse to the accusation mounted by Georg Lukács in the Preface to the 1962 reissue of his *Theory of the Novel*, originally published in 1916. Speaking from his position within the Hungarian *nomenklatura*, in which he intermittently served a never less than precarious role as official spokesman of Soviet cultural politics, Lukács levelled a picturesque charge against the politically inert members of western leftist intellectual circles:

A considerable part of the leading German intelligentsia, including Adorno, has taken up residence in the 'Grand Hotel

Abyss' which I described in connection with my critique of Schopenhauer as 'a beautiful hotel, equipped with every comfort, on the edge of an abyss, of nothingness, of absurdity. And the daily contemplation of the abyss between excellent meals or artistic entertainments, can only heighten the enjoyment of the subtle comforts offered' (*Die Zerstörung der Vernunft* [*The Destruction of Reason*], Neuwied, 1962, p 219).[43]

For Lanning, there is hardly any aspect of Adorno's thinking that is not in conflict with Marxist orthodoxy, but his critique often turns out to devolve on relatively few points of substantive contention, as is the case with his assessment of the interpretive use to which Adorno puts Marx's theory of exchange value. Lanning claims that Adorno reduces all labour to a hypostatised, statically undifferentiated category in the exchange mechanism, retaining none of Marx's own elaborations of the different kinds and contexts of labour, as between classes, the differential status of skilled and unskilled labour, or the varying levels of technical complexity. There is nothing to support such an interpretation in Adorno's work, which repeatedly, throughout his career, empha-sises the baleful social effects of the division of labour. If labour had been homogenised in all its aspects in Adorno's theory, as Lanning charges, there would be no division of it to point to. The homogenising element comes in the notion of the abstract exchange of equivalents, which mendaciously governs not only commodity transactions themselves, but the exchange that takes place between employer and worker for the latter's labour-time. What is needed in the just society is not to abolish the principle of equivalence, but to realise it justly, so that nothing was withheld from workers, either as workers or as consumers. If qualitative differentiation in labour is to be asserted above equality, what Adorno calls 'recidivism into ancient injustice' would be the result.

From olden times, the main characteristic of the exchange of equivalents has been that unequal things would be exchanged in its name, that the surplus value would be appropriated. If comparability as a category of measure were simply annulled, the rationality that is inherent in the exchange principle – as ideology, of course, but also as a promise – would give way to direct appropriation, to force, and nowadays to the naked privilege of monopolies and cliques.[44]

Lanning isn't having this. For him, it doesn't take account of the differentiated aspects of different kinds of work. 'How can exchange be seen as an exchange of equivalents without also considering the possibility of these differing conditions?'[45] he wonders. But this is exactly what would be guaranteed under the conditions of the non-fraudulent, non-exploitative labour relations that Adorno envisions: 'our critique of the inequality within equality aims at equality too, for all our scepticism of the rancour involved in the bourgeois egalitarian ideal that tolerates no qualitative difference.'[46] The negative dialectics of identity, which aims at the nonidentical, the residue or remainder that is left when concepts fail to subsume the objects at which cognition directs them, has its origin in the principle of abstract exchange that governs all social relations, but the goal of a liberated thinking, as of a liberated society, would be to realise true identity, to restore the organic relations between things and their concepts. In the world of work, this would mean restoring to labour-power its full value, *whatever the context* – and it is that last clause that ought to salve Lanning's doubts. 'If no man had part of his labour withheld from him any more, rational identity would be a fact, and society would have transcended the identifying mode of thinking.'[47]

When the simple barter economy, in which objects are exchanged for their use value based on the perception of need, gives way to capitalism, money becomes the objective third element that mediates the exchange, and which, by being strictly indifferent to the two primary entities, becomes more powerful than either of them. What matters is making money, for bare subsistence at the bottom end of the scale, for limitless luxurious accumulation at the top. Observing that Marx describes the monetary value of a commodity as enjoying a special existence alongside it, mysteriously divorced from it in its ontological status, Lanning accuses Adorno of subsuming the money element into his general account of the exchange process. If capitalist exchange produces only the appearance of equivalence, there can be little or no space for the distinction between the commodity and its monetary definition. It is precisely the existence of such space, however, that produces the opportunity for the false equations of capitalist exchange relations. Adorno is in entire agreement with Marx that consumers only become aware of the nature of the exchange process at its endpoint, the commodity, which is thereby cut loose from the actual historical development inherent in it. This is what guarantees the separation of the exchange relation from other aspects of reality, and results in a form of social consciousness that sees nothing else as having the functionally legitimate authority in which the exchange principle itself glories.

More than anything else, though, what undermines Adorno's analysis for Lanning is that his diagnosis of the operations of false consciousness fatally lacks an explanation of how it might be overcome. Invoking the Lukács of *History and Class Consciousness*, Lanning asserts that '[f]alse consciousness is not a permanent state of the individual or the class as a whole but a discoverable condition that can be altered'.[48] Any diagnosis of its existence must be provable by a quasi-scientific veridical methodology, one that, ironically given Lanning's fastidious insistence otherwise on the specificity of context and the differentiation of conditions, ought to be demonstrable under any circumstances: 'to be a valid claim it must include a demonstration of the error by an explicit and systematic method of analysis that can be repeatedly applied in different contexts to establish its veracity.'[49] What he has supplied here, despite himself, is a precise definition of how false consciousness itself works, by being applied as an ironbound principle in all cases, regardless of what individual circumstances might indicate. His criticism of Adorno is the familiar one that a fatalist insistence on the prevalence of false consciousness in many different contexts as a result of the victory of identity-thinking results in hopeless defeatism, because it denies the potential for the false consciousness eventually to stand revealed to itself and become true. The imputation that false consciousness is wrong in Adorno's theory, because it is not seen as potentially self-correcting, is to pull the carpet from underneath the very notion of false consciousness. How could it be false in the first place if its own resolution is always potentially contained within it? If all social problems were susceptible of their own solutions, there would be no need for any form of political education, or indeed of political agency at all. The history of the century-and-a-half since Marx wrote *Capital* has been a history of false consciousness becoming more and more deeply ingrained into society, to the extent that people eagerly embrace it as an expression of their own most dearly held values, and absolutely not of the progressive liberation of true insight promised in Lanning's formulation.

An even more egregious misinterpretation of Adorno's account of Marx is offered by Nigel Gibson, who manages to turn a not especially complex thought about the exchange relation completely inside out. Here again is Adorno's proposition: 'Once critical theory has shown it up for what it is – an exchange of things that are equal and yet unequal – our critique of the inequality within equality aims at equality too, for all our scepticism of the rancour involved in the bourgeois egalitarian ideal that tolerates no qualitative difference.'[50] In Gibson, this is read as follows: 'Even Adorno, known for rigorously pursuing non-identity, insists that the ideal of identity, even if it is a "bourgeois egalitarian ideal" that brooks no qualitative difference, must not be discarded.'[51] Quite apart from the fact that the immediate proposition in Adorno concerns the principle of exchange in economic relations, not that of identity in conceptual thinking, for all that the one ultimately results in the other, the bourgeois egalitarian ideal, which is none such, is exactly what Adorno is scorning, not rehabilitating. The editorial pen only needed to correct the clause 'even if' in Gibson's text to 'other than where' and fidelity to the original thought would have been restored. As it is, it stands as a cheaply wilful misreading of the source. Even cheaper is his characterisation of Adorno's theoretical orientation as a kind of anarchism, or, as he noxiously maligns it, 'an anarchist regurgitation of Lukács' subject/object identity'.[52] If Gibson means this as a characterisation of Adorno's political position, it sits uneasily with his arraignment at the end of the same essay of an Adorno who made 'rotten compromises with the state' during the unrest of 1968, an eventuality that must have made him as sorely disappointing to the other anarchists as he evidently was to party Marxists. If intended merely as a metaphysical satire on the absence of categorical structures in Adorno's theorisation of what eludes conceptual thinking in materialist dialectics, it is more or less functionally illiterate. Adorno no more intends to achieve in theory a totalising identification of subject and object, as does Lukács in his conception of the proletariat as the unified subject-object of history, than does he wish to bring into being a wholly *laissez-aller* political vacuum in the Proudhonian manner.

Gibson accuses Adorno of having flattened Marx's notion of alienated labour to its purely social character, in which social relations become the reified relations among things, and nothing more, so that it has no remaining revolutionary potential, is therefore strictly nothing according to Marx's celebrated dictum that the proletariat is revolutionary or it is nothing. This is once again to elide the evident historical fact, all but indigestible though it be, that the proletariat, by ceasing to be revolutionary, has indeed become, if not nothing, since poverty and exploitation reign unchecked, then at least, as Adorno accurately puts it, invisible. Gibson is right to conclude that Adorno diagnoses capitalism as being able to absorb contradictions within itself, even thrive on them by putting them to productive use, rather than ultimately being undermined by them. It assimilates oppositional movements, in politics as in the arts, quite effortlessly, especially where they have no particular content, and is quite capable of priding itself on its own capacious tolerance in doing so. What Gibson dislikes about this diagnosis, however, is precisely its accuracy against what were the political prognostications of the 1860s, in which, as Marx argued, the dual character of labour as both abstract and concrete, alienated by its transformation into the commodity of labour-time and yet still meaningful in the sense that it constitutes labour for use value, through the employment of specific skills on the part of the worker, is what leads to the possibility of socially progressive forces being liberated in it. One should not stop at the fetishism of the commodity, as Gibson thinks Adorno does, but note that it reflects this dual character of labour, and that thereby from within the false consciousness that it generates, a true one might be released. Nothing other, however, is what Adorno still hoped in the conclusion to the essay on class theory, that reification might have reached its limits. For Gibson, the Lukacsian tenor in Adorno's thought is complemented by one indebted to Max Weber, who in the generation before Adorno, read Marxism as a critical account of the progressive rationalisation of capitalist society. This latter was indeed a misreading, as even the most minimally attentive study of the mature Marx demonstrates, but Gibson's reason for extrapolating this to Adorno is that he charges the latter with overemphasising the category of reification, which becomes the force that flattens and neutralises everything, as did Weberian rationalisation, ensuring that capitalism can no longer be seen as containing the potential for its own overcoming by the proletariat. On which note, '[t]he category of reification,' says Adorno, 'which was inspired by the wishful image of unbroken subjective immediacy, no longer merits the key position accorded to it, overzealously, by an apologetic thinking happy to absorb materialist thinking... The total liquefaction of everything thinglike regressed [in existentialism] to the subjectivism of the pure act'.[53] Without the category of something alien to the subject, there would be no possibility of any experience other than that which mere immediacy offered to it. Truth must be something outside the subject, whether the individual subject or the occluded class subject of Marxist history, otherwise it would be confined for eternity to pure immanence, helplessly hoping to generate its own liberation out of its own given conditions, as in the perennial image of Baron Munchausen attempting to pull himself out of the swamp by his own pigtail. 'Yet the surplus over the subject, which a subjective metaphysical experience will not be talked out of, and the element of truth in reity – these two extremes touch in the idea of truth.'[54]

Gibson closes his essay with a familiar caricature. He approvingly quotes Peter Hohendahl, who contests that Adorno's thinking is 'predicated on his concept of a totally administered society, which leaves its members with the futile choice between a revolution that would not change the structure of domination, on one hand, and individual passivity, on the other'.[55] Certainly, the past century has been strikingly deficient in revolutions that put an end to the structures of domination, which reproduced themselves at the micrological level even where they were officially disavowed at the institutional level, as in China's Cultural Revolution, and anyway generally preferred the institutional version in the form of an ideological irreproachability to which all were expected to submit – 'die Partei hat immer recht' (the party is always right), as it was expressed in the words of the national anthem of the German Democratic Republic. But the latter half of Hohendahl's equation, the individual passivity, is absolutely wrong. Nothing in Adorno's thought counsels passivity, as opposed to a determinate thinking in opposition to the prevailing consensus, the refusal of participation and acqui-escence at the level of critical consciousness. This is only passivity if you happen to think that obstructing tourists from getting into the cathedral, by squatting in its entrance wearing comedy-masks like frolicsome children, constitutes an activism likely to bring down the rule of capital.

The charge that the first generation of Frankfurt School thinkers had relapsed into a state of despairing acquiescence with existing conditions was sufficiently familiar already in February 1969 for Adorno to give a short radio lecture, published under the title 'Resignation', to address the charge. The unity of theory and praxis, already blocked in Marx's own day, Adorno argues, all too easily has the tendency to become a predominance of praxis, imitating the mindless bustle of the world of bourgeois accumu-lation. A Confucian impulse on the part of activists, that any activism is better than none, condemns militant praxis to the status of pseudo-activity. 'One clings to action for the sake of the impossibility of action.'[56] If the eleventh thesis on Feuerbach overturns the earlier promise in Marx of a 'ruthless critique of everything existing', the primacy of practice has the effect of cutting it loose from critical reflection. As Adorno puts it, it culminated in the Eastern Bloc in a body of political law in which the only critique permitted was that the production targets had once again not been met, that people were still not working hard enough. By contrast, Adorno asserts, '[i]t is up to thought not to accept the situation as final. The situation can be changed, if at all, by undiminished insight'.[57] Spontaneity of action, to be sure, can sometimes be good, but cannot be absolutised as a virtue in itself, or divorced from the objective situation. An impatience with theory is what prepared the ground, in the 1960s, for the return of anarchism, which in forgetting thought, falls below the level of what thought has attained. Pretending that a reformed society is within reach amounts to ideological repression, and constitutes what Freud would have recognised as a real renunciation of the actual goal of desire. On the other hand, the insatiability of thinking is precisely what refuses resignation. As to party discipline and all delineations of the correct line, thinking is more akin to a transformative praxis than compliance for the sake of praxis. Unlike the latter, 'thinking has the element of the universal'.[58] This leads to one of Adorno's most striking formulations of political dissent. 'Whoever thinks is not enraged [*Wer denkt ist nicht wütend*].'[59] Rage is the confession of the impotent.

Susan Neiman correctly notes the insistence on transcendence that continued to animate the first generation of the Frankfurt thinkers but, in tune with the critical consensus, draws the wrong conclusion from it:

The *Dialectic of Enlightenment* can seem to describe the worst of all worlds: we have no-one to blame for our misery, but the process is so swift and self-maintaining that we cannot stop what we started. After such a diagnosis, the appeal to transcendence can quickly become an excuse for inaction. The Frankfurt School's response to such criticism was always unclear.[60]

On the contrary, transcendent thought, defused in conventional wisdom into the bits of Kant and the idealistic philosophers that one could safely jettison, after the secularisation programme of the Enlightenment was more or less complete, is what keeps the realm of possibility alive. Even organised religion itself, in the period of its self-defeating demythologisation, gives the impression that it could probably do without the vision of what comes after, as long as it can train itself to a functional quotidian ethics in the present. In a section of the *Negative Dialectics* entitled 'Neutralisation', Adorno repositions metaphysical and philosophical speculation side by side in their refusal to accept that the merely existent is the limit of possibility: 'for the chance of the right consciousness even of those last things [i.e. the 'Last Things' of classical Christian belief] it will trust nothing but a future without life's miseries.'[61] It is these miseries, after all, that disguise what existence might be, confirming its present status as a 'metaphysical authority'. There is no use in saying, à la Schopenhauer, that the whole of existence is in vain. Hardly anybody, in their heart of hearts, will disagree with that. The pessimism that writers like Neiman too readily attach to Adorno could scarcely be further from the truth. If it is true that Adorno maintains the right life cannot be lived in the wrong circumstances of the present, that does not in any way license the acceptance of the wrong circumstances as an end in themselves which, when all is said and done, there is no escaping. It is the very neutralisation of which he speaks, the dissolution of metaphysical matters to mere indifference, that has prevented the disasters of modern history from doing what existentialism thought they would, forcing humanity to confront its most radical imperatives. Instead, a functional administrative society emerged intact from the wreckage, encouraging conformity to the prevalent state of things as the safest bet. Nothing else mandates the necessity to change the way things are, which, Adorno concedes, is not solely a theoretical viewpoint. 'No rebellion of mere consciousness will lead beyond that... The metaphysical interests of people would require that their material ones be fully looked after. While their material interests are shrouded from them, they live under Maya's veil.'[62] The section ends with one of Adorno's most gnomic, yet crystal-clear, political formulations. In the German, it reads with the metre of a poetic couplet: '*Nur wenn, was ist, sich ändern lässt, ist das, was ist, nicht alles*'. Neiman gives this as: 'Only when that which is can be changed is that which is not everything'.[63] Ashton's much-criticised English version of 1973 gives this a distinctly more elegant epigrammatic turn: 'What is must be changeable if it is not to be all.'[64] It is only if what is may be other that it ceases to be all.

These thoughts ought to throw into relief the now notorious summation of Terry Eagleton in the chapter on Adorno in his *The Ideology of the Aesthetic* (1990) to the effect that, in common with the other Frankfurt thinkers, Adorno was guilty of an 'overre-action to fascism' that resulted in a willingness 'to court impotence, deadlock and failure rather than risk the dogmatism of affirmation'.[65] Overlooking the stumble into obscenity that seems to beckon when one might try to calibrate what a reasonable measure of dismay might be at fascist depravity – crimes considered unprecedented enough that their public denial is now itself a criminal offence in some of the countries in which they were committed – the statement misses what is most funda-mental about the change that fascism produced in European consciousness, particularly in the immediate aftermath of the revelation of its full extent. Fascism had achieved nothing short of redefining death itself from a traumatic event that marked an end to an individual life, to something that hardly mattered, a piece of administrative business, on the way to which the victims would undergo what was more insufferable than anything death ever had to threaten. Adorno's thinking doesn't 'court' impotence and failure, as opposed to reflecting the context in which recent historical events have cast speculative thinking. Affirmation, an apparent end in itself in Eagleton's formulation, is more readily put to nefarious ends than what he calls deadlock, which is any case not a characteristic of negative dialectics, which seeks precisely to undo the bonds into which affirmationist thinking has led the desire for change. The one dictum that everybody knows of Adorno's, which originally appeared at the end of a 1949 essay, 'Cultural Criticism and Society', that '[t]o write poetry after Auschwitz is barbaric',[66] was not a derogation of poetry as such, but of the lethal ideological assumption that everything, led by an affirmative culture putting up fairy-lights amid the ruins, could just carry on after the second world war as if nothing had happened. After standing by the statement in the early 1960s, he eventually retracted it in *Negative Dialectics*: 'Perennial suffering has as much right to expression as a tortured man has to scream.'[67] Thinking must incorporate what Adorno often simply calls in Conradian fashion 'the horror', as another of the ways in which a partial justice might be rendered to those for whom justice never came. This at least would be preferable to the current degrading of remembrance into a minimally pious schematism. Interminable memorialising, which encourages everybody to keep remembering traumatic events according to the calendar only, serves notice that the present day has nothing to say about such events other than to make itself aware, according to the logbook of history, when they happened. No illumination arises from knowing that so many people were killed on such a day that could not be outshone by insight into why they were killed. Such chronicling reduces historical experience to the equally meticulous recording of trivia, such as which celebrities have their birthday today, itself the secular survival of the ecclesial system in which every day is a saint's day. History, which did not proceed according to a schedule, no more conforms to one by means of the diary than it did in the programmatic systems of universal historiography.

The yielding of metaphysical experience to the materialism of the brute fact, celebrated in the fetishism of scientific thinking and the gleeful excoriation of religion in the present era, has not, according to Adorno, freed humanity from its enslavement to material insufficiency, only masked the experience of what Hegel had already diagnosed as the unhappy consciousness. A vitalism that decries the medieval stuffiness of speculation is in the nature of blithe medical advice to the depressed that they ought to take up jogging. When metaphysical thinking breathed its last at the end of the nineteenth century, it gave way to analytic logic and its concrete exempla. What was left to those who still wondered about the course of human history was the dismantling of the old theological categories in favour of an ideology of the present moment, some of it at least derived from the kind of misprision of Nietzsche's materialistic metaphysics that might furnish advertising slogans for fitness clubs, with their insistence, against the evidence, that only a healthy body can guarantee a healthy mind, so that the triumph of vulgar materialism was indissociable from an impulse to vanquish, predicated on the subsumption of the individual into the mass. The horror was prepared in such institutions as the boys' military academy depicted from life by Robert Musil in *The Confusions of Young Törless* (1906). 'I like these mass movements,' says Reiting, one of the orchestrators of the relentless bullying of a homosexual boy caught stealing money. 'No one intends to do anything in particular, and yet the waves grow ever higher until they crash together over everyone's heads. You'll see, no one will stir, and yet there will be a raging storm. It gives me extraordinary pleasure to stage something like that.'[68] 'You have the fire in your muscles,' the Führer, ratifying the point thirty years later, told a rally of the Hitlerjugend, 'that we only have in our minds.' By the time demented persecution had at his bidding gripped a whole nation, they were the same thing.

If it is true enough that Adorno's body of thought is not a blueprint for radical action, then it was no less true of those of Hegel and Marx. It is not the prerogative of a philosophy of history to become the manifesto for a recommended course. If, to work a variation on Schlegel,[69] a philosophy of history usually lacks one of two things, the philosophy or the history, Adorno throws the two terms into a mutually contextualising relation with each other, so that while philosophy attempts to address what humanity has become in its recent history, and in its comportment to that history, history itself produces the theoretical categories in which, as Marx would concur, it can be thought. Meanwhile, a state of affairs has come about in the post-war consensus in which the most tasteless parodies of true change are taken for signs of its vital dynamism. One secretary of state succeeds another. A bestselling book is adapted for the screen. A new computer system allows a company to make a phalanx of its workers redundant, while the remaining ones cope unaided with its periodic dysfunctions. What has become of the hope for change in such a society is not to be expressed in symbolic actions merely, in sloganeering and the circulation of memes online. It resides at the level of thought itself, which unless it takes up opposition to the entirety of what there is – a ruthless critique of everything existing, one might call it – only wilts in accommodation to it, for all its appearance of implacable hostility.

In light of the undeniable failure of transformative praxis, what remains for the time being is not optimism but radical hope, even where it expresses itself in the most hopeless circumstances. An evil triumph over evil, such as the post-9/11 world has witnessed, is no cause for hope, but only begets more evil. In one of the aphorisms of 1945 in *Minima Moralia*, Adorno reflects on the paradigmatic melancholy of the Grimms' telling of the fairy-tale of Snow White (1812), in which the justice of the victim's case seems scarcely served by her restitution to life, choking out the poisoned apple in the glass casket in her own cortège. For her malfeasance, the Queen who tried to kill her is made to put on a pair of red-hot shoes and dance herself to death, for the enter-tainment of Snow White's wedding guests. Appending the moral in the fashion of Aesop, Adorno writes that the darkness of the fable speaks of the obstinate moment of hope that irrationally persists amid conditions of overwhelmingly obstinate cheer-lessness:

So, when we are hoping for rescue, a voice tells us that hope is in vain, yet it is powerless hope alone that allows us to draw a single breath. All contemplation can do no more than patiently trace the ambiguity of melancholy in ever new configurations. Truth is inseparable from the illusory belief that from the figures of the unreal one day, in spite of all, real deliverance will come.[70]

Three

Metamorphosis of the Dialectic

Dialectics is the consistent sense of nonidentity. It does not begin by taking a standpoint.
Negative Dialectics

Dialectics has its origin in the intimation that what appears to be the case might not be the truth, or the whole truth. Histories of philosophy that begin from the establishment of naïve realism, the postulate that there was once in intellectual history a concrete objective world that was incontestable and undeniable – a position already belied in pre-Socratic thinking – explicate the succeeding philosophical tradition as having derived from the introduction of disputation into it in the Athenian classical period. Aristotle attributed the invention of the dialectic to Socrates' precursor, the Eleatic Zeno of the famous paradoxes, so that the notion of proceeding heuristically towards the truth by means of reasoned argument did not even have to wait until Plato's Socratic dialogues. Reason is rooted in a dialogic form, the supposition that a predication about reality may well turn out to be false, if its extrapolation ends in self-contradiction, or if it proceeds in the first place from an unfounded presupposition, or a prejudice that is the result of pathic or emotional manipulation. Contending positions do not reflect an entity as possessing a dual nature, but rather that the truth about it is distributed unevenly between different perceptions of it, which can be reconciled through the form of reasoned interlocution, resulting in one side achieving predominance over the other, or of the more accurate elements of the two blending into a reliable whole view of the matter. Its aim is veracity, and it progresses towards its aim by the elimination of what fails to conform to that principle.

The dialogues of Socrates, as recreated by Plato, take ideal moral concepts as their thematic matter. Determining where the right life or just action are to be found not only oriented the bulk of western thought towards the ideal realm, but also instated in the dialectical method itself the primary instrument for the establishment of knowledge. For Aristotle, on the other hand, knowledge might just as easily be knowledge of the material world as of the spiritual; his body of work prepares the separation of the two realms into speculative philosophy and science. What could eventually be explained through the elimination of error then departed from philosophy's purview and became a phenomenon of scientific deduction, which thereby enshrined the principle of demonstrable results as science's golden rule. By contrast, at least until the later stages of the German enlightenment, the thematics of philosophy proper involved ruminations on the nature of consciousness, on its relations to the empirical, on what it could know and how it could know what it claimed to know, whether it could establish any basis for its responses to what it found it liked or disliked, and on what the responsible individual ought to do in a range of exemplary circumstances. All these matters were decided by setting contending propositions in opposition to each other until something satisfactory emerged, which would implicitly become the truth about the world until it too was subverted by another view. Thus was philosophy confirmed paradoxically as the domain of what could not be known. If it could, it would just be scientific fact. One strand of intellectual history insists that the Socratic method is the forerunner of experimental validation in science, in which every hypothesis is tested either to destruction or confirmation, but the Dialogues never entirely close any topic in such a way. Their conclusions are seeming conclusions, which are implicitly open to challenge by the next interlocutor. Dialectics is thus not a progress towards its own closure, but an exposition of the evident truth that every thought-form, every proposition about the state of nature or the human soul, is contestable, and that truth emerges through successive approaches to it. This remains the best explanation of Socrates' own most famous apocryphal dictum, in Plato's *Apologia*, that he did not imagine he knew what he knew he didn't know, often paraphrased into the deceptively self-effacing admission that the only thing he knew was that he knew nothing.

The contestatory form of philosophical reasoning was preserved in the methodology of Descartes, for whom what survives after the elimination of that which can be subjected to doubt must be the truth. The thinking subject may doubt just about everything, but what it cannot doubt is that it itself is thinking, and therefore, in an imperious utterance of its own primacy, must exist. Kant took a dimmish view of dialectical thinking, practically equating dialectical thought in the *Critique of Pure Reason* with what would later come to be called ideology in the pejorative sense. Reason's pretensions to know the world that exists beyond or above what is apparent to the senses are misleading, for all that it can illuminate empirical and scientific understanding and speculate on its own grounds and limits. Anything else is illusion. This conception would be rejected as too static by one of dialectical logic's greatest adventurers, Hegel, whose system is predicated on the phenomenological mechanism that moves all knowledge, that of determinate negation. Thought advances by becoming aware of the contradictions within itself, out of which a new thought supervenes, potentially *ad infinitum*, a procedure that controverts the Socratic-Platonic presumption that contradiction is the dead end in thought. Contradiction, negation, are in Hegel the supremely productive potentials of thought, and not only of thought, but of the impetus of human history. What is crucial to understand, though, is that a victorious contradiction does not simply obliterate what came before it, but retains something of it in its overcoming of it. The German term for this process, *Aufhebung*, usually translated in English

Hegelese as 'sublation', combines three semantic values at once: negation or cancellation; preservation or retention; and a rising up or surmounting. By determinate negation, thought corrects itself, retaining the truth moment in the original thought, but supplanting the remainder by what it perceives as a more accurate thought. Negation is 'determinate' in that it addresses specific problems that arise in response to, or against the historical background of, specific circumstances, rather than having the purely arbitrary speculative nature they have in the Platonic dialogues. Cognitive development is thus an immanent process, in that it proceeds according to motivations that arise out of itself, rather than in response to elements that are parachuted into it from outside. There is nothing extraneous in the dialectical process, says Hegel.

Furthermore, because every new concept is an amalgam of preceding concepts, and also implicitly of all those preceding the preceding, the tendency of thought is to give a progressively richer and more complicated view of reality. What the dialectic achieves in its innermost working is what Hegel calls in his *Science of Logic* 'the identity of identity and non-identity'. The disposition of subject and object in speculative thinking rests on a dual sense of identity between the two terms. There is a formal or relative identity between them, in the sense of a dependent causal relation between the two, and also an absolute identity, by which the different qualitative aspects of each side of the equation are respected, in a process that Hegel calls 'reciprocal determination'. Subject and object are bound together in that one cannot exist without the other, and yet they are distinct entities in that they are different from one another, each constituting a substantial unity in its own right. What dialectical thought aims at is the predominance of the latter aspect over the former, in that a wholly articulated unity of both elements can only be arrived at through the reconciliation of identity and difference. If the two terms are only seen in oppositional form, thought remains marooned in the finite, but where they are conceived as being mutually determining in their difference, thought is liberated to progress towards what Hegel theorised as Absolute Knowing. In this procedure, identity is not just the forcing together of opposed principles, nor the tautological equation of identical principles, but productively brings about a unity of their common and opposing moments – the identity of identity and difference.

It is precisely the idea that there is nothing extraneous in the dialectical process, nothing other than what it produces out of itself by its own movement, that will be confronted head-on by Marx. If the objective idealism of the Hegelian dialectic insisted that the development of thought in the objectification of consciousness, in its *self*-consciousness above all, produced the events of human history, resulting in a progress towards self-realisation as we saw in the previous chapter, for Marx this is exactly – and simply – the wrong way around. It is the material circumstances of social and economic life that produce the thought-forms. Consciousness itself developed when humanity began producing the means for its own subsistence and survival, rather than merely depending on the principle of chance in the natural world. The control and exploitation of natural resources in order to fashion an existence, and then with the advent of forms of ownership and the willingness to defend them, a more privileged existence than that eked out by the others, created the forms of consciousness that established social structures. It is these social relations, for Marx, more than the elaborations of religion, morality, law, and even programmatic politics, that produce consciousness. In other words, instead of moving from general and universal elements to particular ones, as Hegel does, it is the latter that generate the former. The dialectical principle, as expounded in Hegel's *Science of Logic*, is absolutely right according to Marx; it is only that he uses it to look at human development through the wrong end of the telescope. A celebrated passage from the Afterword to the 1873 edition of *Capital* puts this point most succinctly:

> My dialectical method is not only different from the Hegelian, but is its direct opposite. To Hegel, the life process of the human brain, i.e. the process of thinking, which, under the name of 'the Idea' he even transforms into an independent subject, is the *demiurgos* of the real world, and the real world is only the external, phenomenal form of 'the Idea'. With me, on the contrary, the ideal is nothing else than the material world reflected by the human mind, and translated into forms of thought... With him it [the dialectic] is standing on its head. It must be turned right side up again, if you would discover the rational kernel within the mystical shell.[1]

Marx adds that dialectics in its idealist form had become paradoxically popular in Germany in the wake of Hegel's work, just because it was misread as an ideology of the existing state of society. What such a misinterpretation missed was the all-important dynamic principle of movement, the fact that all states of affairs are subject to their own negation, their own eventual demise and transformation into another form that retains something of the old, but in radically altered guise. Whatever the captains of industry and their political apologists and champions may be expecting, the movement of capitalism towards its universal crisis will drill the real dialectical process into their heads regardless.

The opening essay of Adorno's three studies of Hegel of 1963, 'Aspects of Hegel's Philosophy', addresses some of the fundamental misconceptions that had traditionally plagued critical reception of Hegel's work in Germany. Not the least of these is the notion that mediation between two opposing concepts – say, freedom and necessity, lordship and bondage, theory and praxis

– somehow implies a moderating compromise position between two extremes, as opposed to its actual role as the mediation of the extremes themselves. What happens between the two poles of any binary opposition is of scant interest to philosophical thought, compared to the transformation of the poles themselves in relation to each other. No aspect of reality is at all meaningful, can become subject in Hegelian philosophy, without its opposite, without that which helps constitute it, by virtue of being what it is not. The search in traditional metaphysics for an ultimate cause from which everything may be derived, which might be the intellect, the will, the struggle for power, as much as it was once unquestionably God, is brushed aside by Hegel. The dialectic, therefore, is not a mere methodology, a mechanical system through which everything may be processed like ground meat being turned through a sausage-machine, and nor is it a philosophical outlook, like fatalism or pantheism. It is, instead, a description of a process, in intellectual affairs as much as in human history. Contrary to the simplified triadic view that has often been used as a way of propounding Hegel's logic – that every thesis is opposed by an antithesis, and their opposition then results in a synthesis – what the dialectical process consists in is the confrontation of the objective world with the accepted conceptual account of it, or as Adorno puts it, 'the unswerving effort to conjoin reason's critical consciousness of itself and the critical experience of objects'.[2] Against those who would claim that the dialectical construction of history, for example, is entirely arbitrary – why should we assume that every movement of historical affairs proceeds against a countervailing impulse? – Adorno adduces one of the central events of twentieth-century European history. Hitler's war, the attempt of capitalist interests to eradicate the spectre of Bolshevism by unleashing a reactionary mass movement against it, resulted in the domination of half the continent by the Soviet power bloc. Dialectical thinking might well empower the anticipation of such eventualities, rather than being merely a static prophetic gaze into the future in the fashion of Nostradamus.

The problem with Hegelian dialectic, an insight in which Adorno endorses Marx, is that it remains wedded to idealism. It is a philosophy of the spirit, of the primacy of the subject. In a sense, it misses its own moment by not extrapolating from the reciprocal conditioning of the subjective and objective moments in consciousness what would be the illuminating realisation that there can be no fixed subjective position from which everything is determined. Absolute Knowing is not absolved of its grasp at absolutism simply because it has become conscious of itself. Despite the fact that it wants to do away with the fixed principle, the starting-point, Hegel's logic cannot help enthroning the spirit as its constitutional monarch. 'When the contemplating spirit presumes to show that everything that exists is commensurable with spirit itself, with Logos and the determinations of thought, spirit sets itself up as an ontological ultimate, even if at the same time it grasps the untruth in this, that of the abstract a priori, and attempts to do away with its own fundamental thesis'.[3] The unity of subject and object for which the Hegelian dialectic strives is a relic of eroded idealism. It still intends, in the last analysis, that everything be seen from the subject's point of view, and its effect is to enshrine the Absolute as a final principle, no matter how suspended and provisional it appears. Its truth moment is that what spirit really is, what one could counter-intuitively conceive as its concrete material reality, is social labour, which is what the young Marx conceded to be the great achievement of Hegel's *Phenomenology*. In its postulation of negativity as the motor force and creative principle of human development, it had grasped, did it but know it, the true nature of human self-production through labour. Humankind is the result of its own labour because labour, among other things, makes human beings contingent on each other, and thus mutually socially dependent. That in itself ought to pull the rug from under an imperial, or for that matter haplessly contingent, individual subject, and thus from idealism. As Adorno writes, 'labour only becomes labour as something for something else, something commensurable with other things, something that transcends the contingency of the individual subject'.[4]

In his restatement of Marx, Adorno argues that the unity of human beings reproducing their lives through labour constitutes society, in which objective tendencies are produced without reflection, which is to say independently of the authorship of the human spirit. Society as the context of social labour, however, makes no acknowledgement of the specificity of types of human labour, of the labourer's experience, or of the resulting products, which are subjected to the principle of false equivalence in bourgeois exchange relations. In this respect, society has taken on the lineaments of what Hegel calls the emphatic notion of the concept, in that it is both absolutely real and absolutely abstract. Everything human beings think and do runs up against the total functional context of social relations, so that experience itself becomes the experience only of fantastical relations among things. The labour that goes into the social product is reflected back to the workers as their own alienated form, so that nothing in social reality is external to them, and yet the incorporation of that labour as exchange value into their own habits of consciousness reproduces external reality as blind compulsion, rather than the empirical realm upon which the worker could potentially act. Identity, the aim of the Hegelian dialectic, is thus an act of brutal coercion for those who are subjected to it, and anything but a metaphorical effect. If all labour originates in the attempt to dominate nature, that attempt has long become an autonomous function of labouring, making the true nature of labour opaque to itself. The disservice that idealism does to human experience is in casting human labour as just such an autonomous entity, an eternal verity, instead of seeing it for what it truly materially is, which is the totality of human suffering. The

Hegelian spirit is the moment of social labour that has come adrift from its roots in physical labour, in nature. Despite their separation, ratified into an absolute during the industrial era, nature and spirit are mutually dependent, distinct from one another but mediating each other at the same time. Bourgeois sanctimony, in its tribute to its labour force, acknowledges that labour is the source of all wealth, and therefore of culture. Marx, in his dialectical critique of the social-democratic Gotha programme, flays this piety as deliberately eliding the origin of labour in nature, of which human labour power is another of the many manifestations. When humankind takes up a dominant position towards nature, treating it as its own, labour becomes the source of use value, so that when economic conditions create a class that has no other property than its own labour-power, it suits those who own the material conditions of labour to pretend that wealth flows in some supernatural way from pure labour itself, in the manner of divine creation. This is none other than what the Hegelian dialectic does when it incorporates labour into the realm of spirit, rather than explicating spirit as one of the by-products of labour. Its untruth is constituted for Adorno in the fact that it glosses over the economic reality that labour is always labour for others, for those who have appropriated it for their own profit, which they can only do when labour itself has become a metaphysical concept. 'This social relationship dictates the untruth in Hegel,' Adorno states, 'the masking of the subject as subject-object, the denial of the nonidentical in the totality'.[5]

Dialectical thought aims, as is only proper, at the truth, but as Hegel already asserts, the truth is not a fixed quantity that remains sufficiently inert to be grasped, but is in constant movement. Thinking itself is a moment of the absolute towards which Hegelian reason strives. What should be achieved by reflection, which is to say the reflection of reflection on itself, is an awareness of the untruth within its previously held conceptions, for the sake of which, in Hegel's system, the movement of thought tends towards reconciliation. As Adorno puts this, 'Perhaps nothing says more about the nature of dialectical thought than that self-consciousness of the subjective moment in truth, reflection on reflection, is to effect a reconciliation with the injustice that the operating subjectivity does to immanent truth in merely supposing and positing as true something that is never wholly true'.[6] If all thought were merely a true thinking of what was true, it would be an overwhelming tautology, and would helplessly falsify, by marginalising it, a reality that is riddled with falsehood and deceit. Adorno more than once berates those who insist that all criticism ought to be 'constructive', that nothing should be denigrated unless one has a better idea, which he scorns as the pure ideology of affirming what already is. The dynamic aspect of Hegel's philosophy, by contrast, is that, despite itself, it contains an anti-idealist moment, in that its negative consciousness of what is untrue is what constantly subverts the idea, the pure product of the mind. 'If the idealist dialectic turns against idealism,' says Adorno, 'it does so because its own principle, because the very overextension of its idealist claim, is at the same time anti-idealist'.[7] As soon as reflection reveals a moment of untruth in what appears as the truth, its claim to ideality is broken. Everything turns, as Hegel has it, on grasping the true not only as substance, but as subject, as a moving potency in itself, not simply as an object to be cognised. The Kantian method, in which the subject remains external to the matter of cognition, is what his own philosophy has moved on from. Reflection is not just a question of consciousness, but a dynamic insight into what happens within truth itself or, as Adorno characterises it, '[t]he dialectic is a process in terms of the immanence of truth as much as in terms of the activity of consciousness: process, that is, is truth itself'.[8]

At the end of the Preface to the first German publication of the Hegel studies in 1963, Adorno appended a single sentence that was to become a manifesto commitment: 'The work as a whole is intended as preparation for a revised conception of the dialectic'.[9] This undertaking would unfold through a lecture course in the mid-1960s at Frankfurt, and culminate eventually in the publication in 1966 of the chef d'oeuvre, *Negative Dialectics*. What Adorno intended with this gargantuan, monumentally complex body of thought was to reorient the emphasis of philosophy from the transcendental constitutive subject in Kant, who insists 'that the objects must conform to our cognition... to establish something about the objects before they are given to us,'[10] to a stance in which the object assumes primacy, not in the sense that the subject becomes subordinate to it, like the medieval philosopher trying to decipher the secrets of the created world of God, but that the subject discovers its own contingent, historically determined nature in an objectivity that it does not attempt to master. Speaking of the final chapter of the book in its short Preface, Adorno says that what he is attempting in the negative-dialectical approach is 'by critical self-reflection to give the Copernican revolution [i.e. the Copernican revolution in philosophy] an axial turn'.[11] Such a move will displace the subject from its imperious position as the founder of all knowledge, and reconceive it as the product of an empirical world in which the significance of subjective experience is restored to it, as opposed to its being the ahistorical source of all perception. The project will be '[t]o use the strength of the subject to break through the fallacy of constitutive subjectivity'.[12] In other words, a subject rendered impotent by the combined forces of calamitous history and the total context of reified bourgeois society is not conceivable as a transcendental subject, but a focus on the experience of its own suffering at the hands of these forces, which is reflected in the objective world, might restore to philosophy the capacity to say something about experience that would not distort and falsify it.

Adorno is quite clear about those aspects of traditional philosophical method that have to be discarded. The first and most egregious of these is thinking in rigid dogmatic concepts, which subsumes the dimension of sensuous particularity under abstract generality. This does not mean, as is often thought, that he advocates dispensing with concepts altogether. A thinking that does not proceed conceptually cannot be any form of thinking, because thinking is always a thought of something, and its medium is the conceptual apprehension of the world. It is, however, important to purge philosophy of the hypostasis of the concept, its elevation to the level of a self-sufficient and self-authorising totality, which then becomes a unit of speculative thought, what one might conceive as the nominalist fallacy. A concept is only originally a bit of the reality it seeks to conceptualise, and because it emerges from reality, it is therefore dependent on it, not an autonomous entity. 'In truth, all concepts, even the philosophical ones, refer to nonconceptualities, because concepts on their part are moments of the reality that requires their formation, primarily for the control of nature'.[13] What needs to be retained in the concept is what traditional philosophy has tended to jettison from its operations as the unwanted trash, the minute, fragmentary, peripheral elements of existence. The drive in the concept to enfold the reality it indicates into its own comprehensive signifying mechanism is the drive to identity, identity in the sense of making two or more heterogeneous aspects of the empirical world identical with each other. 'To change this direction of conceptuality,' Adorno writes, 'to give it a turn towards nonidentity, is the hinge of negative dialectics. Insight into the constitutive character of the nonconceptual in the concept would end the compulsive identification which the concept brings unless halted by such reflection'.[14] To make reality conform to the concept is to do violence to what in reality most needs to be given expression, the corporeal side of human experience that, through being repressed for the sake of the abstract collective machinery in which all are enmeshed, produces historical suffering. In one of his most celebrated formulations, Adorno declares: 'The need to lend a voice to suffering is the condition of all truth. For suffering is objectivity that weighs upon the subject; its most subjective experience, its expression, is objectively conveyed'.[15]

The traditional medium of fetishised conceptualisation in philosophical history has customarily been the system. Theoretical thought has been a system-building enterprise ever since it began to be realised that the natural world conformed in many respects to intuitable laws. The system that philosophers from Descartes to Kant, Hegel and Schopenhauer announce themselves to have perfected is a structure into which the world is expected to fit, and becomes the template for the workings of society itself, which if it can be conceived as a system might measure up to the standard of rationality that it sets itself. Adorno acknowledges that the lure of system-building is not difficult to explain. 'Systems elaborate things; they interpret the world while the others keep protesting only that it can't be done'.[16] They allowed the thinker to reconceive administratively a reality over which he otherwise had no power. Nietzsche, mounting the first sustained critique of systematisation in the western tradition, observed sardonically that they were a compensation reaction on the part of intellectuals for their political impotence. Systems were the means by which bourgeois society indemnified itself against the incompleteness of its own emancipation. The truth about them, however, lay in the fact that they contended with each other like the different factions at court, or the political parties in the era of bourgeois enfranchisement. Each new system had to be offered as supplanting all the inadequate ones that had preceded it, regardless of whether they explicitly grew out of one or other of them. Refusal of foregoing theories was the lifeblood of philosophy – Schopenhauer excoriated the Hegelian system before replacing it with his own – but if every system was overturnable by the next, the systematic principle itself, more even than the positive conceptual content that it comported, was the problem. Where it depended on a scientific postulate later exposed as gibberish, from the geocentric universe to the pineal gland of Descartes, the system convicted itself of untruth more succinctly than any subsequent polemical exercise that came to be directed against it. When the philosophical systems decisively crumbled in the first half of the twentieth century, politics reappropriated the systematic impulse with more lethally comprehensive results than the absolute subject of transcendental apperception knew how to. Every aspect of a system is implicitly already in place in order for it to be a functional system, which is why systematic thinking is reified thinking. It presupposes its own definitions. Everything in it is already preconceived, so what it offers are merely definitions in accordance with its own principle, rather than insights into what is properly heterogeneous to it. The antidote is a fully immersive mode of thought, one that surrenders itself to the objectivity within the object in order to understand it immanently in all its moments. This may appear phantasmatic under conventional conceptions of thought, but that alone would honour the true potential of thought. 'If the thought really yielded to the object, if its attention were on the object, not on its category, the very objects would start talking under the lingering eye'.[17]

The principle that moves thought is, as Hegel had already demonstrated, that of negation. What is not the case is left behind in the movement of the self-realisation of the human spirit, but the intention is always to produce something positive. The Socratic dialogues proceed by negation to establish a positive conclusion. Hegel would call this procedure the negation of the negation, the cancelling of what was already wrong. For Adorno's reconception of dialectics, the idea that a negation of the negation, like adding or multiplying two negative quantities in mathematics, would result in something positive has become pure ideology. What his own dialectics wishes to do is 'to free dialectics of such affirmative traits without reducing its determinacy'.[18] In other words, rather than aiming at a resolution in thought of the antinomies of contemporary existence, negative dialectics will go on relentlessly pursuing their negative character. Reality is not made right by reconceiving it harmoniously in concepts, but can be faithfully reflected in its treacherous inadequacy by immanent reflection of it through its own categories. This is only possible, however, without reifying thought into the static conceptualisations and arid systematisation that dialectics should always already have relinquished. Adorno is careful to point out that if his theory is not an ontology, neither is it a systematic methodological anti-ontology. It does not simply replace the postulates of identitarian logic with an anti-identitarianism. It is not a standpoint, not a transcendental subjectivism, but not a vulgar-materialist objectivism either. It is not a methodological determinism because it does not anticipate its results prior to discovering them. If the report on knowledge that it delivers tends to be overwhelmingly negative in its provisional conclusions, that says more about knowledge as it is presently constituted than it does about its own tendency. That said, it is not immune to self-reflection, which is its lifeblood. 'It lies in the definition of negative dialectics that it will not come to rest in itself, as if it were total. This is its form of hope'.[19] The key, far from critiquing things from above or outside, bringing extraneous criteria to bear on what is heterogeneous to them, and to which they already thereby contain their own resistance, is to unravel them according to their own concepts and categories, immanently, in their own terms. In this way, thinking retains both its determinate force and its suppleness. '[W]hat would apply to it once more is Hegel's dictum that in dialectics an opponent's strength is absorbed and turned against him, not just in the dialectical particular, but eventually in the whole'.[20]

The objective structure of society looms over all

consciousness, and has to a great measure succeeded in imprinting itself in the forms of consciousness, the better that they might lend support to the total structure. For philosophy to achieve insight into the social structure, it must simultaneously immerse itself in it while not accepting it as its like. The absolute otherness that society itself constitutes, even while claiming to be composed of nothing but preciously individual human units, must remain other to a non-identitarian thinking if it is to retain the hope of illuminating it, even if the goal of consciousness is to achieve the reconciliation of damaged subject and reified object. The contemporary therapeutic notion of 'tough love', in which the parent or partner in a relationship must be prepared to be unsparing in her practical attitude towards the other, if the other is to be brought to a condition of honouring the relationship and thereby fulfilling his own potential, might serve as an image of a negative-dialectical approach to social critique, if it could be persuaded to renounce, that is, its apparent teleology, its assurance that it already knows the right outcome. Whatever happiness dialectical thinking wishes for, it must recognise that its own conception of it is likely to be as faulty as everything else in mutilated consciousness. What it can do, meanwhile, is rigorously identify delusive versions of happiness, including those that suggest that it is within the grasp of all individuals, if only they want it enough, as much as those that appear to posit the reconciled life as a final state, immune to the dialectic of historical contingency. 'Happiness is not invariant; to be always the same is the essence of unhappiness alone... To this day, all happiness is a pledge of what has not yet been, and the belief in its imminence obstructs its becoming... The thought's position towards happiness would be the negation of all false happiness'.[21] It was for the sake of understanding what was not like itself that philosophy began its historical enterprise in the first place, and even where it concluded, in the fatalistic Sophoclean fashion, or with Hegel's assertion that history was not the soil of happiness, that there was nothing to be wrested from objective tendencies that could be conformed to the individual's own psychological needs, it nonetheless wanted its own reflection to reconcile the hapless subject to the world in being. What negative dialectics claims is that as long as peace is declared to have broken out on the terms of the existent, which is not fundamentally concerned with reconciliation as long as the racket itself keeps going, it amounts to the very hostile delusion of which a sensitive consciousness instinctively convicts it. Experience already tells it that this is not the right world, and a thinking that produces the positive from the sum of negativity hopelessly belies that experience.

If the reality that non-identitarian, anti-systematic thinking tries to reflect refuses the essentialising of concepts, however, it does not follow for Adorno that it can yield its historic project of seeking truth. Truth for Adorno is a profoundly emphatic motivation of theory. Even if there is no truth in history, he declared in an early essay, there is by contrast certainly history in truth. There are no eternal verities, either of the rational or the factual variety, for philosophy, which despite centuries of attempting to conform its procedures to those of the exact physical sciences, properly has its domain where the sciences declare there is nothing further to be found. 'Its history is one of permanent failure insofar as, terrorised by science, it would keep searching for tangibility... Philosophy will not dispense with truth, however, but will illuminate the narrowness of scientific truth'.[22] If one superficial misreading of negative dialectics sees in it nothing more than a morbid fatalism, another even more persistent current accuses it of wilful obscurantism and the appearance of erecting a self-defeating irrationalism, rather than accepting the bracing clarity of empirically verifiable knowledge. These are the nothings that lie furthest from truth. What there is in experience that science cannot account for is not just the metaphysical, which neuroscience is anyway drawing under the capacious canopy of mere brain chemistry, but everything that inhabits the gap between what is and what ought to be. When scientific truth assigns ethical conviction to the realm that lies outside its proper purview, even while insisting that those convictions too are probably just the effect of neural activity, having previously conceded them to psychology, it does philosophy the honour of declaring that it too has a substantive domain, for all that it struggles to express what goes on there. Paradoxically, it is the rigorism of science that philosophy appropriates when it aims at truth by eliminating the untrue. Even if it can no longer express it in the tabular schematic form with which Kant and Hegel presented their systems, it still seeks a consistency and a fastidious stringency in the movement of thought that enables it to be the thought *of* something, and not just abstract mentation. Unlike the contentless ontology of Heidegger, its most obvious antipode, Adorno's thought is not non-committal. 'Philosophy seeks stringency in that which it is not, in its opposite, and in the reflection on what, with a poor sort of naïveté, is viewed as binding by positive cognition'.[23] The achievement of insight, however, can only be arrived at negatively. Much as it cannot confine itself to the pleonasm of expressing à la Wittgenstein what seems to be the case, neither can it confine itself to the airy realm of ideas, for all that this realm is what raised dialectics to its highest potency in the first place. There is perhaps no more forceful paradox than this in the relation of negative-dialectical thinking to reality. Without a grounding in the corporeal and sensory roots of knowledge, philosophy is left only with ethereal abstraction, but it is precisely when it abandons the former, when it renounces its own conductivity towards truth, that its ambition collapses to nothing more than the operations of verificationist science. 'Unless the idealistically acquired concept of dialectics harbours experiences contrary to the Hegelian emphasis, experiences independent of the idealistic machinery, philosophy must inevitably do without substantive insight, confine itself to the methodology of science, call that philosophy, and virtually cross itself out'.[24]

To Adorno, the classical drive to find a concept that encompasses all living things – Hegel's World Spirit, for example – only results in untruth, in that it necessarily circumscribes what will not be homogenised into the concept: in short, contingency. The transcendental concept is the hallmark of the identity-principle; it is the symptom of philosophy's misguided search for an ahistorical certainty. Because the concept is generated from out of a contradictory empirical reality, however, it ineluctably includes that which cannot be conceptualised, and yet exists. The philosopher's trust in conceptualisation may lead him or her to believe that, because nothing can be known about reality without it, a semblance of autonomy may be conferred on it. It is from this belief that the identity-principle arises. Since meaning is never invariant, it is not exhausted by the concept, and it is this mutability that guarantees the nonconceptual moment within any concept. The tendency of the concept is to depart from materiality as soon as it becomes an idealised unit of philosophy, a reflex that is only countered for Adorno by a movement towards the nonconceptual, and to that which is not identical with the established concept – in a word, nonidentity.

To ignore the nonidentical element is to reify conceptuality, according to Adorno, and to make it palpably inimical to the dynamism of thought. It is the nonidentical that acts as the hinge for negative dialectics; by deictic reference to the circumstances of material reality, conceptualisation is demythologised and rendered self-reflective. A discourse that only offers modification of the established thought-structures of philosophy cannot release the potential for the advancement of consciousness, which has to be achieved by relinquishing the notion of thought-as-structure in itself. Adorno suggests that for negative dialectics to have at least this demythologising effect would be a modest beginning. It must focus its attention on particularity, contingency, nonconceptuality within the concept. This involves it inevitably in attempting to express the inexpressible, an impulse that seems to harmonise with the desire to attain that utopia of which we have learned that all we can positively know is that it is unattainable. To this end, philosophy is urged to forgo the systematic character that seeks to make the phenomenal world explicable by the application of formal categories, as if in quest of a fully comprehensible existence which would then prepare the abolition of philosophy as sheer unnecessary tautology. Adorno seeks to rescue the notion of the 'infinite' as that which precisely resists systematisation, and is equivalent to the subjective experience of reality. The infinite, as such a notion, transcends all discursive totality. Systematicity demands a formal totalising language that can be expounded in order to come into being as system at all, but experience will always eventually negate it. Against the system, Adorno proposes – a marker of the early influence of Walter Benjamin on his thought – thinking in constellations, in which a linear supersessionary progress from one thesis to the next is replaced by a structuring of disparate elements of thought around a stable centre, from which they are all roughly equidistant, so that the discrete points in an argument bear the same relation to the theme as do the individual stars to the constellation. Instead of being a fixed construction to which one keeps adding another layer, dynamic thinking produces something like an orrery, its component parts moving in relation to each other, as well as around the central star. This procedure imitates the classic form of the essay, which offered a series of propositions around a thematic nucleus without aspiring to the condition of a totalising theory.

'The whole is the untrue,'[25] Adorno announced in *Minima Moralia*, in a classic inversion of Hegelian doctrine. Rather than being a formal credo, the statement acts as an ironic refutation of the totalising impulse, implying that any conjugation of objective reality as an invariant totality will inevitably surrender subjective experience to the identity-principle, colluding in the reduction of the individual subject to a single component of a homogeneous whole, to which exchange relations have already relegated it. An ideologically delusive society, which is constituted by individual subjects who have forgotten themselves as such, and which it was once thought their prerogative to change, gives deadly licence to the identity-principle.

In the context of prevailing economic relations, as Adorno diagnoses it, following Lukács, individuals live under the 'spell' of reification. Against Lukács, though, he claims that this spell is also the means by which dynamic thought is blocked and acquiescence in the status quo is ensured. Under its power, the subject's consciousness, far from being spurred to revolutionary action, is prevented from imagining that things might be different. It may appear that Adorno fetishises the notion of the very reification he seeks to negate, allowing his text to slither into the very totalising statements against which negative dialectics is conceived, as when he declares that '[p]eople, of course, are spellbound without exception'.[26] It is as though the desire for negation had here begun to make an ideology of the despair that is engendered by any reflection on the extent of ideology's influence, but readers of Adorno need to become viscerally responsive to the moments at which only a strategic rhetorical exaggeration, a hypertrophy of the negative impulse, can best express the enormity against which thought contends. The chief form of the spell in western society, indeed its most enormous instrument, as we shall see in greater detail in the next chapter, is the commercial culture industry of late capitalism, which has made works of art into fetishised commodities along with philosophy itself. In this climate, all theories must simply compete against each other in futile debate and none may have practical efficacy. The clamour of this debate is adduced as evidence of the pluralism of bourgeois democracy, as though

democracy consisted merely in the right to call a self-perpetu-
ating ideology inadequate without ever being able to alter it.
Thus does the marketplace extend its sway to embrace philosophers, along with those labourers who have known its influence
for rather longer.

If philosophy strives to express universal truths, Adorno
argues, as art once characteristically sought to do, it posits a false
identity of subject and object in the life of the mind. Instead of
perceiving reality at a distance by means of objectification, its
goal becomes the introjection of all phenomena in a comprehensive act of cognition. In a sense, reality would thereby be no
more than what the transcendent mind understood. This is the
source of Adorno and Horkheimer's contention in the *Dialectic of
Enlightenment* that the rationalistic conception of enlightenment
is totalitarian. To jettison the hermeneutic moment in philosophy,
however, would be to put an end to philosophy itself. Not to
think at all, as may be retorted by those who are adjured in their
everyday lives that their problem is that they think too much,
implies subsumption to the existent. The act of cogitative
reflection objectifies all strata of experience, down to the least
apparently significant; it offers the individual the potential to
resist the tiny catastrophes that confront him in everyday
consciousness. Without such a possibility, Adorno states, '[w]e
could not conceive the simplest operation; there would be no
truth; everything would be just nothing'.[27] This is why, notwithstanding the shallow misapprehension of bourgeois liberal – and
indeed many mainstream Marxist – responses to Adorno,
negative dialectics is not ultimately a despairing philosophy.
Despite the sombre aspects of many of its pronouncements, it is
founded on a dialectical dynamism that has constant flexion as its
mobilising principle. The point, of course, is to change the world.
A theory that deals in immutable, idealistic thought-forms cannot
address itself to this task. It grows untimely, and thus
inapplicable, as soon as it insists on transcendence over the realm

of the practical. This is the reason that Adorno readily embraces those artists – Schönberg, Kafka, Beckett – who sought to shatter the decayed apparatus of the forms in which they practised, making formal dissolution truer to modern experience than classicism was any longer capable of achieving. Only its acquiescence in the prevailing division of intellectual labour, by which it humbly accepts its handmaiden's role in the palace of science, blocks philosophical thought from engaging with what should be its most pressing concern, the decay of experience. Simply usurping science's role, however, is hardly the solution, since it would only reinforce the division of labour in inverted form. As Adorno and Horkheimer put it:

> The status quo compels human beings not merely by virtue of physical force and material interests but also through its overpowering suggestiveness. Philosophy is not synthesis, and it is not the fundamental or master science. It is the attempt to resist this suggestiveness, the determination to hang on to intellectual and real freedom.[28]

The cause of dialectics was not helped in the twentieth century by its petrifaction into an approved methodology in the Soviet system. To Adorno, this was consummate absurdity, because the function of dialectics is to illuminate the wrong state of things. If society were to be truly pacified, freed from the dominative structures of present oppression, it would have no need of dialectical thinking, and in any case, dialectics, as Engels himself defined it, is an account of the total dynamics of a system, its ebbs and flows, its risings and fallings away, the permanent state of becoming in which it existed. It isn't simply a language to be learned, or a rhetorical mode to be adopted and applied to any phenomenon that falls within its ambit.

In a reflection on dialectics towards the end of *Minima Moralia*, Adorno already anticipated the arguments he would put in greater depth and intricacy in the *Negative Dialectics* twenty years later. He begins by tracing a lightning history of its development. In the Sophist tradition of ancient Greece, it represented a means by which an apparently ingrained position could be overturned by argument, so that what started out as the weaker position became the stronger. In the Platonic dialogues, it has become a perennially applied procedure, the principle by which the normativity of received opinion can be tripped up. It is already, Adorno notes, an instrument of domination, if all it does is prove one of two thinkers right. Whether it contains anything of truth, therefore, derives not from the method itself, but from the motivation with which it is put to use at different historical junctures. He states that its bifurcation into left and right schools after Hegel's death reflected not only the prevailing political contest in Germany in the period leading up to the liberal revolutions of 1848, but also the fact that it was in itself profoundly ambiguous in nature. If it had high-minded historical purpose in the Marxist version, in which the proletariat would transform itself from the object into the subject of history by overturning bourgeois society, thereby abolishing itself as a class into the bargain, it also had a ludic, satirical side. He references a cartoon by the French illustrator Gustave Doré, in which a surviving representative of the old order pompously remarks that, really, Louis XVI is to be credited with the Declaration of the Rights of Man, because without him, there would have been no revolution. This is not just an ironic squib, but also an impeccable piece of dialectical thinking, perhaps recalling Brecht's observation that nobody who lacked a sense of humour would understand dialectics. That much ought to be straightforward enough. From this point on, however, Adorno subjects the operation of the dialectic itself to a dialectical analysis.

Dialectics, it will be recalled, is predicated on the notion of sublation, the simultaneous overcoming and retention of the contending terms in an opposing pair. Not only the old form of

an argument is liquidated, but so is the means by which it is liquidated. 'Negative philosophy, dissolving everything, dissolves
even the dissolvent.' In Marxist terms, the proletariat, in
dissolving bourgeois society, dissolves itself as well. 'But the new
form in which it claims to suspend and preserve both, dissolved
and dissolvent, can never emerge in a pure state from an antagonistic society.' As long as society remains a mechanism for the
reproduction of relations of domination, the dialectically
sublated form in which its immediately preceding stage now
manifests itself still contains an element of the old, which is still
active. 'As long as domination reproduces itself, the old quality
reappears unrefined in the dissolving of the dissolvent: in a
radical sense no leap is made at all. That would happen only with
the liberating event.' If the old remains within the new –
sublation, synthesis, call it what we will – it has not yet been
surpassed. In a discomfiting thought for those who accuse
Adorno of lacking a conception of praxis, he declares that only
actual concrete change would have the liberating effect that
Hegelian-Marxist dialectics claims for the movement of dialectics
itself. If the persistence of dialectics is the indication that the right
state of affairs has not arrived yet, then it is always in a sense the
embodiment of conflict between its own critique of existing
conditions, which imply a reconciled better world, and the fact
that no such world yet exists. The objectivity it addresses, which
it rebels against, is precisely what it cannot help but accept as the
truth, because, even though it knows it to be faulty to the core,
there is as yet no other. This is what keeps dragging it back to
what already exists, the abolition of which would also abolish
dialectics. Dialectical thinking is an incomplete liberation, a
partial progress towards what would obviate the need for it, but
which keeps being thrown back upon itself by its asymptotic
character, and which in certain quarters – the Stalinist nomenklatura, pre-eminently, at the time of Adorno's writing – is turned
by drear necessity into a virtue. As Adorno expresses it:

Because the dialectical determination of the new quality always finds itself referred back to the violence of the objective tendency that propagates domination, it is placed under the almost inescapable compulsion, whenever it has conceptually achieved the negation of the negation, to substitute, even in thought, the bad old order for the non-existent alternative. The depth to which it penetrates objectivity is bought with complicity in the lie that objectivity is truth.[29]

In the late 1940s, Adorno already sees the misuse of dialectics atrophying into nothing more than a rhetorical mode, worse still a stance. It is in the nature of a conventional thinking that prides itself on its intellectual sophistication, its non-naïveté [*Unnaivetät*], to relapse into apologetics for the status quo, because the reaching for something else that is constituted by opposing it so often ends up looking childish to those who have accustomed themselves to what there is. A pliant, conceptually supple thought must resist this, and be unceasingly vigilant against it. Dialectics that has congealed into a point of view conforms to the bluntness of the very totalising impulse against which it sharpened its edge. 'The threatening relapse of reflection into unreflectedness gives itself away by the facility with which the dialectical procedure shuttles its arguments, as if it were itself that immediate knowledge of the whole which the very principle of the dialectic precludes'.[30] The weight of facts, constituted as non-negotiable and ahistorical, is allowed to press the life out of conceptual fluidity and self-reflexive agility, while choking off rival negative judgments at their source. What ought to move dialectical thinking is its passage to the logical extremes, the idea that nothing should be regarded as settled, which is what motivates thought in the first place. Arguing from a position that one has already determined in advance is death to it. 'The harm is done by the *thema probandum*: the thinker uses the dialectic instead of giving himself up to it. In this way thought, master-fully dialectical, reverts to the pre-dialectical stage: the serene demonstration of the fact that there are two sides to everything'.[31]

The reception of negative dialectics in critical commentary has been marked by a patchwork of partial understandings, affronted indignation at its wilful inconclusiveness, doomed attempts to subject it to the analytical logic of the Anglo-American tradition, threnodies of despair from those who see only despair in it and, on the left, a continued worrisome sifting of its ideological impli-cations for those elusive flashes of scarlet that might indicate trace elements of a residual Marxism. Andrew Douglas percipi-ently notes the lineage in the dialectical tradition that may be followed through from the negativity of the Hegelian procedure that first attracted the young Marx, itself driven by the need to question how the presuppositions and axioms of pure reason in the Kantian system came to be. Douglas is astute enough to notice that Adorno's negative practice is not a method, and that its *telos*, which is hardly a *telos* at all in the classical philosophical sense, is driven not by the urge to bring the elements of thought into a reconciled state of identity, but to provoke recognition of the nonidentical. Not the least of the ways in which this is achieved is a rhetorically explosive linguistic technique, in which the objects of knowledge, consensual apprehensions of the empirical, are pushed towards the logically self-destructive extremes implicit in them. Douglas poses this interrogatively: 'Is it simply that dialectical thinking, riding in on the backs of exaggeration and hyperbole, is best suited to shock our thinking, to awaken the critical imagination from a state of late-modern lethargy?',[32] before going on to supply the response that this is certainly one of its tactics, for all that it cannot be characterised as 'simply' that, or only that. Something of this is captured in Adorno's suggestion that 'thought need not be content with its own legality; without abandoning it, we can think against our thought, and if it were possible to define dialectics, this would be a definition worth suggesting'.[33] Noncontradictoriness, if consti- tuted as the first requirement of subjective reflection, will inevitably miss whatever is contradictory in the object, which may well not conform to the rules of thinking, its very noncon- formity very often being what mandates thinking about it at the outset. If dialectical thinking is generated by the antagonistic society, it has itself once come to be and will pass, but its own practice is to reflect on itself, to reflect its own motion and its own context of immanence, as much as it engages with the elements of antagonistic society. The attempt to reconcile itself to those elements is what results in a defensive ideology of faked recon- ciliation. 'It is precisely the insatiable identity principle that perpetuates antagonism by suppressing contradiction. What tolerates nothing that is not like itself thwarts the reconciliation for which it mistakes itself. The violence of equality-mongering reproduces the contradiction it eliminates'.[34]

In an attentively critical essay on Adorno's relation to Hegelian dialectics, Mauro Bozzetti observes that, if there is to be no false reconciliation of subject and object in negative dialectics, neither is there to be any traditional synthesis in the Hegelian sense. No such outcome can be presupposed. There is no philo- sophical solution to the noncorrespondence of concept and reality other than for philosophy to think further. And yet Bozzetti's worry is that in its negative movement vis-à-vis the dialectics of consciousness and of history in the Hegelian system, Adorno's thinking is in itself dependent on an inverted system- atics:

[W]e must ask whether a philosophical perspective that justifies itself through the antithesis of another system of thought does not also inherit that system's problems. Adorno does not in fact resolve Hegel's weak spots, morality and history. Rather, he problematises them in a more thoroughgoing way. His negative moral philosophy and apocalyptic view of history are clearly no attempt to solve the practical moral problems of philosophy, and his sociological critique takes insufficient account of the category of intersubjectivity... Adorno's logical arsenal is consciously too weak. He remains fragmentary in form, yet he was both systematic and anti-systematic in content. He was understandably fascinated by Hegel's all-encompassing logic and could not release himself from its spell.[35]

Only an empty formalism could mistake a critical relation to the object of scrutiny as being immanently reflective of that object in all its antinomies. If the only successful attempt to immunise itself against the inadequacies of what it addresses would be to bear no relation to its object, critique would have fallen at the first hurdle. Indeed, there would be no such thing as immanent critique, and thought would be locked forever in a Kantian transcendentalism of the pure intellect. Thought itself in Adorno is anything but autonomous with regard to the objects it thinks, and nor is the goal of negative dialectics a 'resolution'. This would be the very *thema probandum* against which Adorno warns in the section we looked at in the *Minima Moralia*. As for the charge that Adorno takes insufficient notice of intersubjectivity, this is scarcely sustainable in light of his consistent critique of what has become of relations between social subjects in conditions of reification. Again, the idea that traditional logic, by its very force, should be able to meet what it criticises head-on and refute it belongs to the dominative impulse of instrumental reason. Far from not being able to release himself from the 'spell' of Hegelian logic, Adorno everts that logic into its own self-critique, so that the categories and compulsions of idealist thought are returned to their roots in the historical process, in which not just the objects of history are caught, but the reflective subject too. Bozzetti ends by siding with the traditional desideratum that critical assessment of a system of thought, as Adorno applies to Hegel's oeuvre, remains duty-bound 'to present alternative perspectives', which is precisely what would handicap critical thought at its inception. It finds itself under the dual obligation to respect heteronomous systems unless it can think of anything better, and to know in advance what it intends to advocate before it sets about criticising them. A critique of traditional logic, in Bozzetti's view, 'runs the danger of lapsing into the irrational', a suggestion that misses the irrational moment in traditional logic itself, its claim to totality. 'Despite Adorno's relentless critique,' he assures us, 'we cannot do without a form of systematic construction in philosophy,'[36] to do justice to the demands of knowledge and present a criterion of truth in a quasi-theological but non-ideological manner, even if, as Bozzetti elsewhere in his essay appears to suspect, systematic construction may itself be ideology.

In his critical introduction to Adorno of 1998, Simon Jarvis correctly points out that the traditional characterisation of the Hegelian dialectic as a forward motion from thesis to synthesis pays scant regard to the reverse movement that is also crucially implicit in it. Dialectical reasoning is not simply a progress from crude sense-certainty to the refinement of absolute knowing, but always involves a working back through the political, social and cultural conditions of what is apparently certain and immediate. In other words, everything is mediated. Adorno is a sufficiently subtle thinker to know that the dialectical procedure cannot simply be sieved out of the morass of identity-thinking, so that it can then be applied new-minted to the same problems, now with improved results, not least because that would leave identity-thinking itself intact. The point, however – as ever – is to change it. Just as the logic of exchange can only be made good when the principle of exchange itself is honoured by free and fair exchange, thereby doing away with the fraudulent transactions currently practised in its name, so a conceptual thinking making an approach to objects of knowledge needs to recognise the inadequacy of what is currently surrendered to fallacious adequation. Adorno's notion of affinity as against identity in the relation between concept and object gives Kant's schematism a decisive turn, from pure concepts of the understanding being applied to pure appearances to impure concepts interpreting impure objects, with which they are not identical. If consciousness can never know the thing-in-itself in Kant's terms – the so-called Kantian block on thought – then it is always implicitly committed to whatever preconstituted limiting apprehension of it is provided by conceptuality. Such thinking is only ever knowledge of the appearances that can be moulded into the forms of a classificatory conceptuality, whereas what Adorno seeks, via Hegel's command that 'essence must appear', is an attempted knowledge, however partial and provisional, of whatever it is that conceptuality has been content to leave behind. Jarvis spies a slight paradox in this:

> The idea of a thing as it is in itself bears witness to what Adorno himself has... called 'the nonidentical' – although since the thing as considered in itself is necessarily devoid of all qualities it does not fully correspond to Adorno's own notion of the nonidentical. But if we do not admit the possibility of knowing things as they are in themselves, Adorno thinks, we are in fact committed to a kind of scepticism, in which the object is always preformed by conceptuality – in which the object must always remain a logicised object.[37]

In the classical philosophical system, thought creates what it thinks by subjecting it to the systematic process, the grist to its mill being the phenomenal appearances of objects. What it passes over as unknowable, the Kantian thing-in-itself, must be devoid of apprehensible properties, otherwise they would be manifest to consciousness, but that does not trip up Adorno's postulate that the priority of the object is the path that will lead to a truer knowledge of what eludes conceptuality. Jarvis is right to say that the thing-in-itself cannot 'fully' correspond to Adorno's conception of the nonidentical, about which cognition must be able to apprehend something, if is to have thoughts at all, but Kant himself conceded that the limitless progress that reason ought to be able to make in the age of enlightenment found its stride checked when it came up against what could not be conformed to itself. 'Kant had already held that the emancipated *ratio*, the *progressus ad infinitum*, is halted solely by recognising nonidentities in form, at least',[38] or in Jarvis' tidier translation, by the 'formal recognition of the nonidentical'.[39] For Adorno, this is precisely where a non-identitarian thinking might start.

The relation of negative dialectics to epistemology is a question raised by many who have been sceptical of the possibility that a thinking conceived against the norms of identifying logic can establish anything reliable about empirical experience, let alone about the objective world of phenomena to which such experience responds. Roger Foster has sought to counteract these hesitancies by referring Adorno's dialectical technique back to the withering of contemporary experience, and the disenchantment from nature from which it arises. The consequences of a transcendentalist approach are all too obvious, but epistemology, unlike the physician, cannot heal itself within the decayed parameters of instrumental reason. Any transformation of the faulty world would require a wholesale transformation of the conceptual distortions to which reified consciousness submits it. As Foster summarises this:

> [B]ecause Adorno believes that the epistemological problem is a symptom of the social-historical process of disenchantment he does not think that the problem can be solved *within* the terms of epistemology. It is this insight that makes it necessary to carry out the critique of epistemology as negative dialectic,

rather than as a positive theory. Negative dialectic is grounded on the idea that *every individual concept is false*. This is not a sceptical thesis, it is rather an awareness of what our knowledge has become under the conditions of the destruction of experience.[40]

What matters is the propulsive movement that is encouraged by the self-reflection of concepts, not the assertion of a partially reconstituted new conceptual structure, another autonomous theory to replace the old discredited ones.

In a daring move, Steven Helmling recasts Adorno's procedure of immanent critique as 'dialectical mimesis', that is, as a rescue of the mimetic tendency of thought, famously corrupted by its demythologising tendencies into the ideology of a reified science, according to the theory of the *Dialectic of Enlightenment*, by means of its transformation into a thinking that might reliquefy the conceptual basis of thought, rather than simply statically reflecting, and thus repeating, precedent reality, or 'what is'. Thought should be pre-eminently critical, but critical of its objects within their own historically determined terms:

Adorno's immanent critique turns to critical account the mimesis that remains implicated in (or immanent to) it, even as it grapples to surmount, to make conscious on the model of 'transference', all the pathological ruses by which 'mimesis' becomes compulsive, defensive, abreactive against the 'new' and the unknown: all the ways, in short, that resistance to the new becomes ideological.[41]

Abstract rationality constructed itself as an objectifying opposition to reality, but its mathematising approach, which acts as a succubus on whatever is new in experience, by making it the indicator of a pre-existing analysable tendency, isolates thought in its own domain. An immanent procedure, by contrast, stands a chance not only of revealing the untruth in what are presented as the unquestionable facts of the matter, but also of offering restitution to the old, the archaic, and what has been damaged within it by ideological thought-forms.

Attempts to codify what Adorno argues into a schematic or summary form ought to seem fraught with peril, but have not always missed the mark. Alastair Morgan suggests that the (re)construction of experience outlined in negative dialectics, for all that is a process and not an adopted posture, might be summarised as three options for counteracting modern reification. These would be: (i) aesthetic or philosophical interpretation, where such hermeneutics is content with an open-ended procedure typified by the essay form, and by thinking in constellations; (ii) what Morgan terms a 'negative redemptive moment', a breakthrough in consciousness in which reconciled life is figured anti-mimetically as the mirror-image obverse of the present damaged life; and (iii) a positive redemptive moment, an access of potentiality in which a life lived without domination is predicated on 'the trace or figure of a reconciled experience that opens the subject to a different experience of life… the experience of possibility itself',[42] always given the proviso that it remains problematic at best to try to tie such a vision to a practical politics in present conditions. The futural demand that life be different contained within this third form of thinking represents the utopian moment that negative dialectics salvages from decayed metaphysical experience.

Not everybody is convinced of the value of immanent critique, nor – in the case of Fabian Freyenhagen – believes that even Adorno himself was. In a study of the pragmatic implications of Adorno's social criticism, Freyenhagen is troubled about where immanentism might lead if taken too far: 'even if one successfully mounted an immanent critique of our current social world… such critique could only demonstrate the cost of holding on to a value or ideal'.[43] This rather spectacularly misses the point that an immanent critique would not be any sort of critique at all if all it were required to do was uphold the value of an existing state of affairs. Precisely such is what a conservative, restorationist thinking has in mind, that despite all the manifest failure, things are not so bad after all. Freyenhagen is attentive to Adorno's argument that what a critique of bourgeois democracy ought to aim at is shaming its institutional apparatuses into acting in accord with its own ideals, but fails to see that overturning the current 'values' that sustain it, all the way to the lies of ideology, might be indispensable to that end. 'Secondly,' he goes on, 'in certain contexts, we might be able to criticise a social or thought system internally, but would not want it to realise its aims – perhaps the Nazis failed sometimes to live up to their ideals... but it would be rather problematic to criticise them internally for that (instead of welcoming the discrepancy)'.[44] Immanent critique is not a question of establishing whether an ideology succeeds in achieving the aims it sets itself, but in exposing the internal contradictions that lead it to aspire to such a course of action in the first place. Its antinomies do not emerge only in its less than perfect practical efficacy, but in the delusiveness that underpins what efficacy it strives for. A critique of Nazism that pointed out that, despite the best efforts of the SS, not every Jew in occupied Europe was exterminated after all, the logic on which Freyenhagen's paradigm is founded, would not in fact be an immanent critique, but one that compared a programmatic ideal to its concrete external results, something on a par, in the more innocuous modern context, with the banal complaint that politicians are too much given to saying one thing and doing another.

What Adorno's vision of dialectical reflection most insistently breaks with, as is encapsulated in a late essay that originated as a radio talk in 1964, 'Notes on Philosophical Thinking', is the cliché that thought should be optimally constituted by 'a purely logical and rigorous development from a single proposition'. The essence of philosophical rigour is not found in arriving at and emphasising conclusions that mark territorial bounds within the subject-matter, but in the incessant self-renewal of thought. 'Truth is a constantly evolving constellation, not something running continuously and automatically in which the subject's role would be rendered not only easier but, indeed, dispensable'.[45] Paradoxically, thinking must be at once autonomous from its subject-matter, in the sense of being able to objectify what it apprehends, the gesture that marked the great advances in philosophical history, and yet at the same time, it must guard against paying for its autonomy in the currency of reification. In regard to the latter tendency, Adorno makes a strikingly prescient observation about the relation of intellect to the computer, at a historical moment – the end of the 1960s – when the eventual cognitive potential of computers was barely more than a blink in the eye of their users. By becoming significantly more powerful at instrumentalising formalised knowledge than their users can ever be, computers demonstrate the 'nullity' of such formalised thinking when it is abstracted from its contents. The office worker inputting sales transactions into the accounts database of a company computer system is nothing more than the machine-minder of the nineteenth-century factories. What has happened in the era of computerisation is that intellect has modelled itself after the cybernetic processes that were once modelled on it. 'Should thinking subjects passionately transform themselves into the instruments of such formalisation, then they virtually cease being subjects. They approach the machine in the guise of its imperfect replica'.[46] Not every assertion of thought's own independence from machine data need be as critical for human survival as was that of Stanislav Petrov, the Soviet duty-officer who, in the now famous incident of September 1983, overrode the erroneous report of the computerised early-warning system at his nuclear command centre that a multi-weapon strike had been launched by the United States. Petrov's presumption to know better than the computer, which had been fooled by a pattern of sunlight on clouds at high altitude, prevented the accidental outbreak of a nuclear war. There seems all the more reason for speculative thinking not to conform itself to the widely fetishised algorithms of cybernetic data-processing. Indeed, such thinking would only truly begin where it had liberated itself from predictable cognition, from which absolutely nothing emerges that was not already there. This is not an argument against computers, only for the insight that the present-day worship of what are known as Knowledge Organisation Systems has missed the properly emancipatory potential in them. 'The humane significance of computers,' Adorno wrote, at the moment that their power over humanity was beginning to be celebrated as a liberating force, 'would be to unburden the thinking of living beings to the extent that thought would gain the freedom to attain a knowledge that is not already implicit'.[47] The computer can apply analytical logic more potently than the whole of scholastic reasoning could summon through the successive ages of enlightenment. It cannot, however, think dialectically. Only human beings, in what remains of their liberty, can do that.

Four

Aesthetics and the Promise of Happiness

Art is the social antithesis of society.
Aesthetic Theory

A central misconception in much of the most recent generation of Adorno commentary has characterised his later work as describing a movement away from direct sociopolitical inter-vention towards the solace of aesthetics, in which authentic works of art – notably those committed to modernist formal and discursive innovation – become exclusively paradigmatic of the hope for a better world. Indeed, a substantial proportion of writing on Adorno these days is concerned only with his aesthetic theory, not least, one suspects, because its philosophical strategies are more immediately graspable than are those of his more abstract texts. Adorno himself is reported to have remarked to a fellow dinner-guest one evening in 1966, shortly after deliv-ering the final manuscript of *Negative Dialectics* to Suhrkamp, his publisher, that from now on he intended to write only on aesthetic themes, a resolution that would quite likely have been honoured more in the breach than in the observance, had he lived beyond the completion of the *Aesthetic Theory*, his last, not quite finished, major work.

Theorising about the arts came to a head during the course of the 1960s. Movements in conceptual art, minimalism, perfor-mance happenings and Pop had swept aside the last of the sterile academic air of abstract expressionism. Political commitment in the theatre was in the hands of a new generation of engaged dramatists and directors following the death of Bertolt Brecht in 1956, and while European cinema was on the brink of a new wave, the American film industry was in a state of creative ferment too, with the arrival of a generation of young new directors. Popular music, hovering between formal experimentation and polemical engagement as the hippie movement gathered pace amid the great showpiece festivals of the era, was shedding what remained of its adolescence and progressing to a kind of incipient maturity, and a phalanx of European avant-gardists, many of whom had been schooled in the twilight of the serialist age, was transforming contemporary classical music with the aid of electronic equipment and freer principles of composition, frequently founded on chance. Novelists had lost their plots, even characters too in some cases, in favour of a self-referential linguistic practice that drew attention to the unloosing of language from its traditional semiotic functions. The signifier was set afloat and soon found itself becalmed in a sea of what new critical theories would call 'discourse'. Poetic discourse acceded to cut-ups and fold-ins, gnomic iterations of haiku-like brevity, ludic anti-intellectualism, confessional incontinence. Brutal functionalism was the mood in civic architecture, with leavenings of a more formally adventurous modernism for well-funded individual projects. In the culinary arts in France, *nouvelle cuisine* set out to reduce the ancestral gastronomic tradition to its highly concentrated spartan fundamentals.

Adorno observed most of this with a relentlessly critical attention. He had been writing about music since the 1920s, when he was a student of composition under Alban Berg in Vienna, and the volume of his published works on music outweighs that on any other single topic. As well as his writings on music theory, the sociology of music appreciation and the psychology of musical taste, there are book-length monographs on individual composers – Wagner, Mahler and Berg – as well as several volumes of miscellaneous essays on musical themes. His first engagement in the United States, on arrival from pre-war exile in England in 1938, was his eventually aborted participation in the Princeton Radio Research Project, which attempted to construct a sociologically comprehensive picture of the listening habits of American radio audiences, the contexts in which they heard classical music, what they gleaned of it and whether they might be amenable to being lightly educated about it. As well as the corpus of writings in musicology, Adorno wrote three volumes of literary essays, on topics from nineteenth-century lyric poetry and twentieth-century modernism to the significative attributes of punctuation marks and the essay form itself. The late *Aesthetic Theory* ranges across all these areas, constructing a multivalent, anti-systematic body of thought in philosophical aesthetics, drawing on aspects of his social critique to outline a conception of artistic practice that, by faithfully reflecting an impoverished contemporary experience, would hold out the hope of trans-forming society via a transfiguration of consciousness. More than any other thinker of the modern era, Adorno sought to reconnect aesthetic questions to the history of philosophy on a scale not quite attempted since Kant's third Critique. At the heart of it is the theory, first propounded by Horkheimer and himself in a chapter of the *Dialectic of Enlightenment,* of the culture industry, his unremitting derogation of which is the source of much of the institutional distaste there has been for Adorno's aesthetics as a whole. In this view, he emerges in caricatural motley as a fusty old relic of high modernism, incurably scornful of the garbage on which the masses undiscriminatingly feed, as they disregard the obviously liberating nourishment of Schönberg for a bulk diet of cultural carbohydrate in the cinema, on television and at pop festivals.

Possibly no aspect of Adorno's corpus of theory has become more widely apprehended than his aesthetics of the autonomous artwork. In its popular manifestation, this notion has tended to become hardly anything more than a fastidious insistence that art deserves to be treated on its own terms, in isolation from anything that might soil its claim to distinction in respect of the mundanity of social reality. Even in the hands of more sensitive critics, as we shall see, the autonomy theory is a direct index of Adorno's abandonment of faith in practical political involvement, as though a social disposition that has seeped incontestably into every crevice of contemporary experience, paralysing human faculties as it goes, can at least be escaped by retreating into the realm of the fine arts. There is a place in Mahler that is sacrosanct from the hubbub of commerce. Such ideas were naked ideology long before the catastrophe of Auschwitz laid them bare.

The first reason that art does not exist in a hermetic realm of its own is that it is nothing without aesthetics. It requires a philosophical grasp as well as an ordinarily hermeneutic one; indeed, the two go together. Aesthetics, Adorno cautions, cannot just be a method for pumping out of art what the artist pumped in, as though its 'idea' should remain eternally the same. It is susceptible to developments in historical social consciousness, whose expression, directly or indirectly, is what art is. The heritage approach, founded on the idea that the test of time is what determines quality in artworks, commits the naïve error of distrusting its own judgment in the here and now. Work that once stood at the sharp edge of social consciousness takes on a different cast when the problems it illuminated are subjected to positive ameliorative policy, which is not to say, in some philistine fashion, that it becomes outdated, but that its social value changes in relation to the present day. Notwithstanding that, Adorno does also make a complex point that artworks die a certain death, not for what they contain or illustrate, but with regard to their ontological status, as soon as they become universally accessible. The cultural heritage becomes paradoxically alienated from art consumers as soon as they are able to claim it as their own. An authentic artwork does not wish to be possessed as cultural capital, and yet none of them is capable of resisting such possession in the final analysis, however long that may take.

Prior to its appropriation by the canons of artistic taste, an artwork undergoes a profoundly ambiguous state in which it is no longer the property of its creator, but has been only imperfectly assimilated by its potential audiences. This is in fact its period of greatest dynamism. While not hesitating to perceive truly magisterial performances and moments throughout art history, Adorno nonetheless dispenses with the bourgeois notion of artistic genius as the false hypostasis of individuality, the idea that society bestows its gift of talent, ultimately the gift of expressive freedom, only on certain privileged individuals, at whom the rest look on admiringly. If the artwork's significations are not to change over time, it becomes inert, a reified cultural commodity that can no longer speak to those whose consciousness it passes through. This much of Adorno's aesthetics recurs in French poststructuralism, with its insistence on the fluidity of textuality and on the uncertain nature of the signifier.

Where poststructuralism and deconstruction contented themselves at this way-station, however, Adorno pressed on. All art, he contends, is polemical. 'The idea of a conservative artwork is inherently absurd,'[1] he states, for all that the proclivities of their creators may have been profoundly non-oppositional. The fact that art as a practice is separated from the empirical world, that it need not strictly exist, empowers it to bear witness to the conviction that the world should be different. This is the germ of the proposition that authentic art is autonomous art; the artwork 'transcends the antagonisms of existence without perpetuating the deception that they no longer exist'.[2] More, 'art becomes social by its opposition to society'.[3] It achieves this effect, where it does, by translating the perception of injustice into an inner recognition, perhaps an emotional response, perhaps a more intellectual appreciation that the reader, viewer or listener is in the presence of truth. In this, it faithfully reflects a Marxian precept that a rectified social existence can only be achieved through the truthful realisation of what it falsely claims to be practising, not through the abolition of such aspirations as unrealistic. 'The source of art's power of resistance,' Adorno declares, 'is that a realised materialism would at the same time be the abolition of materialism, the abolition of the domination of material interests'.[4]

One of the ways that art accrues its liberating force is through a certain memorialising, a refusal to forget the exigencies of suffering. Historical amnesia is the work of reification, whereas artworks both concretely and metaphysically recover the traces of past experience and use them to illuminate the way towards a redeemed existence that is not yet. What might be can be recovered through determinate remembrance of what was. Nor would such a tendency guarantee the obsolescence of art in a reconciled world. 'Even in a legendary better future, art could not disavow remembrance of accumulated horror; otherwise its form would be trivial'.[5] According to Adorno, there is an implicit discursive character in all artworks, which is what enables them to express truth in both senses of the verb – to press it out and give it voice. Art partakes of the status of writing, even in non-literary forms such as visual art and music. 'In art, universals are strongest where art most closely approaches language: that is, when something speaks that, by speaking, goes beyond the here and now'.[6] This point should not be confused with the character of tendentious art, that it possesses a hidden message that only has to be decoded for its secret to be unlocked. This latter was very much the bourgeois view of socially critical dramatic works in the period following the second world war. What was its message? What was the author trying to say? In contrast, the linguistic nature of art posited by Adorno refers to something like the deep structures of signification contained in dialogic linguistic utterance, where the semantic resonances are nonpropositional, but are capable of pointing beyond themselves to unexpected strata of meaning. Aspects of a work's mood can in this sense often be emphasised antithetically, by their concealment, and not just in the context of the discursive decorum of a sensitive age like the nineteenth century, but in modernist works also. The artwork's expression is not obligated to reflect the expressive subject directly, as the philistine cultural optic has it, but can be wholly antithetical to it, but it can also be the faithful reflection of the sense of lack or loss that permeates a frozen society. Moments of tenderness, in music for example, are more likely to be expressive not of a present state, Adorno writes, but of the artist's own yearning towards such a state: 'subjectively, all expression is mediated by longing'.[7] For many engaged in the left critique of Adorno's aesthetics, this apartness from the immediate material concerns of politics is what fatally weakens it, but Adorno himself already anticipated this argument and met it head-on, both in the *Aesthetic Theory* and elsewhere.

For Adorno, the primary status of all art is its relation to reality, from which everything in it is generated, and to which it takes up a stance, either in overt or implicit form. On this note, his essay 'Commitment' of 1962 represents a further engagement in a debate that had been begun with Walter Benjamin in the 1930s. He begins by acknowledging the belatedness of this latest intervention, in view of the changed political reality that obtained in the era of the Cold War, in the context of which all scholastic debate about the life of the mind seems an epiphenomenon to the possibility of total catastrophe. He acknowledges Sartre's theoretical motivation in *What is Literature?* (1948) for the call to political commitment in art as an attempt to prevent artworks from being degraded to the status of fetishised cultural commodities, but against this he argues that the committed work represents a surrender of the possibility for pure objectification of existent reality. In this latter respect, committed writers join forces, despite themselves, with conservative cultural critics in demanding that, through assimilation to the existent, a work of art should 'say something' immediately perceivable, that is, should be clearly and unambiguously reducible to a definite effect of meaning. Thus what he calls atelic or autonomous art is derided as unintelligible. He does, however, draw a distinction between what he calls tendentious and committed art, under which the former – represented, for example, by Ibsenite naturalism – seeks to bring about change in a specific area such as sexual morality or domestic patriarchy, while the latter, Sartre's own work as well as Brecht's Epic theatre, wants more generally to alter social consciousness of the entire structure of the given. Commitment for Sartre is an injunction to individuals to take sides for or against a propositional view of social reality; Adorno argues that, by this injunction, subjects are implicitly urged to overlook what they are actually being offered in this apparent act of choice.

The theatrical works of Sartre, Adorno contends, make a fetish of aesthetic immediacy, like all naturalistic theatre, which is to say they collapse the distance between form and expression, so that the drama simply becomes a statement of existentialist *Weltanschauung*. 'Hell is other people': there you have it. The first problem with this is that it could just as easily have been a proclamation from a philosophical work, such as Sartre's own *Being and Nothingness* (1943), and thereby subjugates the dramatic form to a function for the utterance of a worldview, rather than respecting it as an aesthetic form in its own right, and secondly, by acting as the effective punchline of a play – *Huis Clos* (1944) – it makes the act of philosophical reflection an interchangeable commodity. Adorno asks what difference it would have made had the line been 'Hell is ourselves'.

By contrast, Brecht is for Adorno at least a better dramatist. His theatre is antithetical to the philosophically based theatre of existentialism in the sense that it seeks to show objective economic tendencies in didactic and simplified form – almost as cartoons. The problem Adorno sees here is that the cartoons functionally have to become the social reality they really only satirise, in order to theorise about it. Thus the mythicised form of reality gives the impression, for the sake of agitatorial and propa-gandist simplicity, that the catastrophe is easily soluble. He takes the example of Brecht's parable play about the ascendancy of Hitler, *The Resistible Rise of Arturo Ui* (1941), in which an otherwise historically precise account of the advent of fascism in Germany is recast in the mode of the antics of a gang of protection racketeers who take over the greengrocery trade in Chicago. While in many ways operating to a sustained degree of metaphorical continuity, the play sows the seeds of its own failure precisely by trivialising the reality that obtained when Brecht was writing it. The question is begged: how could an indubitably malevolent group of gangsters running an extortion racket possibly create Auschwitz? To be sure, the extent of fascism's crimes was only fully known four years after the play was completed, but all Brecht did was to add an epilogue of six lines, which tells of Hitler's defeat and is somehow intended to confirm the thesis of the resistibility of his rise. As an adversary, Ui is diminished in stature, since this is after all propaganda. The play's first audiences in neutral Switzerland chortled at the Hollywood-influenced machinations of a comic villain, even while the Nazi gas chambers were in full operation. As political reality is trivialised, social effectivity capsizes. This raises the always already answered question as to whether drama, or art in general, can ever engineer social change. Sartre frankly doubted that it could; Brecht is said to have admitted once, in a moment of heresy, that the theatre as an institution was finally more inter-esting to him than any changes in the world it might promote. He therefore absolved himself of taking any interest in the workers' uprising in the German Democratic Republic in 1953, being occupied as he was at the Berliner Ensemble in directing his proletarian version of *Coriolanus*. The positive moment in his work, for Adorno, is that it at least invites its spectators to think about social reality, rather than presenting them in the Sartrean fashion with pre-packaged conclusions. He accepted Benjamin's contention that for art to have any political effect, it has to be successful as art. The paradox in Brecht, however, is that, in order to communicate with the proletariat of the day, he sought tirelessly to adopt its linguistic and expressive habits, dismissing high culture as 'dogshit', and missed the point that these habits are precisely an effect of capitalist reification in themselves, only perpetuated in their mimicry.

In the notorious pronouncement of his essay 'Cultural Criticism and Society', Adorno had stated that writing poetry after Auschwitz was barbaric. For the time being, in the 'Commitment' essay, he clings to it against critical admonition, on the grounds that in representing suffering, art raises the possibility that it might be appreciated in its aestheticisation. Lyric poems can only seem self-satisfied contemplation of a reality that must be unequivocally negated. The paradox is that, as he was to concede by his eventual retraction of the statement in *Negative Dialectics*, art remains a necessity because it is often the only form in which a protest against suffering can be registered. Nonetheless, there is the ever-present risk that in reifying suffering as an aesthetic commodity, it is at best forgotten in its reality, and at worst rendered purposeful. Since narrative is always implicitly didactic, it is assumed by its recipients that pointless suffering may have a message, perhaps that authentic humanity only shines forth in extreme situations or, at its most crass, that there is always someone worse off than ourselves – someone trapped up to her neck in earth perhaps, still persuaded after all that life is a blessing.

Autonomous, that is to say, overtly non-political, works of art are, in the Marxist aesthetic tradition, accused of being unpopular. For Adorno, this is their point. They have not subjugated themselves to the prevailing definitions of legitimacy; they do not say what is expected of them. Above all, they do not adapt to market forces. Their abstraction is a response to the abstraction that objectively dominates society in the form of reified consciousness, because there is finally nothing in art that does not originate in social reality. The point, however, is to transcend that reality by means of critical objectification, rather than accommodating it with a discourse that speaks its language. Only where it seems to be politically dead, then, does art carry the potential for subverting the power of ideology, because only here does it escape the need to degrade itself by speaking ideology's language, and only here does it evade the functionalist view of it as the motor of revolutionary political praxis. A conundrum inevitably arises in the realisation that a Marxist aesthetic practice could scarcely speak the language of the people, since this language would not yet be a revolutionary one. Lurking in the background of the debate about commitment in art, furthermore, is the troubling thought that whether art might offer a critique of value in late capitalist society, through assuming a directly political character, can only be raised after it has been decided whether art has a right to exist at all. Having, for Adorno, demonstrated the untruth that was inherent all along in the notion of art's civilising and enlightening influence, its continued existence as such can only perpetuate its ideological character. Paradoxically, however, he concedes that any strident call for an end to culture would resemble the very barbarism against which it was articulated. 'When I hear the word "culture",' said Hitler's culture minister, 'I reach for my gun.' The dilemma is compounded for Adorno in that the retreat into silence that represents the third and final option is also an admission of defeat.

Against the notion of autonomous art, and before we come to consider the theory of the culture industry in greater detail, one might question whether all popular cultural forms are as affirmative as Adorno suspects. If it remains hard to see how critical consciousness could find itself nurtured in an individual saturated in video games, downloaded playlists and ketamine, nonetheless there are oppositional currents within the mainstream from time to time, even if only brief ones. Punk rock, in its first year at least, articulated something like the summary judgment from *Negative Dialectics* that all post-war culture is garbage, giving expression to the ultimate negative, and thereby emancipatory, thought-form. Then again, when the impulse of refusal fizzles out, negative works find themselves absorbed into the canons of stylistic history. Even Beckett's virtually mute late dramatic fragments eventually found a home on Broadway.

Adorno's aesthetics is animated to a great extent by a thoroughgoing formalism that has long since dropped out of favour in philosophical approaches to art. If there has been a tendency to the restitution of the subjective experience in art in postmodernist theorising, an insistence that the reception of even the most apparently valueless productions of the entertainment industry can be subjected to transgressive and potentially trans-formative readings that take little or no account of their generic identity, the *Aesthetic Theory* remains committed to an interro-gation of what has become of such genres through historical social transformation, and the ways in which a work's generic morphology relates to its objective contents. The content of artworks for Adorno is not just a question of the objective material of their plots, their pictorial subjects and so forth, but the question of how these materials are treated and thereby trans-formed. So many of the canonical aesthetic genres court the immanent threat of failure according to their own concepts, an effect Adorno detects in forms as diverse as epic, classical tragedy, abstract painting and the realist novel. Like many another commentator, Adorno notes the liquidation of the tragic at the dawn of the modern era – '[i]t succumbed in the denoue-ments of the second acts of Budapest operettas'[8] – but attributes this not simply to secularisation and the loss of a sense of the heroic, as does George Steiner in the reactionary thesis of *The Death of Tragedy* (1961), but to the fact that artistic means grow organically from the social relations in which they are rooted.

Simply put, it isn't that art must fail to live up to its own ideals in a society that has ceased to be responsive to them; it is rather that that society generates a revised artistic practice that reflects the antagonisms presently latent in itself. This holds true especially for the contradictions inherent in social consciousness. In a suggestive passage, Adorno suggests that it was the realisation at the outset of the twentieth century that art could now neither embody pristine nature in the fashion of the Romantics, nor incorporate the industrial processes that had, as he puts it, 'scorched' the natural world, as the Italian Futurists briefly attempted, that was more responsible than anything else for the transition of modern painting towards nonrepresentationalism. 'The object of bourgeois art,' Adorno states, 'is the relation of itself as artefact to empirical society'.[9] The more dialectical view sees art as an integral product of that society itself, its autonomous status underpinned by its critical apprehension of society, not purely by its artefactual museum character.

Adorno's aesthetic theory has been crudely characterised as a kind of pessimistic hermeticism. In a world where direct political interventions have become futile and tasteless, only art retains the potential for a true liberation of consciousness, standing in the way of reification by means of its inherently oppositional semantics, provided that it is draped in the livery of modernist technique, which, like Henry Ford's Model T, is available in any colour the consumer would like as long as it's black. Among the many valencies this blunt caricature misses is Adorno's own acknowledgement, made regularly throughout the *Aesthetic Theory*, that art itself is an insufficient vehicle for opposition to social reality. There must be some level of philosophical precipitation in the artwork, but that does not equate simply to reducing each individual work to its own idea, nor does it move within the classical definition of Aristotelian catharsis, to which Adorno's theory is not hospitable on the grounds that all it achieves – if indeed it ever worked at all – was the reconciling of audiences to a status quo of which art was implicitly supportive, making it not the dissolvent of repression but its ally. If there is an all-important 'truth content' to the most valuable works, this property remains something evanescent, ephemeral, historically mutable. What matters is not whether what an artwork overtly asserts about reality is accurate, but whether, for the time being, it is itself true or not in the philosophical sense. There is a necessary connection between the veridical potential of art and a higher concept of truth, but it is a troubled and ultimately fragile affinity. '[A]rtworks stand in the most extreme tension to their truth content,' Adorno insists.[10] What undermines their claim to permanence is their relation to a realm figured as the Absolute, not in the Hegelian sense of a secularised God, but as a state of existence beyond what is concretely known, and for which artworks surrender their right to be under present circumstances. 'Radical art today is synonymous with dark art; its primary colour is black... Still, black art bears features that would, if they were definitive, set their seal on historical despair; to the extent that change is always still possible [es immer noch anders werden kann, things can always become other] they too may be ephemeral'.[11] For all that Beckett may grasp at the truth about the impoverishment of experience in the era following the catastrophe of the last global war and the Shoah, the transformation of empirical reality in some hitherto unimagined fashion – unimagined, precisely, by art – would render it obsolete at a stroke. Peter Uwe Hohendahl makes a sensitive case for the internal aporias of the artwork in Adorno's conception: 'Adorno maps a double trajectory for art: on the one hand, he stresses the special stakes of art, its autonomy vis-à-vis social reality; on the other, he contrasts the truth claims of art with the unknown and hidden absolute, thereby emphasising the artwork's transience'.[12] There is what he calls a theological element in Adorno's aesthetic and social theory, to which we shall return in the final chapter, which he is intent on rescuing from both the propositional forms of positive religion and also the transience of artistic expression. True enough, as Adorno also claims in the *Aesthetic Theory*, 'what has once been said never fades away completely, neither the evil nor the good,'[13] but what remains of it may reappear in the messianic light of that transfigured society envisioned in the final aphorism of *Minima Moralia*, while its original context in the artwork fades to nothing under the radiance of the new.

Hohendahl offers a useful perspective on Adorno's assimilation of the concept of the ugly into his aesthetic theory, which forms part of a dialectical lineage traceable back to art's liberation from primordial ritual. In Adorno's analysis, art began when it became detached from purely instrumental propitiatory cultic practices, but in the manner of a Hegelian sublation, it typically retains an element of the cultic in its transformation of it. It is precisely that residual mythic moment that is what enabled the return of ugly and archaic components in art during the onset of modernism in the early twentieth century. Cubist figurative forms, atonal dissonances in music, the unsparing depiction of urban squalor in the naturalistic novel are all made possible by the marginalising of the traditional ideals of beauty that had obtained in Romantic aesthetics. In the century of the world wars and the industrialisation of administrative murder, ugliness in art at the most obvious level does no more than reflect the horror of modern history. In so doing, however, it also calls into question the ideological illusion of the beautiful, but not with the aim of restoring the mythic element in art, as Nietzsche advocated, but of empowering modern art with its critical function. Hohendahl teases out the divergence between Nietzsche's argument in his early work, *The Birth of Tragedy* (1872), and the analysis inaugurated in the *Dialectic of Enlightenment* and sustained into the *Aesthetic Theory*:

Nietzsche makes the loss of myth and the rise of Socratic rationalism responsible for the decline of Greek culture and therefore calls for a rebirth of myth... This means that in [his] schema, myth and art are on the side of the transfiguration of unbearable suffering... Adorno and Horkheimer... differ sharply from this analysis. Myth denotes the realm of bondage (*Unfreiheit*) that characterises the archaic and barbaric, and its return in totalitarian political systems does not hold a Nietzschean promise of aesthetic reconciliation.[14]

The result of that latter was nothing other than the wholesale legitimation of human suffering.

'If one originated in the other, it is beauty that originated in the ugly, and not the reverse,' Adorno suggests.[15] The beauty that Romantic aesthetics held art to have noticed in the natural world, but which nonetheless paid for its assimilated status by being formally abolished from aesthetics after Hegel, has indeed become ideology, but as a construct, the beautiful must have been conceived out of the ugliness of archaic ritual, as its antipode, and as a speculative category against the rule of abstract terror in death. This current is what lends art its flimsiest character, as mere escapism, down to the present day. In the culture industry, even what seemed like natural manifestations of the beautiful, in tropical sunsets and the warmth of smiling faces, have been as internally commodified as they have been overtly commercialised in the images of travel brochures, but it may be, to extend the implication of Adorno's aesthetics, that the ugly too has been incorporated into industrial culture, from its supposedly most sophisticated manifestations to the crassest. Ugliness, revulsion, deformations of all kinds are the stock-in-trade of the kind of conceptual art that draws packed audiences to the gigantic new galleries, in the disfigured portraiture of Francis Bacon and Lucian Freud too, but also in the disgusting tasks to be undertaken by celebrity contestants in the jungle, and in the limitless proliferation of the horror-movie genre, which productively allied itself with comedy just as its audiences had stopped taking it seriously anyway.

The totem around which much of Adorno's aesthetic theory circles is the question of what relation art has to the empirical totality of the social world. How does it best critique the menacing tendencies of a societal apparatus characterised by irrationality and blind domination? The consistently false solution for Adorno, at least since modern history took on this threatening character, is realism, the mirroring of objective conditions in the content of the artwork. In the postmodern era, this may now seem a significantly outdated concern, but aesthetics in the mid-twentieth century, at the nadir of the Cold War, was dominated by an ideological contestation between the obligation to straightforward photographic reflection of reality in the Eastern Bloc, the officially prescribed style known as socialist realism, long since vanished but still current at the time of Adorno's death in the summer of 1969, and the formal experimental modes that had come to prevail in advanced western art, and which Soviet ideology, most prominently in the person of Georg Lukács, contemptuously rejected as not only appropriate to a decadent stage of late capitalism, but also as decadent in themselves. Adorno's essay 'Extorted Reconciliation' (1958), a review of Lukács' literary study *Realism in Our Time*, pours scorn on the notion that an officially fully harmonised social settlement having been achieved in the Soviet sphere of influence, its apposite aesthetic genre was a mirror-like realism. The problem with artistic realism in any social context, as Adorno puts it, is that simply duplicating reality as it is only propagates all the faults and delusions of that reality, instead of throwing them into critical relief. Socialist realism is always predicated on the complaisant acceptance of reality, which it is then art's task to reflect faithfully, a process that not only insults its recipients with the lie of propaganda, but corrodes artistic practice itself to a bureaucratic procedure. 'Rather no art than socialist realism,' Adorno dismissively contends near the beginning of the *Aesthetic*

Theory.[16] Hohendahl usefully reconstructs Adorno's history of the progress of the classic novel from its beginnings in the English early eighteenth century, when it only incorporated fragmentary moments of concrete life amid the ruminations of its principal characters, through the high-water mark of the realist style in the nineteenth-century French and English novel, in which social reality is a fully integrated aspect of the novelistic form, which now becomes the vehicle for the depiction of that reality par excellence, and on to the disintegration and apparent meaning-lessness of the concrete in modernist prose fiction, typified by the parabolic works of Kafka and the almost contentless terrain of Beckett's treatment of the novel form. In this schema, the evident triumph of realism in the commercial artforms of the mid-twentieth century, which is to say the period immediately following the demise of modernism, is a direct index of the increasing hegemony of the culture industry, when artistic expression has been degraded to the function of 'mere enter-tainment and the loss of truth'.[17]

Since Adorno's death, the predominance of realist modes in the arts has once more been thrown into doubt. If it remains true that most television drama and genres such as detective fiction are still wedded to the ideal of unmediated reflection of reality, the most conspicuously successful cinematic works nowadays are wholly given over to fantasy, in the forms of futuristic science fiction, comic-book adventures, and the magical milieu of children's fairy-tales, recast in faintly more adult mode than was the norm, while the postmodernist novel has been a prolonged exercise in the overt foregrounding of narrative strategies and other framing devices, with a virtual requirement for self-refer-entiality, as though nobody any longer dared risk suspending a disbelief that social reality has otherwise drilled into them as a survival tactic. The postmodern novel announces, 'I am a novel', much as the morphology of the natural world announces itself to the senses. What is achieved thereby, however, is not the return to a naïve realism, but a deep and pervasive ironising of the very act of aesthetic expression, in which even the serious arts have become as much commodities as their kitsch counterparts in the mass market. It would have been fascinating to discover how Adorno might have responded to the work of a writer such as David Foster Wallace, who worked his way through the techniques of postmodernity, incorporating some of the practices of an earlier modernism, such as the affectless repetitions with which Beckett's mature prose work was replete, in which the defiant lack of signification takes over the role of signification itself. Unlike Beckett, however, what Wallace manages to extract from these technical protocols is an unmediated psychological and emotional truthfulness, moments to which Beckett's characters only succumb against themselves, as when Krapp finds himself mesmerised again by his own recorded voice recalling an evidently idyllic romantic moment in a boat on the river, a moment irretrievably lost to present reality. The tax office workers in Wallace's *The Pale King* (2011), or the young tennis players undergoing relentless athletic training in *Infinite Jest* (1996), a little along the road from the recovering substance addicts in their therapeutic groups, are victims of heteronomous discursive and practical regimes, whose subjectivities, at least in isolated cases, are not after all utterly defeated by their institutional enmeshment, but emerge in damaged fragmentary form from within it. Beckett's characters understand viscerally that such moments of apparent pacification are pure mendacity, but there is arguably greater dialectical subtlety in the critical consciousness that is awakened, however fleetingly, by what one could call the immanent critique of which Wallace's luckless figures suddenly find themselves capable. Adorno's unsparing ideological sensibilities would probably not have missed the undoubted streak of social conservatism in Wallace, but nor, I suspect, would he have convicted the work as a whole of the restorationist tendencies he saw everywhere in the appropriation of social realism by the culture industry, and still less would he have seen in it only the empty formal exercises of avant-garde literature that he brushes aside in a parenthetical comment towards the end of the 'Commitment' essay.

How the artwork stands in relation to its recipients became one of the most pressing concerns in aesthetics in the age of reception theory, politically tendentious art, and the ultra-subjectivist turn of poststructuralism. By these means, readers, listeners or spectators construct the text, are awakened to radical consciousness by it, and are provoked by its play of significations to even more complex signifying responses of their own. To those who see Adorno as an immediate precursor of the poststructuralist wave in cultural studies, it may come as a surprise to learn that he was not particularly hospitable to the idea of a projective relation to the artwork, in which one seeks identification with elements such as the characters in narrative works, or allows one's spirits to ebb and flow between vivacity and resignation in accord with the markings in a musical score. What permits a deeper immersion in its meanings is to surrender oneself to them, to allow the artwork its own immanent movement, rather than asking what it is doing for us. In many ways, this is the polar opposite of the Brechtian approach, in which the audience of a didactic drama is encouraged to analyse the events depicted through objectification, engaging perhaps in their own polemical exchanges with each other after the performance. If the artwork itself is to be considered monadologically, apart from the social reality that nonetheless generates it, that in turn best represents the present monadological structure of society, in which the impress of the collective has paradoxically created an ossified social structure bereft of living intersubjectivity. A certain community of feeling, Adorno argues, has been lost in modern experience, which, for example, can no longer comprehend sadness fluently, stranded as it is in the context of universal loneliness. 'As the tears have run dry, this consolation has become inaudible'.[18] What has replaced it in the most recent era is an unstoppable public effluvium of tears, the exhibition of which is intended to fill the gaping holes left by both art and the affectlessness of personal experience. Emotion was an evolutionary adaptation that once encouraged human beings and their ancestors to unite in cohesive societies that had a chance of survival. That was its advantage, but the problem with emotion is that, like physical pain, it can be deliberately provoked and is almost always a yielding to a negative state of mind – terror, fury, jealousy, misery, revulsion, scorn, even simple embarrassment. If the full range of emotional complexity and emotional intelligence is a specifically human trait, the victims of emotional manipulators, by contrast, have too often been dehumanised. Nobody would worry about this question if the emotion that was being wilfully provoked in everybody was happiness, as long as it was a happiness worthy of the name, not mindless glee, idiotic hilarity or childish fun. It is the unavailability of any concept of what happiness might look like on the social scale that confines it to people's private lives, while the expression of the negative emotions is permitted free public rein.

At the heart of the aesthetic impulse is what Adorno, following Stendhal, calls the *'promesse du bonheur'*. In Stendhal's essay *On Love* (1822), it is beauty that is the promise of happiness, and even then the emphasis is negative – 'beauty is only the promise of happiness' – with the implication that the promise, like many another such spiritual commitment, may be broken. A less attractive lover may turn out to be truer and more fulfilling than the more obviously ravishing option. Adorno's topological adaptation of this trope converts the point to something about the relation of art to empirical reality, which at once directly retains its negativity – 'Art is the ever broken promise of happiness'[19] – but also, precisely through its negative operativity, sustains the element of hope in the promise that empirical reality cannot keep:

Stendhal's dictum of the *promesse du bonheur* implies that art does its part for existence by accentuating what in it prefigures utopia. But this utopic element is constantly decreasing, while existence merely becomes increasingly self-equivalent. For this reason art is ever less able to make itself like existence. Because all happiness found in the status quo is ersatz and false, art must break its promise in order to stay true to it.[20]

This complex dialectical point bears careful scrutiny. Adorno is claiming that what traditional art, say the novel in the era of Stendhal, gestured towards was a vision of a transformed state, in which happiness would be realised through the righting of wrongs and the advent of social justice. In this respect, aesthetic production is covertly doing reality a favour, by locating the emancipatory potential within it, which everyday existence all too easily suppresses. However, in the industrial era, and with the onset of reification on the societal scale in the totally admin-istered world, reality increasingly does no more than reproduce itself, or ensure that its human components, who have become its functionaries and servants, do so, with the result that there is ever less utopian potential within it for art to gather in. The first duty of art, therefore, in the modernist era and since, is to be as little like a degraded reality as possible. Not only would that merely perpetuate the present delusion, but it courts the risk of replacing true happiness with the illusionary happiness that is the culture industry's cheapened stock-in-trade. That leads Adorno to conclude that art has to break its promise in order to keep it; in other words, it must apparently abandon any impulse to drawing positive comfort from present conditions, and implicitly draw what hope it can from the inference of a totally transformed state unimaginable – literally, unimageable – in current circumstances. What this results in on the part of the culture industry's mass consumers is not a yearning for bleak dramatic works and the cheerless stuttering of atonal music, but an irresistible desire for immediate material gratification, which is hardly unjustified of course, but in which the industry has descried its best chance of seeming to answer their needs. 'The culture industry has its element of truth,' Adorno concedes, 'in the fulfilment of a need that originates in the ever-increasing renunciation demanded by society; but the sorts of concessions it provides render it absolutely false'.[21]

The theory of the culture industry is probably the Frankfurt School's most widely known – and widely misinterpreted – postulate about the apparatuses of advanced capitalist society. It first emerged in fully extrapolated form in the fourth chapter of Adorno and Horkheimer's *Dialectic of Enlightenment*, 'The Culture Industry: Enlightenment as Mass Deception'. The first point to note about it, then, is that it fits into a narrative of the progress of the ideals of the enlightenment. In the opening chapter of the work, as we have seen, the authors argue that enlightenment, in freeing itself from mythic thought-forms by way of instrumental rationality, returns to the mythic in the belief that everything in natural existence can be referred to the dogmatic regularities of science and of deductive logic. In the two excursuses that follow, one on Homer's *Odyssey*, the other on the contiguity of Sade's work with the transcendental subjectivism of Kant, enlightenment is shown to be profoundly ideological in its effects. In the figure of Odysseus stopping the ears of his crewmen and lashing himself to the mast to avoid hearing, or being seduced by, the siren voices of a primordial nature from which humanity has become alienated, western culture constructs its image of the proto-bourgeois individual, while in the encyclopedic blasphemies and obscenities of Sade's libertines, Kantian rationalism contemplates the disavowed other of its own self-policed ethical fastidiousness. By the first half of the twentieth century, when civilised society had succumbed to an orgy of barbarism, when fascism had demonstrated that even the monsters of irrationality could be subjected to the procedures of the rational in the carefully planned administration of hysterical persecution, intellectual liberty produced consummate disaster. The apparent failure of proletarian revolution to found a society rationally consecrated to fulfilling human needs left the ground open to, on the one hand, murderous totalitarianism of varying complexions, and on the other, a slumberous, ostensibly democratic liberal settlement, construed not as freedom from oppression so much as freedom to consume, a system that keeps the market economy churning by recruiting its subjects to participation in the imperatives of commerce, which it achieves both through round-the-clock advertising and through inveigling consumers into its value system through a vast apparatus of prescribed distractions and entertainments. Enlightenment under the aspect of fulfilment, allowing each individual to realise his or her full potential, has thereby chiasmically reversed into its opposite, the cauterising of individual aspiration in a system of full-blown lies, some so overt that everybody can see their mendacity for themselves, but politely choose not to notice it, others so insidious that people are quite capable of believing that what official discourse is saying to them is precisely the opposite of what it is. The culture industry is not, despite what academic cultural studies have long believed, solely about the products of mass culture, as they were delineated in the mid-1940s – Hollywood films, commercial radio, hit songs, swing jazz, the coming hegemony of television. It also took in leisure activities, sports events, political clubs, fashion, modes of locomotion and human converse, greeting cards, public lotteries, housing, household gadgets, personal hygiene – everything, indeed, that goes to make up the exemplary modern citizen of late capitalism.

The chief contention of the theory is that the rationalised industrial process, which resulted in streamlined automated factory production, its individual workers reduced to tiny interlocking components of the machinery, has been applied to the world of culture and leisure as well. Everything that moves has been commodified, but it has also been subjected to maximally efficient mass-production methods, so that a seamless weave is spun around every individual, who is as enmeshed in it at home, or when out on the town after work, as he is in the factory or office. Not only the means to reproduce his own existence, but the techniques by which he is distracted when not immediately engaged in earning those means, is part of a gigantic manufacturing enterprise, which, to the extent that it needs him to play an integral and willing part in it, flatters him that it is created with just his particular interests in mind. The fact that his interests are conceived as being identical to those of everybody around him, when the boundaries between him and the others are precisely what constituted his individuality in historical social existence, is an anomaly that every client of the culture industry is encouraged to overlook, rather in the way that everybody will recognise the ersatz psychological profiling of astrology as being specifically about them, even when the self-same profiling is offered to everybody else. While the industry appears to be reflecting popular will in all its variety, it is actually insidiously creating it, engendering a soporific consensus around its products and its leading personnel, so that everybody finds themselves caught up in the vicissitudes of the drama serial plots, the marriages and divorces of the celebrities, the public pronouncements of newspaper columnists and sports managers. There are, to be sure, those who don't watch the soap opera or take an interest in Lana Turner's latest break-up, but they are made to feel like outsiders or, worse, dissidents, people who refuse to join in, and can only remain pitiably mute while the others chatter. The consensus woven by the culture industry is not necessarily about ensuring that everybody has the same opinions, although the undertow of the cultural blandishments addressed to them is always in the direction of a conservative or liberal-conservative political orientation; what matters more is that everybody responds to the same stimuli, reacts in accordance with the same paradigms, and peacefully forgets that it was ever possible to take a critical stance towards what they are being offered. The myth of consumer choice sustains the vast proliferation of cultural goods on the market, but much as there is no particular difference between the automobiles produced by Chrysler and those of General Motors, so Adorno and Horkheimer argue, neither is there anything to separate the ideological proclivities and techniques of aesthetic construction of the respective productions of Warner Brothers and MGM. Apologists for the industry already pointed out in the 1940s that a mass society needed a mass cultural apparatus, that there was no way to satisfy the needs and interests of millions of people through the media of large-scale publishing, film distribution, radio broadcasting and the recording industry other than through rationalised processes of mass production, since that is what the various technologies now made available. 'The result,' the authors write, 'is the circle of manipulation and retroactive need in which the unity of the system grows ever stronger.' To point to the existing state of technology is already to admit that the system is one of domination, in that technology by definition is controlled by the most powerful economic forces in society. 'A technological rationale is the rationale of domination itself. It is the coercive nature of society alienated from itself'.[22] There was no particular reason that technology should have been enslaving rather than liberating, as was its promise, but that is the function to which it has been put in advanced capitalism, and with its subsumption of the forms of distribution of mass culture, technology has recreated its more or less willing clients in its own image.

Despite what many commentators have believed, Adorno and Horkheimer allowed that it was possible to see through the junk offered by the culture industry – indeed, most people arguably did just that – but one of its most impressive achievements is that it has persuaded people to accept it anyway, partly because there is no alternative, but also because there is something intriguing about its operation that makes absorbing the blockbuster film or the ubiquitously reiterated hit song compelling, rather in the manner that watching the churning pistons of the factory machine can be peculiarly hypnotic. In the last generation before the culture industry assumed its hegemonic sway over collective consciousness, the Italian Futurists had wagered that the relentless pounding and belittling power of automated technology could be energising to the switched-on spectator, who would find in it a galvanising release from the sluggish irregularities of the organic. The world was speeding up, according to the ideology. In fact, what was happening was that the world was becoming conformed to the robotic pulse of mechanisation, which no more permitted a thrilled acceleration into dynamic living than the natural limits of the physical organism did. In the European cinema, the metropolis depicted by Fritz Lang delineated a brutally hierarchical society in which a privileged elite was served by a toiling underclass, a mass of what were effectively androids moving in regimented formation, though not above being reminded of their fleshly origins by brutal maltreatment, but Hollywood, despite opening its doors to Lang in 1936, was not in the least hospitable to socially critical messages such as these, and his American films exhibit only the pale shadows of expressionist technique as surface features. Instead, audiences accepted the unvarying templates of commercial culture in the manner that Victorian readers expected the neat resolutions and happy endings of popular novels, as obligatory formal requirements that did nothing to undermine the entertainment of the stories themselves. What was lost between the cultural life of earlier eras and the output of the culture industry was the expectation that cultural products would speak individually to those who received them, and where the Kantian expectation of mature aesthetic judgment had once prevailed in idealistic aesthetics, there was now the construction of culture as a matter of functional public provision, the consumption of which ideally required no ruminative reflection at all, as opposed to programmed autonomic emotional gratification, yelps of laughter one minute, floods of rueful tears the next. Everything was geared to the production of a belief that what already was could not be any different. The objectification of empirical reality carried out by serious art, whether popular in its reach or not, which made artworks constitutively critical of the societies that produced them, was replaced in the culture industry by bland acquiescence, ensuring the absorption of its production processes into precisely those socioeconomic structures in which they were implicated, the ideological system of which they faithfully reproduced. In this way, culture, instead of throwing everyday practical life into relief by standing in opposition to it, is forcibly merged into the mundanity of practical life, so that it surrenders its status as culture, and becomes another of the indomitable forces that hold people captive in a totalising administrative system. In the classical Marxist conception, culture was part of the superstructure that was shaped by the imperatives of the economic base, whereas by the era of mass society, culture has been subsumed into another of the indispensable foundational means by which capitalism reproduces itself. Its shameless consecration to the generation of surplus value goes hand in hand with its manufacture of ideological consensus, which latter is all that remains of the spiritual values to which cultural artefacts were once oriented.

The happiness that the culture industry promises its clients, and apparently efficiently provides to them, is only a tasteless parody of the real thing, which if it were the real thing would not lend itself to being dished out in precisely calibrated uniform portions. Exactly its prodigious reach is what persuades people that the culture industry must be successful, must be fulfilling needs and granting wishes on an unprecedented historical scale. The favourite advertising slogan to the effect that millions of people cannot be wrong, a claim that was never pressed to the exigency of explaining why not, is the only rationale it adduces in its own legitimation. If it didn't work, it wouldn't be popular. In this fatal logic, it announces the amalgamation of what remains of culture and of society itself, whose discursive mouthpiece it has become. 'Everyone can be like this omnipotent society,' Adorno and Horkheimer declare. '[E]veryone can be happy, if only he will capitulate fully and sacrifice his claim to happiness. In his weakness society recognises its strength, and gives him some of it. His defencelessness makes him reliable'.[23] The contract involves a recognition that the innate idea of happiness, to which people might still privately cling unless their fingertips are prised from it by a process of seductive adaptation, is not available, but that what industrialised culture can supply without interruption is not just the next best thing, but eventually a more tangible version of happiness, precisely because its provision can be guaranteed. This will involve a learning process, to be sure. 'Life in the late capitalist era is a constant initiation rite. Everyone must show that he wholly identifies himself with the power that is belabouring him'.[24] Once fully habituated, however, the consumers relish the sense of belonging, avidly consuming the substitute satisfactions on offer as though they were what they had their hearts set on all along. There is something of the air of a factitious religious cult to mass culture as it is theorised in this essay. It proffers an escape from dreary reality, which it replaces with a reality whose own dreariness is disguised beneath surface glitter, the better to conceal the fact that it is nothing other than the self-same original dreary reality. Its own linguistic and rhetorical practices are learned and fully internalised, like the mantras of devotion chanted in plenary meetings of the cult, and the long hours of working in the fields, which cult members have been persuaded are a release from the backbreaking labour of the rat race, are matched by long hours spent in front of the television, watching game shows, situation comedies and commercial messages, as a liberation from long hours spent in front of the machines at work. Consumers begin to imitate the vocal inflections and gestural habits of the screen stars, and everybody adopts the American linguistic idioms of the giant corporations, no matter where they were born. Once learned, these aptitudes form a dense cocoon around their users, insulating them not only from the crimes and misdemeanours of the capitalist racket, which rattles on unchecked, but from any genuine contact with each other that is not already mediated by the thought-forms and turns of phrase generated by the integrated system. 'The lying words of the radio announcer become firmly imprinted on the brain and prevent people from speaking to each other; the advertising slogans for Pepsi-Cola sound out above the collapse of continents'.[25] Communications media, theoretically a means of joining people together in a globalised world as never before, succeed only in isolating them from each other, not as an unfortunate side effect but as a deliberate tool of control. One should remember that this was written sixty years before the advent of social media networks, nothing about which would have surprised the authors of the theory.

At roughly the same time as the composition of *Dialectic of Enlightenment*, Adorno wrote a further essay entitled 'The Schema of Mass Culture', in which he restated the theory of the culture industry in an intellectually denser and more concentrated form. The piece begins with a restatement of the thesis that mass culture has the intended effect of dissolving the demarcation lines between culture and social life, which were once so vital to the dignity of culture and provided it with its critical capacity. 'The commercial character of culture causes the difference between culture and practical life to disappear... On all sides the borderline between culture and empirical reality becomes more and more indistinct'.[26] This should be understood in its full literal force. The ideals the culture industry holds out to socialised humanity are those which it is encouraged to adopt as the goals of life. Indeed, the culture industry itself is not merely the instantiation of such ideals, but their very incarnation. Adorno suggests this is one way in which one might read the story of Robinson Crusoe, who no sooner finds himself marooned on an almost uninhabited island paradise, thousands of miles from the bustle of bourgeois society, than he begins recreating from it a bourgeois society in miniature. The ersatz becomes the real because people have been swindled out of the real. 'Reality becomes its own ideology through the spell cast by its faithful duplication'.[27] Adorno posits that the true way to read the notorious incident of Orson Welles' radio production *War of the Worlds* in 1938, which provoked an undoubtedly exaggerated number of people to telephone the radio stations and gather in the streets in frantic panic at the imminent invasion of Earth by hostile Martians, was as a test by positivistic culture to determine the extent of its influence. The interpretation is lent credence by the resonantly unconvincing apology that Welles issued in a press conference after the event, and by the fact that soon after-wards Hitler, swallowing the fabulations of the American press whole, cited it as proof of the chicanery to which a democracy in an advanced state of corruption was prepared to sink. If the stories of mass hysteria had been true, the production would have stood exposed as crudely manipulative. That the hysteria itself was a hyperbolic construction after the event demonstrated that the manipulations are nothing if not subtler than Hitler would have given them credit for, but that manipulation is nonetheless the only game in town. Art becomes parasitic, Adorno argues, when it forfeits its opposition to empirical reality, whereupon its thematic matter becomes nothing other than itself. Despite the overt experiment of *War of the Worlds*, mass culture more typically lives off the pretence that there is still a separation between culture and everyday practical life, while the artworks of the past pass into the museum. In an era when the status of classic works protects people from having to read them, the culture industry's confection of them produces artefacts that relate back to culture as its own object. Not what Wells' novel says about the course of human history, but the novel itself as a cultural commodity, is what now matters.

In a particularly provocative passage, Adorno argues that mass culture has taken upon itself the deep structures of meaninglessness that attend the presentation of large-scale sporting events. 'Sport is the imageless counterpart to practical life. And aesthetic images increasingly participate in this image-lessness the more they turn into a form of sport themselves'.[28] The blockbuster costume dramas of TV, stadium pop concerts, even the star system of conductors and soloists in the classical music seasons all partake of the nature of the Super Bowl or FA Cup finals, showcase events whose content is practically incidental. Sport itself is robbed of its competitive unpre-dictability by being turned in advance into the ritualised celebration of subjugation. Much is made of the gruelling sacri-ficial training regimes undergone by the competitors, who thereby re-enact through the residual freedom they have to dispose over their own bodies the violence already done to them in their day-jobs, if they are still unfortunate enough to have them. The mindless repetition of sports training, even at the most humble level of pounding out circuits in the municipal gym in order to keep fit, is the best school of obeisance that mass culture has so far dreamed up. One of its functions is to localise general social anxieties into the possibility of injury on the field of play. Willingly incurred suffering is always more endurable than the heteronomous kind. 'While the act of repetition schools obedience, it absorbs the fateful damage in the perpetual potential for anxiety, and so it continues. At the same time the borderline between acting and suffering, between internal and external force, is eliminated in the symbolic performance'.[29] On the spectators' side can be seen the sublimated political power that has succeeded in turning the powerless into 'a band of applauding hooligans'. Real competition, fair play, a clean contest according to strictly defined rules are what is officially promised in the economic life of society, which having long since abolished such principles in the monstrous appetites of obese corporate entities that destroy competition by devouring their weaker rivals, now offers them back in the form of football, 'the colourless reflection of a hardened callous life'.[30] Adorno allows the evanescent possibility that the virtues of team solidarity, pulling together to help others, even the spontaneous enthusiasm that little else in mass culture evokes, might one day prove useful at some critical juncture in the life of society, but he despairs of seeing any such impulses in the spectators, whose role is not after all to aspire to a fractional approximation of the fitness and virtuosity of their heroes, but simply to respond on cue to the meaningless action, chanting in blind devotion, taunting the visiting supporters as bitterly as if they were class enemies incarnate. Sport thereby takes on the character of practical life itself, losing the dignity it once possessed precisely by being the interruption to the common round. Weekend sport is expected to be taken as deathly seriously as the misery of the working week, the loss of its properly recreational quality mirroring the vanishing of aesthetic semblance in the artistic products of the culture industry. The precariousness of labour conditions in the globalised economy are offered a false restitution in the ironbound regularity of the sporting calendar, which has gradually expanded to fill the whole year. Supporters whose obsession with their teams has taken over their entire nonworking lives have found a substitute for work, albeit one that costs rather than pays. The degree to which sport, and mass culture generally, structure the vacuumed-out lives of their devotees is the precise index of the failure of a social life that must resort to such hypnotic distractions:

Under monopoly conditions, the more life forces anyone who wishes to survive into deceit, trickery and insinuation and the less the individual can depend any longer on a stable profession for his living, on the continuity of labour, then all the greater becomes the might of sport in mass culture and the outside world in general. Mass culture is a kind of training for life when things have gone wrong.[31]

Adorno ends the essay on an inflamed rhetorical note. The voices of the culture industry, from radio announcers to television presenters, promotional videos to the celebrities' press releases, are voices of absolute authority, speaking directly to their clients in a way that parliamentary politicians and trade union leaders no longer know how to do. They are voices that go unchallenged, the more so when they appear to be offering some fake challenge to authority themselves. If technology is truly the determining factor in modern social consciousness, and the relations of production that it makes possible continue to have the advantage over the potentially liberating impetus of the actual forces of production, the culture industry's appropriation of technology leads the way. In its surrender to the rationalised instrumental uses of technology, culture itself becomes as slippery with deceit as the lubricated gears of factory machines are with oil. The moment of truth in its untruth rests in the open avowal of its own transformation into part of capitalism's socioeconomic base, an avowal that does nothing to absolve it, but illuminates the blinding calamity towards which society is careering:

The neon signs that hang over our cities and outshine the natural light of the night with their own are comets presaging the natural disaster of society, its frozen death. Yet they do not come from the sky. They are controlled from earth. It depends upon human beings themselves whether they will extinguish these lights and awake from a nightmare that only threatens to become actual as long as men believe in it.[32]

The notably angry revolutionary voice in which 'The Schema of Mass Culture' is written undoubtedly disappeared from Adorno's writings after the war. Once back in the German academic context, he would hardly ever revert to the fervour in which this essay was couched, a rhetorical shift that leads many, even today, to accuse him of a progressive dilution of his radical theoretical commitments in the era of the student uprisings. 'Whoever thinks is without anger in all criticism,' he declares in the peroration of the 1969 essay on resignation.[33] Thinking sublimates the reflexive immediacy of anger, and begins properly when anger subsides. Nonetheless, there is no diminution in intensity of his critique of the culture industry, which he continues to excoriate as tenaciously as he and Horkheimer did in the 1940s. Indeed, with specific reference to the persistence of truculence and anger among the culture-consuming populace, he writes in a 1960 essay, 'Culture and Administration', that the postulate of cultural consumption as the antidote to boorish incivility, as the means of suppressing violent natural instincts, is a total failure. It cannot take root where dignity and freedom are not available to social existence. Consciousness of suppressed rancour is exactly what produces the barbaric outbursts that trouble the surface of a civil polity from time to time, and the precise indication of such a state of affairs is the degree to which people openly welcome the trash of the culture industry while secretly recognising it to be trash. Meanwhile, all that culture in its most elevated definition amounts to is the evidence of unthinking class privilege, the behaviour of those who can afford good tickets to the orchestral recitals through which they will peacefully sleep. There is a slight modulation here from the averral of 'The Schema of Mass Culture' that culture has merged indissociably with the economic base of capitalism. Here, it is an amalgamated, but still discernibly distinct, aspect of it: 'Culture long ago evolved into its own contradiction, the congealed content of educational privilege; for that reason it now takes its place within the material production process as an administrated supplement to it'.[34]

Adorno undertakes a late retrospective look at these arguments in a short essay entitled 'Culture Industry Reconsidered', included in the miscellaneous collection *Ohne Leitbild: Parva Aesthetica* (1967). Here, he recalls how he and Horkheimer came to alter the terminology of the thesis between the first and second drafts of the *Dialectic of Enlightenment* in the 1940s. The originally preferred term 'mass culture' [*Massenkultur*] was dropped and replaced by 'the culture industry' [*die Kulturindustrie*], in order to avoid any misleading suggestion that what was being scrutinised was a culture that had grown organically from the masses themselves, that it represented in any sense a people's culture, as opposed to the so-called high culture of the elites. In the reassessment Adorno offers in this late essay, he concedes that the culture industry may not, as was originally suggested, be an industry in its methods of production, though the conveyor-belt nature of much of what was turned out by the film and recording industries in wartime America certainly bore that stamp, but that it is certainly an industry in terms of distribution, in the organisation of its reception, and the methods of rationalisation to which the industry as a whole is dedicated. In response to the contention of certain cultural critics and sociologists, opponents of cultural elitism, in the German 1960s that the emanations of the culture industry deserve to be taken seriously in themselves, Adorno does not demur. They should definitely be taken seriously, but critically so, not in a way that cowers before their hegemony, making their cultural significance a function of their pervasive ubiquity. The most pressing imperative that militates against the uncritical celebration of the culture industry's products by intellectuals is that the target audiences for them mostly know that they are being force-fed with drivel.

They have learned to desire it because life would be even bleaker without it: 'if it guarantees them even the most fleeting gratification, they desire a deception which is nonetheless transparent to them'.[35] The apparent contradiction of a transparent deception is just what the culture industry has made its own. It is nothing as simple as the Romantic notion of the willing suspension of disbelief, but represents instead a combined suspension of belief and disbelief. People know they are being offered garbage, but they want it anyway. The point recalls Zizek's inversion from *Tarrying with the Negative* (1993) of Marx's dictum that, under capitalist social conditions, people don't know what they are doing but they do it anyway, into the more obviously contemporary application that they know perfectly well that what they are doing is nonsensical, but they do it anyway. Adorno and Horkheimer already argued this about the operations of the culture industry fifty years before Zizek, and Adorno reiterates the point in this late meditation on the theme: 'They force their eyes shut and voice approval, in a kind of self-loathing, for what is meted out to them, knowing fully the purpose for which it is manufactured. Without admitting it, they sense that their lives would be completely intolerable as soon as they no longer clung to satisfactions which are none at all'.[36]

The standard objection to this line of argument has always, from Adorno's own time onwards, been that if the culture industry, or 'popular culture' as it is risibly characterised in the discourses of university cultural studies, was as malevolent as the Frankfurt theorists painted it, it would hardly be popular. Pointing to the overweening efficacy of the industry in people's lives, Adorno counterposes, only underlines how doubly serious it is, rather than sanctifying it in some way as performing a public service. 'The consensus that it propagates strengthens blind, opaque authority'.[37] What is nurtured instead is ego-weakness, reflecting the overwhelming concentration of power at the societal and institutional level, as against the cauterised perception of the recipients. If their consciousness is developed at all, it is retrogressively, so that film producers who already saw their mission in the 1940s as appealing to the average intellectual capacity of eleven-year-olds have only continued to make their own tasks easier by reconstituting relatively aware adults as eleven-year-olds. Hence, in our own day, the preponderance of films that use the forms and techniques of children's entertainment, with faintly risqué jokes, which are funnier for the youngsters anyway, to patronise the adults into believing that they are not being entirely patronised. What kind of escapism is it from which virtually nobody can escape? One only has to imagine what would happen to people psychologically if television were suddenly to be withdrawn from them. In recent times, the film critic David Thomson identifies the manipulative principle that has been learned in the commercial cinema and TV industries:

> the outline of franchising, of taking a situation and repeating it until there was no one left with patience. Give them something they know they like – make it like fast food… The impetus within franchising is the reliable situation in so much television – the sitcoms, the Westerns, the police stories, the family shows. Always the situation endures, like the pitch in the advertising that held such shows in place. That is an endorsement of security in worrying times, just as it is an avoidance of drama or resolution.[38]

Commercial film, the pre-eminent medium of the culture industry, openly relies on the hypnotic effect of the projected moving image, an entrancement further enhanced by using the medium to relay images that are themselves mesmerically spellbinding in character. Discussing the oeuvre of Steven Spielberg, Thomson emphasises the further dimension of metahypnosis that consists in presenting the spellbound viewer with spellbinding images of people looking spellbound:

> Call it the drive to make great shows that are about nothing
> except letting the light play on the screen for a couple of hours
> and keeping the faces of the audience as open and exalted as
> the faces in *Close Encounters of the Third Kind* (1977) whenever
> they face the light... *Close Encounters* can be read as a film
> about the movies themselves and the wonder that light casts
> on a watching face. If ever you doubt the movies, look at the
> faces watching the screen.[39]

Nothing in social development is aided by reducing individuals
to the hypnotised mass that the culture industry deliberately
makes of them. The old adage that nobody in show business ever
went broke by underestimating the intelligence of the public
spoke the truth about the contempt in which show business holds
its clients, but it was disingenuous about the implied separation
of its effects from social existence, which is not purely incidental
but mutually constitutive. To rise to something like enlightened
objective awareness about social relations, human beings would
at some stage need to tear themselves away from the distractions
that simultaneously bewitch them and persuade them that everything is fine the way it is. Despite what cultural studies, in its
craven defence of the means by which people are subjugated,
thinks of the theoretical apostrophising of the masses in critical
theory, it is not critical theory that constitutes them and
imprisons them as masses. 'If the masses have been unjustly
reviled from above as masses,' Adorno asserts, 'the culture
industry is not among the least responsible for making them into
masses and then despising them, while obstructing the emancipation for which human beings are as ripe as the productive
forces of the epoch permit'.[40]

In light of the central critique advanced against the theory of
the culture industry, the charge that it is ultimately a reactionary

assault on popular entertainment *de haut en bas*, it is worth remembering that its roots lie in the exchanges on aesthetics that form the subject-matter of much of the correspondence between Adorno and Walter Benjamin in the 1930s. In the famous lengthy letter to Benjamin of 18 March 1936, in response to the second draft of the latter's essay 'The Work of Art in the Age of Mechanical Reproduction', published in French in the *Zeitschrift für Sozialforschung* that same year, Adorno relates the debate over autonomous art versus mass-produced art, typified by the commercial cinema, to the projected restitution of an organic culture that would truly serve the interests of those who produce society's wealth, instead of merely distracting them from the reifying labour they perform under the unfree conditions of capitalism. Distraction, contra Benjamin's assessment of the function of mass culture, is precisely what needs abolishing, 'if only for the simple reason that in a communist society, work would be organised in such a way that human beings would no longer be so exhausted or so stupefied as to require such distraction'.[41] Against the position that mass culture just is the authentic expression of the proletariat, Adorno counterposes the argument that it ought to be no less subject to dialectical self-reflection than are the most advanced productions of the avant-garde. Culture can be interpreted, like most phenomena, through the internal mediation of its extremes, 'but only if the dialectic of the lowest has the same value as the dialectic of the highest, and not if the latter is simply left to decay'. The extremes are all that is left of culture at the economic stage of high capitalism, its reified social relations, the regressive state of consciousness of the masses, and the division of manual and mental labour. In the most celebrated formulation of this letter, Adorno states of high art and mass culture: 'Both bear the stigmata of capitalism, both contain elements of change (but never, of course, simply as a middle term between Schönberg and the American film). Both are torn halves of an integral freedom, to which, however, they do not add up'.[42] Although there appears no middle term between the two extremes, they do not therefore amount together to all that culture ought to be, but represent the sundered state of the human soul under a system that seduces the intelligentsia with the rarefied esoteric work of aesthetic pioneers, while reserving idiotic dross for the rest. There is a strong streak of Leninism in Adorno's case, audible when he explicitly refers to Lenin's argument of 1917 that the practical task of the proletariat in overthrowing the bourgeois state can only be achieved 'through the theory introduced by intellectuals as dialectical subjects'.[43] While the consciousness of the proletariat remains fogged by alienating labour and its time colonised by the same, it cannot autonomously generate the revolutionary consciousness required to carry out its historic task, which is why the culture industry, which in the theory formulated after Benjamin's death acts as a gigantic mechanism for occluding insight and freezing consciousness into a permanent state of anaesthesia, is anathema to any thought that would look for the awakening of the masses through their exposure to culture. The proletariat is itself a product of bourgeois class society, otherwise it would not be a proletariat, and is not therefore spontaneously equipped, pace Lukács, with the intellective means to work out alone what is to be done. Although he has called into doubt in comradely fashion the revolutionary potential Benjamin's essay identifies in the artworks produced under the technological conditions of mass production, Adorno closes the letter of 18 March with an open-hearted concession to its polemical thrust: 'I cannot conclude, however, without saying that I find your few sentences concerning the disintegration of the proletariat into "masses" through the revolution, to be among the most profound and most powerful statements of political theory I have encountered since I read [Lenin's] *The State and Revolution*'.[44] These are footnote sentences in which Benjamin perspicuously distinguishes between the respective masses as constituted by the petit bourgeoisie, which is characterised by the emotional reactivity diagnosed in mass psychology, and that of the proletariat, whose actions are mediated by the practical tasks of revolutionary politics. The masses, conceived as a homogeneous agglomerate, are the passive victims of fascist crowd manipulation, whereas in a historical situation in which their hour has come, the bonds that form social subjects into a mass have begun to be transformed into organic relations between real, imminently free individuals. 'At the moment when it takes up its struggle for liberation, this apparently compact mass has actually already begun to loosen,' Benjamin argues. '[Fascism] realises that the more compact the masses it mobilises, the better the chance that the counterrevolutionary instincts of the petit bourgeoisie will determine their reactions. The proletariat, on the other hand, is preparing for a society in which neither the objective nor the subjective conditions for the formation of masses will exist any longer'.[45] In the following few years, Adorno and Horkheimer would apply Benjamin's insight into the reified mass addressed by fascist demagogues, who want only to keep the masses furiously ignorant, to the techniques and programmatic intentions of the culture industry, the only qualitative difference in the effect of which is to turn the fury to bliss. This was not exactly what Benjamin had in mind in his theory of the emancipatory potential of technological mass culture, to be sure, but the social analysis on which the outline of the culture industry depends evinces an unmistakable continuity with his own political argument.

The most egregious and tone-deaf objections to the theory of the culture industry can be swiftly dispensed with first. Of these, the most monotonous is the postulate that it is an apologia for cultural elitism, spoken out of the privileges of education and mandarin discernment, in which the Frankfurt thinkers, and Adorno in particular, bewailed the brainless tripe of proletarian audiences who paid little or no heed to the *Kronjuwelen* of high culture. The division between high and low art, as Adorno describes it, is the social bad conscience of serious art. So-called high art's institutional claim to represent the most exalted reaches of the human spirit was already ideology before Auschwitz exposed it as such, but one of the unfortunate by-products of the ideological falsity of elevated art is to lend a false legitimacy to the commodities of mass culture, notwithstanding their freedom from elitism, but in Adorno's conception, it is precisely the division itself that expresses the social truth of an unreconciled society. As we saw when looking at Adorno's essay on class theory in chapter 2, the seamless economic functioning of late capitalism has as one of its tendencies the effect of concealing – and thereby falsely sublating – class relations, which continue undisturbed in their latent form. To claim that mass culture is the antidote to elitism in these circumstances is to overlook the manipulative techniques that it appropriated from the appeal to emotions staged by the totalitarian societies of Nazism and Stalinism. In this structure, the cultural elite of the classical concert halls and art galleries has been replaced by a much less visible bureaucratic elite, who administer the production and distribution of mass entertainments on behalf of corporations that are ruthless in their pursuit of profit and reactionary to the core in their social and political attitudes. When Adorno defends the fragility of autonomous art, art which is independent both of overt political orientation and of the commercial demands of the culture industry, he is speaking up for an impulse of resistance that is stifled by the consensual clamour of mass entertainment, not simply sponsoring a high-minded qualitative estimation of Mahler over Benny Goodman. Nothing would emerge from such a static undialectical construction. An extensive statement of this misapprehension is given in Salvador Giner's *Mass Society* (1976), in which Adorno and his cohorts are represented as aristocrats who despise the rabble, the cultural successors, oddly enough, of an English lineage extending from Matthew Arnold to TS Eliot.

Nothing of the economic analysis of the Frankfurt critique is present in this travesty. Nobody at the Institute for Social Research thought that class exploitation had evaporated in the post-war world. It had rather become obfuscated by the massification of society, in which bourgeoisie and proletariat alike are subjected to the same forms of social and cultural consciousness. Mass society and its culture are not the condescending construction of a mandarin elite, but the objective historical outgrowth of class society in its latest manifestation. To deny, even in the much less totalising media atmosphere of the British mid-1970s, from which Giner wrote, that the mass of cultural consumers was being offered a diet of vacuous television entertainment, soporifically bland pop music, tabloid newspapers that offered full-page pictures of nude women to take their male readers' minds off the news they pretended to report, and so forth, an attitude that is careful not to say anything insulting about these insults for fear of seeming not to sympathise with their recipients, is itself an expression of high-handed elitism. In its anxiety not to seem to be siding with an ossified patrician high culture, it is reduced to crediting the reactionary swill of the media corporations as something more organically democratic. The accusation of elitism is the recourse of a temperament that thinks that popular cultural forms, precisely by virtue of their being popular, speak the language of the people, as opposed to subserving an ideology that everywhere speaks untruths to the powerless. Elitism is the very charge that the spokespeople of a predatory culture in full cry, from tabloid editors to reactionary comedians and mass media micro-celebrities, level against those who scruple to join the pack.

Secondly, the theory is held to be as much of a one-dimensional totalising gesture as the culture it criticises, not permitting any gaps or exceptions in its all-encompassing sweep. This point too disintegrates under even the most cursory examination. In an essay written in English in 1941, 'On Popular Music', which dates from roughly the period when the *Dialectic of Enlightenment* was beginning to be drafted, Adorno speaks of 'the tremendous effort that each individual has to make in order to accept what is enforced upon him – an effort that has developed for the very reason that the veneer veiling the controlling mechanisms has become so thin'. This effort, to be sure, consumes most of the individual's capacity for spontaneous responses, but the idea that people's inner reflexes are totally controlled, as though they were nothing more than insects being tormented, belongs, Adorno states, to a surface analysis that fails to appreciate the counter-vailing impulse to freedom. 'In order to become a jitterbug or simply to "like" popular music, it does not by any means suffice to give oneself up and to fall in line passively. To become trans-formed into an insect, man needs that energy that might possibly achieve his transformation into a man'.[46] Although the culture industry employs the psychological techniques of mass manipu-lation, its ideological base is relatively weak, compared to that which supports the general economic base of society. What is happening, it will be recalled from the point about advertising outlined earlier, is that consumers and audiences agree to buy the products they are offered, despite the fact that they see through them. Deborah Cook puts it this way: 'Adorno frequently described the culture industry's reinforcement techniques and ideology – the frank lie no one believes – as fragile. Moreover, he insisted that consumers of cultural commodities were already aware of the truth'.[47] Their consciousness is accordingly duplic-itous. They suspect, for example, that the cheaper something costs or looks, the less they are being offered, hardly the incli-nation of victims who had been comprehensively hoodwinked. Their attitude is structured in the form of a dual suspicion: 'the double mistrust of traditional culture as ideology is combined with mistrust of industrialised culture as a swindle'.[48]

Despite what many even in the second generation of the Frankfurt School itself have argued, there are dialectical niceties to the theory of mass culture that prevent it from being a non-negotiable account of seamless universal delusion. If people are not socially free, their consciousness may well be susceptible to the fetters in which the culture industry would like to bind them, and the delusion that they are free, which forms a strong under-girding of biopolitical reality, would seem to militate against the likelihood of true enlightenment. Just that false belief, however, is what could provide the light that would illuminate the actual state of affairs to them. Cook puts it succinctly:

> Adorno did acknowledge that in late capitalist societies, liberal ideology provided, if not a 'subcultural' horizon, then at least a prevalent mode of self-understanding that occasionally had the effect of countering the culture industry's messages and techniques. Although individuals in late capitalist societies are not free, autonomous, and equal, they believe they are.[49]

Just as the exchange principle demands that, one day, a just and equitable exchange would, by replacing the present lopsided one, put an end to the universality of the exchange process once and for all, so too the liberal ideology that insists that everybody deserves to be told the truth, and to have their intelligence respected, might one day do away with insulting TV shows, vacuous advertising jingles and horoscope columns.

A third point of contention has it that the culture industry theory is not particularly radical because all it outlines is a theory of escapism, thereby aligning it, despite itself no doubt, with the standard conservative criticism of mass entertainment. People watch trash TV and lap up cheap romantic fiction as a way of diverting themselves from a grisly reality. Here too, a major point is missed. If the products of the culture industry were solely about escapism, they would be admitting that reality was indeed grisly, but that is just what they don't want people to think. What is actually being promoted is a false reconciliation with reality. The stimuli they offer are fundamentally mirages, representing the absent objects of pleasure in the rest of life, and thus not stimuli at all, which is what explains the frequent amalgam of prudishness and mild pornography in mass entertainment. This is a point Lisa Yun Lee productively emphasises in her analysis of the theory. By substituting its own version of stimulation for the real thing, the culture industry does not sublimate desire, as a one-dimensional escapism theory would have it, but represses it. It provocatively invites audiences to gaze on the sexualised bodies of the stars, but only so that the desire so provoked can be cauterised. As Lee writes, '[i]t is not only the products that are inauthentic and degraded, but also – and more importantly – our experience of them. The culture industry effectively destroys the sensuous nature of existence and our ability to experience it sensually'.[50] The pleasure of genuine pleasure has the effect of suspending thought in moments of pure joy. Where these are simulated in mass culture, they intend to have the same effect, even when the pleasure being retailed is that of seeing others suffer for whatever reason. The psychological foundation of pleasure is therefore a willing surrender to a feeling of helplessness, which commercial films and popular tunes have learned to mimic. What is escaped by this mechanism is not reality as such, but any thought of not accepting it. The result is an imaginary state of reconciliation, a caricatural version of social harmony based on instinctual repression, in which not the world outside is left behind but any substantive critical articulation against it. 'It is flight,' Adorno and Horkheimer concede, before adding the qualifier, 'not, as is asserted, flight from a wretched reality, but from the last remaining thought of resistance. The liberation that amusement promises is freedom from thought and from negation'.[51]

A more nuanced encounter with the theory is staged by Espen Hammer, who notes the preformative function that the culture industry's products take on for Adorno. On analogy with the view of a priori rational schematism in Kant, which automatically subjects the elements of sense perception to rule-bound interpretations in a normative sense, the productions of film and television in particular enhance and intensify the mechanisms of social control in a more insidious way than do the more overt repressive social apparatuses such as law and public morality. Hammer feels, however, that there is a hesitancy in Adorno and Horkheimer's theory in the exposition of its relation to the world around it. The authors comment at one point in the *Dialectic of Enlightenment* that the familiar feeling everyone has had on coming out of the cinema, that real life for a while feels like an extension of the film, is not accidental. To the degree that the film studio or TV company is intent on reproducing the life of empirical reality, people's own experience of that reality collapses into a function of the film itself, whose straightforward continuation it now appears to be. This was the point made by Adorno in the opening proposition of the essay 'The Schema of Mass Culture', that the boundary between real life and the culture industry was being progressively demolished. For some reason, Hammer sees an ambiguity in this. 'Is the claim that the judgments we make are adopted from a heteronomous source, leaving the content of experience untouched? Or is it that what we perceive in the "real" world is continuous with the perception we have of persons and objects presented via the industry?'[52] In other words, have the discursive and emotional protocols of the culture industry marginalised modern experience, or have they displaced it entirely by substituting themselves for it? The answer, for Adorno, was undoubtedly the latter. There is no modern experience worthy of the name, which is why the culture industry achieves such an easy sell in providing the semblance of it.

An index of the withering of experience, according to Adorno, lies in the ready resort of the culture industry to comic idioms intended to provoke uproarious laughter. This was an important pillar of the critique in the *Dialectic of Enlightenment*:

> Conciliatory laughter is heard as the echo of an escape from power; the wrong kind overcomes fear by capitulating to the forces that are to be feared. It is the echo of power as something inescapable. Fun is a medicinal bath. The pleasure industry never fails to prescribe it. It makes laughter the instrument of the fraud practised on happiness... In the false society laughter is a disease that has attacked happiness and is drawing it into its worthless totality. To laugh at something is always to deride it, and the life which, according to Bergson, in laughter breaks through the barrier, is actually an invading barbaric life, self-assertion prepared to parade its liberation from any scruple when the social occasion arises. Such a laughing audience is a parody of humanity.[53]

Hammer worries on behalf of some paradigmatic readers of Adorno that sentiments such as these, which he continues to express in later essays such as 'Is Art Lighthearted?' and the essay on Beckett's *Endgame*, 'seem remarkably stern and ungenerous. Is Adorno rejecting all forms of amusement? For how long is western culture supposed to resist the comic mode? Can laughter ever be innocent again? Adorno's sweeping, acidic remarks are not very helpful'.[54] These ventriloquised questioners might be advised that they are framing these queries in the wrong terms. The critique is not of laughter or of comedy themselves, but of what has become of them in reified society and its official culture, where the innocent levity to which they once gave voice has become unavailable. Much as the most urgent questions ought to be asked about the kinds of emotions provoked in audiences by both commercial entertainment and in public discourses in the news media, so too one ought to consider exactly what it is that audiences are being prompted to laugh at, and why. A certain hackneyed current in the politics of aesthetics has always insisted that laughter can be subversive, because it invites the chuckler to see the world at an obtuse angle, a view restated by Simon Critchley, who thinks that Adorno took Beckett far too seriously. For Critchley, laughter is 'a site of uncolonisable resistance to the alleged total administration of society, a node of non-identity in the idealising rage of commodification that returns us not to a fully integrated and harmonious *Lebenswelt* but lights up the comic feebleness of our embodiment'.[55] The cathartic function of laughter for Critchley enables audiences to carry on with their lives, despite knowing that they have become 'absurd'. Scarcely any more precise evaluation, *malgré lui*, of the culture industry's intentions could be conceived. The exact problem with mass laughter is that it is inherently conservative. Not only are audiences so often encouraged to deride what does not conform to expectations, but the function of laughter in reconciling them to circumambient misery is not innocent in its attitude to the misery, which it hopes will prove fundamentally unchangeable. Having their noses rubbed in their own comic feebleness is not in any sense liberating for subjects of the administered world. Indeed, an official culture that enfeebles its clients, and then invites them to enjoy their own helplessness, might be thought to have read its Sade with disturbing assiduity. There are, as is often pointed out, jokes in Beckett – *Endgame* is probably more replete with them than any other of his dramatic works – but the laughter they generate, if any, is of the drily bitter type, a laughter, as Adorno points out, about laughter itself and what has befallen it. Such meta-laughter was Beckett's forte, as witness the joke about the tailor told by the elderly Nagg in his dustbin. What is both funny, and overwhelmingly sad, about the joke is that it was once just funny, a point underscored only moments before in a philosophical reflection by his moribund wife, Nell: 'Nothing is funnier than unhappiness... Yes, yes, it's the most comical thing in the world. And we laugh, we laugh, with a will, in the beginning. But it's always the same thing. Yes, it's like the funny story we have heard too often, we still find it funny, but we don't laugh any more'.[56] This same point already worried Adorno in his criticism of Benjamin's valorisation of mass entertainments in the letter of March 1936. Is the laughter of the audience at the figure of the down-and-out played by Charlie Chaplin in *Modern Times* (1936), whose failure to understand the industrial work processes of the modern factory keeps landing him in jail, an expression of solidarity with the victim of society, or does it mock his hapless misfortunes in the secure knowledge that they themselves are, or would be if they were factory workers, perfectly proficient in them? 'The laughter of a cinema audience... is anything but salutary and revolutionary; it is full of the worst bourgeois sadism instead'.[57]

It has become the critical fashion in the last twenty years to point out that mass culture bears a very different physiognomy to the one it wore when Adorno and Horkheimer first theorised it, and even when Adorno defended it again in the 1960s. In many respects, this argument only plays posthumously into the Frankfurt theorists' hands, because nothing about the culture industry as it functions now is at all discontinuous with what there was in the 1940s. What has happened since, through the proliferation of new digital and electronic communications technologies, is that the industry has taken on acromegalic dimensions. If what the *Dialectic of Enlightenment* and its successive texts anatomised was a picture of the extent and influence of western mass culture, what it has now grown into is truly a global industry. The same menu of prescribed tastes that was once limited to a broad culture area defined by the bounds of North America and western Europe has now extended into what was once the ambit of the Soviet sphere of influence, where it previously lived a precarious subterranean existence while being officially reviled and interdicted by the state apparatus, and into extensive tracts of the underdeveloped world, where the miracle of iPods has often arrived ahead of clean running water. The fact that everybody is listening to the same tunes, watching the same American export TV shows, and going to see the latest iteration of the same fecundating film franchises, from Lisbon to Lilongwe, is ideologically celebrated as a wonderful unifying force in a world otherwise riven by fractious hostilities and violently prescriptive fundamentalisms. For all that liberal voices in the cultural studies departments may try to insist that there is a diversity of address and creative heterogeneity throughout what it calls popular culture, nobody in the popular culture industries, least of all in the handful of gargantuan media conglomerates that own everything, believes any such rubbish, although they are doubtless delighted that somebody does. This is so because what the culture industry is offering is amusement, and the provision of amusement, as distinct from cultural forms that developed organically in accord with the total technical level of attainment they have reached at any historical point, is always a business concern, as is indicated by its inability to do without the sales talk of advertising and the techniques of market research. '[T]he original affinity of business and amusement,' write Adorno and Horkheimer, 'is shown in the latter's specific significance: to defend society. To be pleased means to say Yes'.[58]

Where there may be grounds for finding crevices in the theory, they arise critically at those points where products of the culture industry function as antibodies within it, however transiently. Everybody, including Adorno himself, could think of examples of mass culture that are better than the surrounding dross, depending on personal taste. It remains the case that, very occasionally, work is produced within the official channels that serves the function in some way of subverting them or throwing them into relief, if not into reverse. Recording artists distributing newly released CDs of uncommercial material for free, culturally dissident films that bypass the normal distribution routes and yet manage to acquire an audience, sometimes a whole current that throws the existing industry into a state of jealous panic, as the very early punk movement did briefly in the UK, are clearly not component parts of the rationalised industrial provision of culture, for all that they may soon become assimilated within it. It is just that the dialectics of this are more complex than they might at first appear. Arguably, in their first manifestations, these phenomena are not products of the industry, but are seeking, however forlornly, to sidestep it, but following their absorption into it, they then take on another character. Capitalism finds no problem at all in profiting from attacks on capitalism. The Fox TV network has endured regular attacks on its business ethics and its dictatorial controller by one of its own most successful shows, *The Simpsons*. All this was foreseen in the critical theorists' original argument, although one of the first critiques to be mounted of it in the 1960s, that of Hans Magnus Enzensberger, wrongly imputed to Adorno and Horkheimer a failure to see that modernist works would in due course be co-opted into the commodity system too. This purblind argument is still being put in the present generation: 'Their escape into the realm of high culture reflected their resignation to the continued rule of capital. Their reduction of resistance to artistic works that subverted form was ahistorical'.[59] Adorno's analysis of the relation of autonomous artworks to the culture industry is hardly an escape, since he is never less than wholly aware of how precarious is the status of such works in a cultural apparatus riven by the division of labour, and nothing about the critique of a capital that continues to rule implies resignation to it, even where the potential for resistance to it is wholly impotent. Autonomous artworks do not, for Adorno, successfully resist a totalising system in the sense of preventing it from functioning, but their dispositional impulses will not allow them to give assent to it, which is exactly what commercial culture virtually everywhere eagerly does. To see this case as 'ahistorical' is an embarrassing lapse of judgment, given that it never ceases to attend to the present state of historical development of cultural forces, which in the era of mass communication is what has thrown social dissent back to the almost invisible margins of the mainstream, where Enzensberger and now Ronald Bettig find it. Bettig's essay closes by citing the British cultural critic Raymond Williams, whose book *The Long Revolution* (1961) argued that capitalist economic relations had produced the alienation of cultural production from everyday life, the diametrical opposite of Adorno's case of over a decade earlier that the whole tendency of the culture industry was to collapse the distance between the two, so that mass culture eventually becomes a central component of daily experience, shoring up its ideological enmeshment by subtle and unsubtle means combined.

A more fruitful and thoughtful objection to the culture industry theory might lie in evaluating those of its works that appear to be particularly effective, not despite their engrossment in the industry's mechanism but because of it. Again, it would not be especially helpful to advance specific examples, which would express nothing more than the contingency of personal taste, and also discount the temporal factor in which every commodity has a use-by date, but generically, there may be individual episodes, or indeed whole narrative strands, of soap opera, individual recordings or whole DJ sessions of functional dance music, that are not only consummate paradigms of their particular genres, but actually appear to be doing something distinctly productive with them. For the theorists of the culture industry, something productive would have to be possessed of a paramount critical edge with regard to empirical reality, even if, as in the case of the literary works of Kafka and Beckett, that edge consists in the indomitable refusal of any acknowledgement of empirical reality in its present concretion. Put simply, Adorno in particular was not noticeably hospitable to the idea that mass culture could ever be anything other than deeply embroiled in the reproduction of the status quo, to which end it applied its emotional and attitudinal manipulation techniques to willing audiences. But the same Adorno who eviscerated the sentimental slosh of the film and television industries – and there is more than just gossip value in this – was an avid follower, as was his wife Gretel with him, of the CBS children's drama series *Daktari*, which was syndicated to Germany's ZDF television network in the late 1960s, so much so that friends and colleagues were very much aware that the two of them were not to be disturbed when it was on. Adorno's fondness for animals cannot perhaps wholly account for his absorption in the adventures of Judy the chimpanzee and Clarence the cross-eyed lion, but a passage from the *Aesthetic Theory* perhaps sheds a little more light. Serious art needs to manifest evidence of control of its own most ridiculous elements, unless it is to succumb to the easy condemnation of the philistine. 'If it remains on the level of the childish and is taken for such,' Adorno writes, 'it merges with the calculated fun of the culture industry... In its clownishness, art consolingly recollects prehistory in the primordial world of animals... The collusion of children with clowns is a collusion with art, which adults drive out of them just as they drive out their collusion with animals. Human beings have not succeeded in so thoroughly repressing their likeness to animals that they are unable in an instant to recapture it and be flooded with joy'.[60] Could it be that in the least unpalatable manifestations of the culture industry, which is after all the obverse that the intolerable privilege of serious art must both generate and live by, and by which it is in turn punished, as Adorno puts it, the repressed collusion with a layer of experience that socialisation has imperfectly exorcised from people finds some vestigial belated expression? It cheers the heart in ways that it had not intended to, not self-subvertingly, to be sure, but – just possibly – entirely innocently. There must have been something in the plotlines of *Daktari*, which to the best of the author's own childhood recollection certainly did not depart from the standard diegetic approach of unhappiness alleviated and problems resolved, that the Adornos found oddly satisfying, perhaps even reassuring amid the tumult of the conflict-plagued German academic world. While giving no other detail, Adorno's biographer Stefan Müller-Doohm suggests that there were many other TV shows he enjoyed in what turned out to be the closing chapter of his life.[61]

What might be in operation here is something like an immanent critique, the generative principle of all properly dialectical thinking, applicable to cultural products as much as to social phenomena, in which an item is scrutinised in itself, according to its own principles of construction and ideological motivations, rather than being subjected to a transcendent judgment that holds it to objective criteria from above or outside it. The only problem is that this is a supremely successful strategy when the work of critique is precisely critical, a procedure of immanent determinate negation, but where one is saying nothing much more than 'Say what you like about *Daktari*, but it's good at what it does,' the exercise appears to lose all its polemical stringency, indeed turns out to be a more or less willing acquiescence in the dreary reign of what is. Which may be why there is nothing whatsoever of value in devoting books and seminars to the study of video games and animation films as though there were something culturally progressive about them, or as though – even worse – they were worth analysis at *prima facie* surface level just because so many people were captivated by them. Inasmuch as it reinforces obedience to conservative social habits, and reconciles its clients to life in a world devoted above all to the mad dance of financial speculation, the mad accumulation of profit, and the mad concentration of the world's human and natural resources in the hands of people driven by fanatical belief in their own benevolence, where they are not driven by fanatical greed, the culture industry is a force for evil. It short-circuits consciousness, and makes cross-eyed lions of one and all. The tiny flaw in it, which at times in his work it feels as though only Adorno can see, is that by failing to live up to its own promise, in delivering a pharma-ceutical version of happiness once the natural alternative has been placed in cold storage, to await a final defrosting with the arrival of paradise, the industry creates the conditions in which, from time to time, fleetingly, inchoately, people bridle at the crap.

The established intellectual fashion in recent years, with regard to what is perceived as the broken continuity between authentic aesthetics and a reconciled social reality, is to say that Adorno ceased to believe that any sort of practical action could have anything other than purely symbolic significance in the degraded political condition of the post-war world, and that his conception of resistance to that condition had decomposed to nothing more than an essentially idealised aestheticism, in which only the technical practices of modernist artforms, and the responses they evoke in a dwindling audience of sensitively attuned recipients, retained the potential to stand against the enveloping context of delusion. We shall look at the specific implications of such a characterisation in the concluding chapter, but for now it suffices to turn to the substance of Adorno's late aesthetic theory to see how he conceived art's liberating potential.

In contradistinction to the effect of the culture industry's products, what Adorno consistently referred to as authentic works of art refused acquiescence with the surrounding world, instead of merely justifying it. Even where the discursive subtext of an artwork imagines itself to be reconciling its recipients to a belief that all is for the best, art cannot help in its inscriptive procedures being polemical – inscriptive because, for Adorno, the articulative strategies of artworks always possess something of the status of writing, even in non-literary forms. We recall that he writes in the *Aesthetic Theory*, '[t]he idea of a conservative artwork is inherently absurd.'[62] This is so by virtue of the fact that artworks always separate themselves off from the empirical world, setting themselves up over against it, in order to be artworks at all. Prior to whatever ideological affiliations they may then go on to express, their disjunction from the merely existent cannot help but be an indictment of the impoverishment and falsity of that existence, which if it were truly reconciled would not need art. The institution of art, all the way back to its emergence from religious ritual and the propitiation of the gods, bears witness that the world should be other than it is. That said – and here we appear to enter one of the conceptual aporias that strongly characterise Adorno's late work – it is also the case that there is a conservative side to even the dissenting works. 'Every artwork today, the radical ones included, has its conservative aspect; its existence helps to secure the spheres of spirit and culture, whose real powerlessness and complicity with the principle of disaster become plainly evident'.[63] On the one hand, he is arguing, art is constitutionally polemical, in that it inhabits a discrete zone to the realm of social reality, in which it sees at least something, whether systemically fundamental or glancingly marginal, that ought to be changed. On the other hand, there is nonetheless a conservative component in art that arises from its own participation in the institutional realm of culture, and the role that culture ought to play in the enhancement of the human spirit. It is only if that spirit can survive and persevere in the face of the social totality that there might be any hope for thinking a resistance to that totality. That is the positive effect of art's conservative aspect, which, oddly enough, is more respected by advanced modernist works that are subversive of artistic tradition than it is in the products of the culture industry. The dual potential of this dialectically poised argument finds an illuminating paradigm, as so often for Adorno, in the reception of Samuel Beckett's work. With reference to the then recently established military dictatorship in Greece, Adorno states that the country's 'new tyrants knew why they banned Beckett's plays, in which there is not a single political word'.[64] The foundational polemic in Beckett, that the denuded world should be almost inconceivably different to what it is, does not preclude the existence of a conservative element that continues to insist that, by virtue of the spirit that is being assiduously crushed out of them in the world as it is, people are better than the refuse that a heartless blind tyrant has consigned to his dustbins. The horrible truth of twentieth-century political history is that treating people as refuse is as profoundly radical as hoping to overthrow the rule of capital. By contrast, art at its truest to its own principle, by ringfencing within itself the realm of autonomous spirit, preserves the possibility of opposing the present reality and enabling its victims to influence it in however peripheral a way: 'the principle of the isolation of spirit, which casts a spell around itself, is also the principle that breaks through the spell by making it determinate'.[65]

If art's imperfect containment of spirit is the antidote to social reification, it was in music that Adorno seems most reliably to have heard that principle at work. Already, however, at the outset of his career, he had become convinced that the way even serious music was being heard militated against its liberating potential. In the 1938 essay, 'On the Fetish-Character in Music and the Regression of Listening', he criticised the tendency of communications media to reduce music to a culinary role as a half-heard accompaniment to dinner, in which the famous dominant themes of the great classical works, and the cult of superstar conductors addressed half-ironically as 'Maestro', become the most noticeable aspects of a fossilised elite culture. The corollary of all this is that the way people listen to music has undergone a qualitative shift from the attentive patience of the nineteenth-century concert hall to the blithe semi-awareness to which its mass dissemination via radio has subjected it. This tendency has not brought classical music to a wider audience, as was and is still claimed, so much as degraded it to a half-comic status, in which the labour of the virtuoso looks as strictly pointless as it is. The same effect incidentally reveals the alienation of people from each other as much as from the thematic ramifications of the Haydn symphony. 'All music today can very easily sound as *Parsifal* did to Nietzsche's ear. It recalls incomprehensible rites and surviving masks from an earlier time, and is provocative nonsense'.[66] The alternative is what Adorno calls a 'structured listening' that hears the principle of overall construction in the work, and the relation of its elements to each other, of which he frankly doubts radio listeners to be capable. This was only confirmed for him when he arrived in the United States in 1938 and began work under Paul Lazarsfeld on the Princeton Radio Research Project. Through extended content analysis of such broadcasting strands as the NBC Music Appreciation Hour, in which listeners were invited to hear famous passages of the canonical works in the light of supposedly salient features of the composers' biographies, Adorno charged radio with keeping its audiences ignorant while pretending to educate them, not really the conclusion at which Lazarsfeld expected his researchers to arrive, given that a large part of the motivation for the Project was constructively helping radio to do its job better. It was probably already a lost cause. A decade earlier, while still in his twenties, in an essay dedicated to his former composition teacher Alban Berg, Adorno noted the decay of comprehension with regard to the classical tradition on the part of both listeners and performers: 'The works themselves are starting to become uninterpretable. For the essences that interpretation seeks to access have been wholly transformed in reality, and thus also in the works, which are located in history and participate in living history'. What musical works actually mean has been split off from any formal unity with their structure, so that only fleeting glimpses of their original signification are possible: 'interpretation now wanders aimlessly between fragments and recognises their essences, but can no longer draw them back into the material from which history expelled them'.[67]

Regardless of the temporal state of music in the continuum of history, it remains for Adorno the artform that stands in the most inappropriable relation to empirical reality. The technical means and signifying regimes of music are anything but straightforwardly propositional. They do not make summarisable statements about the world. This is so even where music has an obviously programmatic basis, as in opera and oratorio scores, songs, symphonic poems, thematic and impressionist music. A piece that evokes the dynamism of a summer landscape, or the changing tidal moods of the sea, may set those mental pictures in the minds of its listeners, but exactly how the orchestral or instrumental sounds evoke those images remains obscure. The greatest music in the classical tradition, including the works of those modernist composers that were conceived in direct antagonism towards that tradition, such as the works of the second Viennese school – Schönberg, Berg and the early Webern – serves to throw the unreconciled world in which they arise into relief. In the early essay 'Night Music', Adorno says that the precise reason people do not want to hear atonal music is that they secretly know that it is telling them some sort of truth about damaged life, and which the petrified works of the established canon now exist to smother. In Mahler's works, there is a tension, sustained throughout his career, between the mellifluous elements that draw on outmoded formal resources and such musical *objets trouvés* as folk tunes, and the moments where his music, driven to the extremes of expression, breaks through those apparently affirmative tendencies to utter tragic and unspeakable truths on behalf of the socially marginalised, the bereft and the forgotten, those who, as Adorno puts it in his 1960 monograph on the composer (*Mahler: A Musical Physiognomy*), only live in the shadows.

At the summit of achievement is Beethoven, subject of a theoretical labour of decades that remained unfinished at the time of his death, who for Adorno expressed everything that was formally and technically possible with the musical resources of his time. Beethoven's works are in one sense supreme products of his bourgeois musical milieu, all the way to the dedications to members of the nobility and – at least temporarily – to Napoleon Bonaparte, and yet what he achieves within, and in sustained dialectical tension with, that tradition subverts everything that is expected of it. The last works in particular, which are the subject of a 1937 essay, 'Beethoven's Late Style', wrench their conventional forms inside out, turn the fugal and sonata forms into autocritiques, and insist in the fury of their rhythmic and dynamic contours on an expression of the profoundest dissatisfaction. To reassure ourselves that this is only music after all, as the works take their place in the reiterable repertoire of classical approval, is to succumb to a spiritual anacusis as all-consuming as the physical version that afflicted the composer's own later years. The essay opens with a provocative non-analogy: 'The maturity of a significant artist's late works is not like that of fruits. They are not usually round, but, rather, furrowed, even ruptured; they tend to lack sweetness, and are prickly in their refusal to be merely tasted. They show none of that harmony that the classicist aesthetic is accustomed to demanding of a work of art, and the marks they bear are more those of history than growth'.[68] It is important to understand that these deformations are not simply products of the psychological temperament of an artist nearing the end, whatever his age happens to be, but are immanent to the laws of aesthetic form themselves. 'The relationship between conventions and subjectivity must be understood as the formal law from which the substance of the late works originates, if they are truly to amount to more than touching relics'.[69] The laconic abruptness that characterises many of the late works is not a direct expression of the wounded subjectivity of the composer, but a tendency that emerges from within the musical language itself and reorients the relation of subjectivity to technique: 'it seeks not to cleanse his musical language of formulas but, rather, to strip the formula of its semblance of subjective control... that places the formula as a monument to what once was, a monument of which subjectivity itself, in its petrified state, forms a part'.[70] The abrupt caesuras that characterise Beethoven's late style, moments where the music suddenly breaks off, are the nodal points where formula and subjective intention enter an expressive deadlock, as though the momentary hiatus is the precise point at which subjectivity most directly addresses the hearer. The greatest eloquence lies in the pause between the sudden halt and the continuation, when the following notes emerge in the shadow of the coarsely hewn break, like a speaker attempting to recover himself after a rhetorical stumble caused by the intensity of his own diction. Subjectivity and objectivity do not harmoniously resolve each other in these works, however, as would be the bourgeois prescription, the two elements to be swallowed medicinally together. 'He does not bring about their harmonic synthesis,' Adorno warns. 'Acting as a force of dissociation, he tears them apart in time, in order that they might, perhaps, be preserved for the realm of the eternal.' The realm of the eternal is unmapped territory, however, to which music, like all artworks, may or may not gain access. Elsewhere, Adorno poignantly notes Beethoven's hubristic boast of his own piano sonata no 23, known as the *Appassionata*, that he confidently expected people would still be playing it in ten years' time. By contrast with that, as Adorno puts it in the celebrated closing epigram of the 1937 essay: 'In the history of art, late works are the catastrophes'.[71]

The *chorismos* between what music retains in its innermost particles and what it confronts in the objective world is of paramount importance to Adorno's aesthetic theory. 'No music of our time was as humane as his,' he says in a late monograph on the works of Alban Berg. '[T]hat distances it from humankind'.[72] This is what he deplores in the homogenised extrusion of commercial music: not only that it is always technically and qualitatively inferior to the advanced artwork, but that it also blends imperceptibly into its social context, smudging what ought to be the lines of demarcation that separate a truly critical work from the hegemonic culture that would encompass it along with all the other commodities. Joseph Weiss articulates this succinctly in an essay when he says of the universal 4/4 tempo of industrial pop that it represents 'the discipline of clock time, posing as music,'[73] a factor that explicitly announces its continuity with the mechanised world of work, from which it emerges and to which it offers up its consumers. Meanwhile, in the disjunct morphology and the dissonances of atonal works, music refuses a social function, precisely by telling the truth about social functionality. 'Dissonance is the truth about harmony,'[74] Adorno writes in the *Aesthetic Theory*, suggesting that whatever aural discomfiture is evoked in audiences by the chamber works of the Schönberg circle is the sonic evidence that the appearance of harmony, the semblance of reconciliation in works of the classical tradition, serves in the modern age as an ideological mask to conceal the reality of antagonism. For this reason, Adorno was virtually allergic to the bulk of Stravinsky's output. Just as other composers were searching for a new musical language that would encapsulate the deterioration of subjectivity within societies in crisis, Stravinsky undertook a wholesale restoration of deceased classical and neoclassical forms, in music that appears to ratify the annihilation of the individual, ritualistically in the *Rite of Spring* (1913), formalistically in the anachronising restitutions of the Italian Baroque and so forth, amid circumstances of universal social regression. This makes his music simultaneously conservative and psychotic, a bulwark for musical tradition that also invites the listening individuals to enjoy their own liquidation, an impulse in which it unwittingly joins forces with the ritualistic mythical elements in Wagner, whose music Stravinsky openly loathed. 'Anxiety in the face of dehumanisation is transformed into the joy of its unveiling, and ultimately into the pleasure of the same death instinct whose symbolism was prepared by the hated *Tristan*... The schizo-phrenic deportment of Stravinsky's music is that of a ritual that means to outbid the coldness of the world. Grimacing, his work makes itself a match for the insanity of objective spirit'.[75]

If there is one aspect of Adorno's music criticism that everybody has heard of, it is his career-long derogation of jazz. Indeed, the course of his disquisitions on the topic describes a baleful chronology. His first short aphorism on the subject in 1933 is entitled, hopefully enough, 'Farewell to Jazz'. Only three years later, in British exile, he wrote a much longer analysis, 'On Jazz', on a form whose rumoured death with its interdiction by the Nazi regime in Germany had clearly been premature. By the mid-1950s, when the miscellaneous essay collection *Prisms* was published, the long piece on the same theme was given the exasperated title, 'Perennial Fashion – Jazz', in acknowledgement of the fact that jazz had not had the decency, unlike other transient fashions, to fade away when its hour was done, in which ephemerality Adorno stated the dignity of fashion to consist, but was still panting on, allegedly reinventing itself for each successive generation of cool cats and hipsters, as though flared trousers, once banished to the back of the wardrobe, were to keep reappearing ad nauseam every season. Despite the retro-gression that was stamped in it from the very beginning, jazz refused – and refuses – to die, clearly because, even by the 1950s, it had become as quaintly indestructible an idiom as Viennese waltz music of the late nineteenth century. If the polkas and galops that were all the five-minute rage in the era immediately prior to the inception of jazz had had the discretion to surrender to the Charleston, the jitterbug and the Lindy hop, the last two at least were still as obdurately evident on the dancefloors of the fifties as the music they accompanied.

Those critics who have construed the early essay, which was a comment on Hitler's ban on radio broadcasts of what the Reich called *Negerjazz*, as a virtual ratification of Nazi policy, have spectacularly missed the point. Adorno observes that the ban naively interpreted jazz as being black music, which had already ceased to be the case on both sides of the Atlantic by the early 1930s. 'Jazz no more has anything to do with authentic black music, which has long since been falsified and industrially smoothed out here [i.e. in Nazi Germany], than it is possessed of any destructive or threatening qualities'.[76] It is neither the degenerate music of racial minorities nor the subversive force of that 'cultural Bolshevism' that the Nazis saw in anything that was not to their regressive aesthetic taste. Indeed, the attentive ear could already hear in the jazz played on the radio a distinct straining, beneath the tired syncopations and the ostensibly liberated passages of triple rhythm, in the direction of military marches, which were scarcely anathema in the Third Reich. Tethering all the airborne improvisational hubbub of the soloists to the ground is the relentlessly marked tempo of the bass drum that drives the beat. Nothing changes in jazz, according to Adorno; it is a static musical form, for all its professed freedom from musical convention. Even the syncopations were hardly new, and were probably done better by nineteenth-century masters of populism such as Brahms and Johann Strauss. There is nothing dialectical in a Strauss polka perhaps, but neither is there in the Paul Whiteman Orchestra doing *Makin' Whoopee!* with Bing Crosby at the microphone. Whiteman, a classical viola student from Denver, converted to jazz after the first world war, and became one of the most successful bandleaders of its early phase, sufficiently to be styled the King of Jazz in the American press. Apart from Crosby, he worked with a succession of other white vocalists including Ramona Davies, whose solo act, Ramona and her Grand Piano, amounted to little more than crisply enunciated parlour crooning with diminished sevenths, but was enough to earn her the honorific, the Princess of Jazz. This was as much the story of jazz as a musical convention by the early 1930s as were Louis Armstrong's scat singing or Fats Waller's syncopations on the ecclesiastical pipe organ. Adorno also heard the classical influences in jazz of this period, the chromatic harmonies of Debussy and Delius, the ninth chords, the augmented sixths, the mildly dissonant stereotypical 'blue chord', whose path into popular taste had effectively been smoothed by jazz: 'it would hardly be exaggerated to observe that this style is making its way for the first time into the broader strata of society through jazz. In Parisian nightclubs, one can hear Debussy and Ravel in between the rumbas and Charlestons'.[77]

Not only was jazz mired in its own lack of development, but precisely its static quality as a musical form had to be parsed into individualistic showmanship and innovation, both in the personalities of its performers and in its basic principle, syncopated phrasing over a metronomically invariant metrical structure. Like many another element of the culture industry, jazz was predicated on the principle of pseudo-individualisation, the raucous trumpet tone or mellow saxophone lilt of the various musicians being the signatures that supposedly raised them above the pitifully meagre framework in which they were constrained. The other variant principle was the arrangement, which often tinkered with the hit songs of the day in order to persuade listeners that not only was the music restlessly creative, but that it had been somehow tailor-made for each specific audience and occasion. Jazz has remained throughout its long history parasitic to the last degree on the popular song tradition, whether it had vocalists or not. Even in the allegedly avant-garde bebop period, audiences were expected to tolerate further highly processed versions of *Sweet Lorraine, It's Only a Paper Moon* and *Lover, Come Back To Me*, tunes their parents would have danced to before the war. Nothing announces its collusion with cultural orthodoxy more brazenly, despite the hope vested in it that it was fundamentally an autonomous subversive current. This and its reliance on the principle of arrangement testify to jazz's 'absence of all artistic ambitions to achieve distance from reality, to the readiness of the music to swim with the stream; this is music that does not fancy itself any better than it is'.[78]

Virtually nothing in Adorno's aesthetic theory arouses as much critical antipathy as the writings on jazz. Much of this is couched in normatively conformist terms, as though there ought not to be anyone in the world who has not been seduced by the sophistication and the limitless creative energy of the medium. To find jazz offensive in its elephantine dullness is to be as perversely out of step as thinking the Beatles were rubbish. For one thing, there were just too many offshoots of it. Within the ensemble of disapprobation, a particular riff has played on the notion that Adorno only ever heard the worst commercial slop that was played on German, British and American radio stations, and that if he had gone to certain jazz clubs on the west coast of America in the 1940s, he might have heard the greater pliability of style that the most advanced groups were offering. None of this subverts the principal force of the argument, that the simulated innovations that the rest of us can hear at the click of a link on YouTube remain squarely within the tradition as Adorno criticised it. When jazz did throw away the crutch of hit songs and show tunes, and light out into the territory of its own modal improvisations, the result was a descent into mere mood music, themes that flow on placidly beneath fragmented bits of solo work, the two-note descants of the trumpet over the honeyed seventh chords and brushed snares of *Kind of Blue* (1959), one of jazz's claimants to the title of greatest recording ever made. The music is monotonously sleepy, the sort of undifferentiated soundtrack that nobody would have the slightest compunction about piping into an airport departure lounge now, the wandering melodic lines not discovering any particular reason to go one way rather than the other, the sonic equivalent of the apathy induced by a marijuana drowse. Max Paddison hits on an important point when he notes that jazz in Adorno's conception 'is apparently not only regarded as a degeneration of the material of serious music, but even as being a degeneration of the material of light music and of the commercial hit song'.[79] Those who find something genuinely affecting and moving in the best performances of the swing vocal period, the rendition of pop tunes by such artists as Billie Holiday, Ivie Anderson or Nat 'King' Cole, may find the limits of their tolerance when the same tunes are subjected to twelve-minute instrumental jams that add nothing to the rendition other than a barrage of standard tricks and clichés.

Robert Lanning makes the boilerplate point that Adorno had obviously just been listening to the wrong types of jazz, before repining into the dog-eared argument that opposing mass cultural forms is ipso facto to be a snobbish elitist, as though mass cultural forms were axiomatically valuable in themselves, precisely because everybody buys into them. 'There is a sense in this of personal attacks made from the conviction of his intellectual and cultural superiority'.[80] Better to be polite and accept that you know nothing more than anybody else does, a stance that would have left oppositional politics, among other intellectual ventures, stranded on the start-line. From a position of hostility to the theory of the culture industry, Lanning misreads Adorno's analysis of jazz as conflating the two elements of cultural production and the capitalist exploitation of it, when the correct Marxist practice is to keep the two separate, not least for what objectifying uses the former may be put to by its audiences. 'Merely concentrating on the commodification of music and its descent into commercialism, as Adorno does, sets up all cultural production as nothing but a manifestation of the structure and purpose of capitalism. Commodification cannot be ignored, but neither can the process that transforms cultural practices into commodities, or the reasons people undertake cultural activity as a means of self-expression, social presence and resistance'.[81] In the case of the process specified, it is hard to see how Lanning thinks this point is a correction of what Adorno argues throughout, and on which the theory of the culture industry

234

rests, while the personal reasons he gives for people consuming cultural products do not in any way undermine the status of those products as commodities. The wager in such an argument is still that a commodity such as jazz emerges from a space outside capitalism, and is then rapidly absorbed into the economic system of the recording and performance industries. Jazz was already well on the way to its assimilation into that system, however, in the 1930s, when Adorno began writing about it, as is attested by critics such as Lanning himself, whose discriminative powers extend to the perception that there was, if not a definitive right jazz in this era, then certainly an obviously wrong one. The point is that once jazz had become packaged for mass consumption, its recordings and performances carefully filtered down to a homogenised pabulum suitable for broadcast in the mass media, it had become precisely what Adorno saw in it, which is what Lanning calls 'a manifestation of the structure and purpose of capitalism'. The fetishism of jazz techniques, which quickly became indispensable stylistic elements of it, contribute like all fetishes to the regression of consciousness. The fetish is a non-living object that stands in for, or entirely replaces, its living antecedent, to the detriment of any spontaneous relation to the original. In the light of this observation, Douglas Kellner correctly summarises Adorno's assessment of jazz – '[i]ts seeming spontaneity and improvisation are themselves calculated in advance and the range of what is permissible is as circumscribed as in clothes or other realms of fashion'[82] – before insisting in a footnote to the passage that Adorno had obviously not heard the right kind of jazz.

Today, the discerning consumer can choose from smooth jazz; acid jazz; dark jazz, an outgrowth of the downbeat ambient electronic music of the 1990s; nu jazz, which incorporates elements of commercial funk; or ethno-jazz, a style that subjects indigenous music from the poorer parts of Europe and the developing world to a thorough jazzing. In a recording of 2013 by an

Armenian ethno-jazz ensemble,[83] brass figures tootle over a metronomic 4/4 beat, interspersed with rockish guitar solos and meandering one-handed keyboard filler, the harshly dazzling production sound over-defining every element of the banality, as though it were saying anything different to the upbeat instrumental jazz of the 1950s renaissance. It sounds about as Armenian as Dizzy Gillespie. This is the auditory equivalent of identical branded food products in the supermarket, and is what is meant by the observation that culture has become, in its relentless formulaic predictability, a branch of the economy, for which consumers magnify their enthusiasm in order to convince themselves that what they are going to be served anyway is another astounding stroke of good luck. 'Jazz sets up schemes of social behaviour to which people must in any case conform. It enables them to practise those forms of behaviour, and they love it all the more for making the inescapable easier to bear'.[84]

'Through language,' Adorno wrote in an early essay, 'Theses on the Language of the Philosopher' (c1931/32), 'history wins a share of truth. Words are never merely signs of what is thought under them, but rather history erupts into words, establishing their truth-character. The share of history in the word unfailingly determines the choice of every word because history and truth meet in the word'.[85] All language is marked, indeed compromised, by the inveiglement into it of the historical development of consciousness, making any grasp at a pure linguistic expression a purely mythical enterprise. That said, there is nothing but language in which to articulate complex propositions that aim at the truth, and in the circumstances all the writer can do is hope and try to hit upon the words that carry the intended meaning at the present historical moment. 'In the absence of unified society there is no objective language and therefore no truthfully communicative language'.[86] It is as though conceptual expression can only proceed crab-wise, sidestepping its way through the rusted jetsam and entanglements of previous linguistic conventions, trusting, half-tactically and half-intuitively, that it will light on the right ways of saying things that would elude the communicative aporias into which everyday language has already fragmented. Its fragmentation, indeed, is in large part owing to the demotion of language to the kind of functional communication in which nothing is actually communicated. If so much of language has disintegrated under the force of reified society, its ruins are nonetheless what the objectifying thinker must work with, arranging them into the best configurations available according to the residual force of truth in them. A philosophical critique can therefore also function as an autocritique of the language in which it is framed. In particular, what Adorno calls 'deceitful ontology', by which he intends the theoretical systems of Max Scheler and especially Martin Heidegger, whose chef d'oeuvre *Being and Time* (1927) had been published only a few years before this essay was written, is to be exposed by means of a critique of its language, which despite what its authors may have imagined, is as historically situated as the chatter of people waiting at the tram-stop.

It was not exclusively philosophical discourse to which Adorno attended, however. The three volumes of literary essays, *Notes to Literature* (1958–65), are augmented by other miscellaneous writings on literary themes *inter alia*. The first volume of the *Notes* opens with an essay about the essay form itself, which lends itself to a micrological focus on the fugitive, seemingly incidental elements of its object, and declines to enter the sealed conceptual order in which theorising has traditionally taken place. 'Because the unbroken order of concepts is not equivalent to what exists, the essay does not aim at a closed deductive or inductive structure. In particular, it rebels against the doctrine, deeply rooted since Plato, that what is transient and ephemeral is unworthy of philosophy... the essay invests experience with as much substance as traditional theory does mere categories'.[87] The essay is an exercise in heretical cunning, by which it seeks to give conceptual orthodoxy the slip, and reveal something of what orthodox thinking keeps obscured. Thus primed, the essays go on to explore themes and techniques in nineteenth-century German lyric poetry, Goethe, Balzac, Proust, Dickens and Thomas Mann. Items on literary theory, such as the role of political engagement in literary works or the formal language of literary realism, are interspersed with some of Adorno's most idiosyncratic excursions, including a physiognomy of punctuation marks. Exclamation points, he writes as early as 1956, have become intolerable, the crude ruse by which writers attempt to impose an external authority on language. They proliferated in works of German expressionism, until they became as superfluous as the zeroes on banknotes during the inflation. The ellipsis (...) has become the disingenuous mark of a writer pretending to a wealth of further unexpressed thoughts that have not yet entered his head. Parentheses, by imprisoning subsidiary thoughts between bars, create enclaves within the flow of thought and militate against dialectical thinking, in which no element should not be integral to the overall structure. In these tiniest details of what writing looks like are contained concrete indicators of the administrative reality in which all writing must take its chances. While use of some has become hyper-inflationary, however, others are fast disappearing into the surrounding void. 'It starts with the loss of the semicolon,' Adorno warns. '[I]t ends with the ratification of imbecility by a reasonableness purged of all admixtures'.[88]

As we have seen, Adorno valued the work of writers who refused explicit accommodation with the prevalent discourses of political engagement, in favour of those whose work disdains to speak the language of the existing culture at all. This point is made with potent emphasis in his dispute with Lukács in the essay 'Extorted Reconciliation', on the Hungarian theorist's *Realism in Our Time*, a study of the realist novel that attempts to disembowel the literary modernism of the twentieth century as so much self-indulgent decadence, the very charge brought against dissidents of all stripes in both Stalinist Russia and Nazi Germany. The opposite of decadence is flourishing healthy growth, a usage that inappropriately applies categories of the natural world to socially mediated artforms. As Lukács puts it, 'the conception of what is socially healthy is equally and simultaneously the basis of all really great art, for what is socially healthy becomes a component of man's historical self-awareness'.[89] These are, for Adorno, pitifully undialectical concepts, and a far cry from the profound theoretical insights into literary production evinced in the earliest works of Lukács, such as the indispensable *Theory of the Novel* (1916), its methodology still germane to Adorno's own era, despite the passage of intellectual history and the reconciliations with the party state which its author had subsequently been browbeaten into making. In that earlier work, the talk was not at all of health and flourishing, but rather the reverse. '[T]he very disintegration and inadequacy of the world is the precondition for the existence of art and its becoming conscious... they [the artforms] have to produce out of themselves all that was once simply accepted as given'.[90] This is the Lukács who exercised such an enduring influence on Adorno, and others of the Frankfurt School thinkers, in the 1920s. In terminology that applies the conceptuality of German idealism to a putatively materialist theory of literature, he speaks of the bounded temporality that undermines the claim to transcendence of even the greatest works, and which must influence their reception in later ages – 'time brushes aside even the eternal'[91] – and seems, in the irony of retrospect, to speak out to a future self subjected to the duty of pretending social harmony has broken out, in circumstances where the reality brands such ideology a socially necessary illusion on pain of death: 'any attempt to depict the utopian as existent can only end in destroying the form, not in creating reality'.[92] Of course, for Adorno, the point applies with equal saliency to modernist works, which is why he favours those that appear more or less to have forgotten that utopia was once a wish, let alone one that could be wished, via literature, into reality. For this, Lukács would satirise Adorno's western cohort of dissidents as having taken up residence in the Grand Hotel Abyss, an establishment sitting in aloof splendour above the chasm, like some crumbling monastery on top of Mount Athos but with better cooking, in a preface to the 1962 reissue of this very work, whose conceptual naïveté its author now obediently disowned. Adorno turned a blind eye to the squib.

The most thoroughly dialectical relation to history was legible in the dramatic works of Samuel Beckett, which flirted with a relapse into final silence in the case of the half-minute fragment *Breath* (1969), and the prose parables of Franz Kafka. On the latter, Adorno had written a piece in constellation form, 'Notes on Kafka', which appears as the closing item in the *Prisms* collection. The hermetic character of Kafka's world at once sets itself in opposition to the material history going on around it, but at the same time produces the truth about that history precisely in its diremption from it. The nowhere in which his characters are stranded becomes the contemporary everywhere that expressionist literature, which was exactly contemporaneous with Kafka, addresses in more obviously vituperative manner. Where expressionism boiled with hopeless rage, though, Kafka's works have the tranquillity of death on them, and his characters, if that is what they are, have no relation to their own subjectivity, which was the animating principle of expressionism. 'What is enclosed in Kafka's glass ball,' writes Adorno, 'is even more monotonous, more coherent and hence more horrible than the system outside, because in absolute subjective space and in absolute subjective time there is no room for anything that might disturb their intrinsic principle, that of inexorable estrangement'.[93] The much-cited meaninglessness of his universe is not the pure absurdity that would be on display in the post-war theatre of Ionesco, but of overdetermined meaning, applied systematically until its rationality splinters under the strain of its own hypertrophic logic. Titorelli, the impoverished painter in *The Trial* (1925), who is also a trustee of the judiciary, explains to Josef K, who has petitioned him for advice on his arraignment, that the best result he can hope for is either a deferment or an 'apparent acquittal', which is followed by rearrest and another trial, leading eventually to another apparent acquittal that paves the way to another arrest and trial, and so forth, the process each time requiring an entire new legal approach to keep at bay the looming menace of a final verdict and sentencing. The fact that there may be hope is what casts the bleakest light over it all. Unexpectedly passionate sexual desire, from the female fan-club that crowds outside Titorelli's door, gasping over his every move, to the adventitious tenderness that blooms between Frieda and Klamm amid the beer-puddles on the inn floor in *The Castle* (1926), is a feature of worlds that are otherwise the antipodes of reality down to the molecular level. 'There is plenty of hope,' Kafka is said to have remarked to his literary executor Max Brod, 'an infinite amount of hope – but not for us.' To the moribund Josef K's failing vision appears a man at a high window, his arms outstretched in apparent solicitude, offering comfort and solidarity to somebody. An infernal punishment machine inscribes the letter of the law they have violated on the bodies of the condemned as it kills them, dispensing a mystical experience that is regrettably passing into history with the introduction of new technology. In building China's Great Wall in its laborious sections, workers are encouraged to try with all their might to understand the orders of their distant imperial leaders, and at the moment their understanding fails, to cease trying. All of social schizophrenia is rooted in these parabolic scenarios, as well as the petrifaction of antique theology. In the firmament is not the God-shaped hole of the deity who never existed, but the empty seat of the *deus absconditus*, of a God who has become totally abstract in his translation from anthropomorphic myth to indeterminate principle of power. 'Kafka's work preserves the moment in which the purified faith was revealed to be impure, in which demythologising appeared as demonology'.[94]

Martin Ryle and Kate Soper have some difficulty penetrating through the top layer of Adorno's critique of realist literature, mounting the standard objection at the apparent paradox that obtains between his conception of the novel as a truth-telling device and the fact that its potential recipients are the very subjects of the state of alienation it depicts. How could they respond to it? 'Adorno's insistence on the fixed, almost irredeemably negative nature of "mass" life jeopardises the claim he nonetheless wants to make about art's redemptive power, because it leaves us wondering who – apart from the critic – is supposed to be able to enjoy or understand art... Even as he illuminates particular writers and works, he often suggests unhelpfully that writing is, or should be, always and only devoted to the representation of negativity'.[95] Unhelpfully to whom? But in any case, aesthetics are negative by their very existence, because they demonstrate that the present world is not enough. Even where they appear to be celebrating it, they must be pointing to an ontological lack in reality that, if it were whole and reconciled in itself, would have no need of art. The essayists themselves, meanwhile, appear to take a fatalistic view of the efficacy of telling the truth in circumstances where the lies of myth and ideology are prevalent. Truth is what illuminates the darkness of mendacity, and Adorno nowhere proclaims that it will inevitably prove hopeless, only that some aesthetic ways of expressing it are more likely to succeed than others. Otherwise, every child must still be puzzling to this day over how Andersen's small boy manages to persuade the crowds that the Emperor isn't wearing any clothes.

The truthful reflection of the world as it is demands not just a changing mirror-image, but a new formal device with which to reflect it. Historical circumstances in the present day mean that the narrative arts cannot just carry on telling didactic stories, as they were wont to do since the rise of the bourgeois novel form in the eighteenth century. David Cunningham captures this point: 'If human reality can no longer be taken to have an inherent meaning or necessity, then the meanings and logical patterns imposed upon it by novelistic narration must necessarily appear as artificial and arbitrary (something clearly foregrounded in, for example, Joyce's *Ulysses*), thus making questionable any conventional claim to realism'.[96] Joyce's ironic reappropriation of the epic form is one of the precise ways in which, for Adorno, literature might reflect a fragmentary modern experience. Photographic realism à la Lukács was already formally defunct in the 1950s, and must seem all the more so to an age used to consuming narratives in screen format. This suggests what Adorno might have made of such micrologically recursive works as Karl Ove Knausgård's autobiographical cycle, *My Struggle* (2009–11). 'Nowadays anyone who continued to dwell on concrete reality the way [Adalbert] Stifter, for instance, did, and wanted to derive his impact from the fullness and plasticity of a material reality contemplated and humbly accepted, would be forced into an imitative stance that would smack of arts and crafts. He would be guilty of a lie: the lie of delivering himself over to the world with a love that presupposes that the world is meaningful'.[97] Where this technique was pushed to the limits of extreme subjectivism in the nineteenth-century Austrian novelist Stifter, and consummately in Proust, the form itself was reshaped by its material. To cling, in the absence of any other narrative technique, to an unquestioned utilisation of the realist mode, was already in the 1950s, when Adorno wrote these words, to practise the same kind of defeated restorationism, and the same kind of ideological obfuscation, as was carried out in the musical realm by the neoclassical Stravinsky. 'The more strictly the novel adheres to realism in external things, to the gesture that says "this is how it was", the more every word becomes a mere "as if", and the greater becomes the contradiction between this claim and the fact that it was not so'.[98] If there is a smack of mendacity to this, it is at least not as culpable as were the efforts of those who tried to keep alive the tradition of lyric poetry in Germany after the full extent of the catastrophe had become known, disgracefully plucking at flowering weeds amid the rubble of liberal humanism. Thus Werner Bergengruen in a 1950 volume, *Die Heile Welt* (*The Perfect World*), shoring fragments against the ruins: 'What came from pain was only transient. / And my ear heard nothing but songs of praise'. 'Bergengruen's volume,' Adorno notes, 'is only a few years closer to us than the time when Jews who had not been completely killed by the gas were thrown living into the fire, where they regained consciousness and screamed. The poet... heard nothing but songs of praise'.[99] Cunningham identifies the same, if less grotesquely tin-eared, error in the widely celebrated work of WG Sebald, a writer for whom a subjective inwardness has assumed a self-sustaining form that fails to bear the same dialectical relation as Kafka's inwardness does to the material world of his day: 'such subjectivism, and the self-consciously "poetic" (even archaic) diction in which it is expressed, may simply result in – perhaps cannot avoid – a problematic disengagement from contemporary social reality altogether, a regression into "literary" solipsism'.[100] The scare-quotes speak accidentally of the fate that such stylistic features as poeticism or literariness have taken on in the age of information, of deceptively unmediated functional communication in the popular press and on the Internet. No form of writing that conforms itself to such discourses has any chance of revealing the antinomies at the heart of present-day social reality, any more than can the radio that pipes out happy tunes to the workers disguise the fact that their work is the source of their unhappiness.

What Adorno's aesthetics found reflected in the terse monochrome world of Beckett, in the aridly rhetorical jokes as much as in the howls of despair, is that the world becomes a hell when there is nothing else beside it, when everything, including even culture, is crunched up into its machine and digested. The negative mimesis that Adorno celebrates in modernist art is the case for the prosecution of such a world. Romanticism mourned the onset of the disappearance of the natural realm in face of human industry and its reconfigurations of consciousness, but the descendants of Fichte, 'who despises the world because it is nothing but raw materials and products,' haven't even that sense-memory left. As Hamm's servant Clov tells him in some exasperation, there *is* no more nature. Beckett never quite lets the matter rest there, however. The notorious pessimism that is all that a myopic cultural theory sees in Adorno receives its ironic refutation in the bickering one-upmanship of those last men who survived Mary Shelley's apocalypse, stumbling through a sickly decrepitude in the shadow of Nietzsche's *Ubermenschen*, to gather on Beckett's stage in their dustbins and wheelchairs. 'He lets a twisted secular metaphysics shine through,' notes Adorno, 'with a Brechtian commentary':[101]

CLOV: Do you believe in the life to come?

HAMM: Mine was always that. (Exit Clov.) Got him that time![102]

Five

Cracking the Shells: Adorno in the Present Day

There is a kind of poetic justice in the fact that Adorno is the great survivor of the Frankfurt School, the only one whose thought retained its full actuality.
Slavoj Zizek

Death is a human scandal, and should be abolished.
Adorno, letter to Thomas Mann

There was a period, roughly from the late 1970s to the early 1990s, certainly in the English-speaking world, when Frankfurt School critical theory looked to have had its day. What little notice was paid to it tended to be on the order of lip service, and it was seen as a body of theory that, while it contained many cogent and suggestive insights, was essentially limited, both by its own historical rootedness and by the severe curtailments that it appeared to apply to the possibility of radical political engagement in an era as desperately in need of engagement as ever. The academic fashion was all for French poststructuralism, in particular deconstruction in the Derridean manner, with its eloquent hesitations, its ramifying investigations of textuality in everything from postcards and national flags to actual literary texts, and its suspension of grand narratives and inductive logic in favour of deferrals and elisions, or outright disavowals, as when Derrida himself carried over from his early reading of Heidegger the technique of placing undeconstructed remnants of the western philosophical tradition, those concepts that were now strictly considered unsayable, under erasure (*sous rature*), which meant having the word typeset with an emending line through it, a fastidiousness for which earlier generations had made do with inverted commas, or scare quotes. The peculiar aspect of this turn to postmodernist irony and incertitude was that, just as the Frankfurt thinkers, Adorno chief among them, were being written off for their political quiescence, everybody was signing up to an intellectual vogue that saw politics as another of the discursive networks that awaited patient unravelling, and morality as another of the generators of inflexible binary oppositions. Derrida was not without leftist commitments, as his allusive text *Spectres of Marx* (1993) eventually demonstrated, but never quite resolved the conundrum as to what, ultimately, the point was of deconstructing everything, still less what anybody was expected to do with the disarticulated components of something like Marxist theory once they lay before us on the dissecting table.

If the widespread abandonment of Frankfurt critical theory at this juncture could be ascribed to one of the ebb-tides of intellectual history, its recovery in the period from the mid-1990s on is altogether more surprising. The work of a number of thinkers in the American academy, among them Martin Jay, JM Bernstein, Fredric Jameson and Susan Buck-Morss, some of which dated back to the 1970s, began to be more widely taken up. Introductory studies proliferated, and improved translations of some of Adorno's key works, by the likes of Robert Hullot-Kentor, Rodney Livingstone and Edmund Jephcott, brought his notoriously demanding German into partial, provisional alignment with the English philosophical habitus. The full corpus of Adorno's work embraced a prodigious range of intellectual reference, from analytical sociology to literary criticism, ethics to musicology, and critiques of existentialism, phenomenology, historiography and psychoanalysis, along with personal memoirs that drew on any and all of these disciplines to reflect on the minutiae of what he continued to envision as a 'damaged life'. The negative composite figure that has emerged, to many present-day students at least, is of a relentlessly intolerant refusenik, a stuffed-shirt elitist in cultural matters whose grimace of demurral at Hollywood romances and jazz marks him out as a humourless drag, and at worst a collaborationist who failed to see the insurgent potential of the dissenting movements of his latter day. These allergic responses, on the other hand, are countered by an appreciation of the protean originality of his thought, his insistence that conformity in virtually any aspect of life leads to spiritual death, his enduring sensitivity to the exorbitant evil of totalitarianism and other forms of repression, and the potentials his work seems to contain for some indeterminate restitution of leftist theory in the postpolitical age. If there is a buzzkill Adorno, there is too an ineffably cool one. If there is an Adorno who allegedly failed to see beyond the end of his culturally privileged Eurocentric nose, there is the Adorno who emerged to plain view at a March 2016 conference in Amsterdam as 'Global Adorno', a thinker for the internationalist and globalising times, whose cultural and political critiques, while eschewing any specifically prescriptive tenor, nonetheless speak eloquently to the moods and conflicts of our own hour. Despite the chants of the desk-thumpers in 1969, Adorno is not after all dead, but has risen to the historical moment to cast an unwavering strigine gaze over the landscape of a dawning third millennium, in which practically nothing surprises him.

What might surprise a sensitively attuned inspection of Adorno's philosophical writings today is the discovery in them of a theological element, deeply interred, to be sure, but occasionally surfacing to take on something of the conceptual apparatus of traditional theology, even, occasionally, its language. Adorno's relation to religion in his own life was tangential to the two related cosmologies of Judaism and Christianity. He was brought up and confirmed in the Roman Catholic church, but had seemingly departed from any commitment to positive belief by his late teens. After the persecution of the Jews in the Nazi period, and during the troubling period of reconciliation that followed in Germany after 1945, he took on a fiercely partisan allegiance to the condition of Jewishness as paradigmatic of the fate of the individual in the administered world, which may have contented itself thenceforward with administrating culture rather than mass extermination, but retained the same jaundiced view of the outsider, the nonconformist. There was a new categorical imperative, as *Negative Dialectics* states, to ensure that Auschwitz should never be permitted to happen again, and which an unfree humanity had no choice but to adopt, if it was to guarantee its own survival in conditions of advancing reification. Nonetheless, Adorno did not adopt a practising faith, nor, as far as anybody can tell, accede to a belief in God. What he did explicitly contend, however, was that something in the eschatology of the Judeo-Christian tradition did need preserving, and that was the immaterial sense of an alternative to the present material world, a futurity in which history might be redeemed. Having chided Benjamin in the 1930s for his attempt to marry elements of the Jewish mystical arcana with Marxist historical materialism, the noumenal with the phenomenal, it was as though Adorno had returned amid the ruins of enlightenment to the very same endeavour. This impulse flashes recurrently like lightning through the enveloping darkness of the constellation of texts that closes the *Negative Dialectics*, 'Meditations on Metaphysics'.

A path towards these late reflections was paved by the essay 'Reason and Revelation' (1958), the published notes of a radio discussion of November 1957 between Adorno and Eugen Kogon, the Christian historian who had survived internment by the Nazis in the Buchenwald concentration camp. The debate took place against the perceived background of a renewed turn to institutional religion, which prefigured something of the widespread interest in the appurtenances of spirituality, if not any wholesale subscription to an entire belief-system, in what has been called the 'post-secular age' of the present. Adorno sets this exchange in the customary terms of the confrontation between revelation, traditionally the central support of religious faith, and autonomous reason, its avowed enemy in the age of enlightenment and its amicable interlocutor in the century that followed. In the era after Hegel, Adorno contends, religion doomed itself by attempting to engage with rationalism on the latter's own terms, which has only resulted in the present-day conception of religious commitment as a mere voluntarism, a decision to be part of an institution rather than an impulsion towards it by revelation. What many people have taken up, therefore, is a philosophy of religion, rather than religion itself. Interestingly, however, at the same time, rationalism itself is being queried on its own terms, not least by the Frankfurt School, just as reason once queried religion.

The objective social tendency at work in the recovery of religious affiliation, according to Adorno, is that people look to it again because they no longer believe, after a century of radical social movements has ended in failure, that the existing world can be changed. The monstrous cathexis of this is the Cold War standoff of his era, in which the world was divided into two opposed power blocs that threatened each other, and the world itself, with mutual annihilation. What could ever overthrow that sclerotic impasse? The problem from the point of the view of the churches is that, instead of holding fast to the principle of revelation and the rich historical theological tradition of which they were the keepers, religion had conspired in its own dilution by offering to be something other than what it was, a practical support like the welfare institutions of society, and precisely that self-reconfiguration is the index of its own desperation. In the present era, the reformed Christian churches, keen to speak the language of administered society, have participated to a large extent in their own demythologisation, in accordance with the minimal demands of rationalism, and although they still require a weekly statement of the Credo, when it comes to such mysteries as the Transubstantiation and the Resurrection, what matters more is a general sense of comfortingly ill-defined spirituality, a concept once entirely alien to revealed religion.

At the heart of the rationalist approach to belief, Adorno argues, is a vicious circle. To use reason to adopt the faith requires that one has already effectively succumbed to it, since no path of deductive reason could possibly lead to it, unless it had already gained authority in relation to the exercise of reason. The same is true if the question of free will is introduced. 'If, as high Scholastic doctrine maintains, my will is added as an express condition of faith, then one does not escape the circle. Will itself would be possible only where the conviction about the contents of belief already exists, that is, precisely that which can be gained only by an act of will'.[1] It was for this reason that Judaism, and those individualised branches of what came to be known as primitive Christianity, such as the variant favoured by Tolstoy, tended to avoid the conscious adoption of the dogmatic elements of belief. Religion cannot claim to be objective without submitting itself to the very criteria of objectivity that it rejects. The paradox with which it is faced is that it is as subject to socio-historical mediation as any other institution of society, just as it reluctantly acknowledges every time it accepts another piece of socially enlightened legislation, or another scientific break-through, that conflicts with its own tenets. If, however, it seeks to disregard those aspects of its material rootedness in the empirical world as the inessential elements, in the light of which only the ineffable remains constant, then it risks its own dissolution by becoming nothing in particular in itself. 'Anything more than this nothingness would lead immediately to the insoluble, and it would be a mere ruse of imprisoned consciousness to transfigure into a religious category this very insolubility itself, the failure of finite humankind, whereas it instead attests to the present impotence of religious categories.' In the light of this final point,

Adorno ends these reflections by stating unequivocally his own distance from any such categories in a kind of ironic credo, avowing 'an extreme ascesis towards any type of revealed faith, an extreme loyalty to the prohibition of images'.[2] The latter, on which Judaic scripture originally insisted as one of the negative commandments, now means refusing the images of the administered world, to which modern religion, only too often, hopelessly offers to reconcile its clients.

In the fourth of the metaphysical meditations from *Negative Dialectics*, 'Happiness and Idle Waiting', Adorno attempts to get a temporary hold on what falls under the concept of metaphysical experience, the numinous entity officially liquidated in materialist dialectics, but which persists beyond the extinction, already intimated in the early Hegel, of its status as a veridical category of thought. The metaphysical, precisely by not presenting itself to objective sense-certainty, is subjective through and through. Idealistic philosophy grasped at what lies outside the deductive categories of thought, what might be given the name of truth, without acknowledging that the theological notions that it disdained represented in themselves, however poorly, the terrain beyond the limits of thought. There is no straightforward other of thought that thought can think, but no more could it simply abolish it as being beneath thought. What there is in the objective world that eludes conceptual appropriation by identity thinking is not just, as vulgar materialism would have it, the residue of concrete historical forces, but also contains within itself whatever that elusive element is, the unknown X on which a properly dialectical thinking turns in asserting that nothing is ever wholly what it seems. The fetishism of pure immediacy, the direct understanding of empirical reality without any mediating intervention, which is raised as the culminating ideal of idealistic thought, would involve relinquishing the very element of otherness that animates dialectics and makes it indispensable in an unreconciled world. Something remains outside the subject, which, as Adorno puts it, 'a subjective metaphysical experience will not be talked out of', and which represents the complement of the ungraspable element within the world of objects. These two elusive sides of subjectivity and objectivity must surely encounter each other in whatever truth finally turns out to be. Truth emerges through the negation of subjective delusion, but it must involve the subject because the notion of a world of truth without consciousness of it is nonsense. 'For there could no more be truth without a subject freeing itself from delusions than there could be truth without that which is not the subject, that in which truth has its archetype'.[3] If human beings and all their delusions were to be subtracted from the world, what would be left would not be truth, just pure reity, an undifferentiated thingliness without qualities of any sort, negative or positive.

A theological temperament might discern in these reflections an asymptotic approach to the divine. Nothing is as simple as that in what Adorno himself terms in these passages a 'negative theology', but he does address what has happened to metaphysical thought in the secular era. Earlier metaphysical experience had a paradoxically substantial air when its underlying tenets were not subject to rational questioning, an air that secularisation has turned 'unmistakably paler and more desultory'. The trace element of the older version lives on in the virtually universal experience of hopeless waiting, the yearning people have for some kind of qualitative change in their lives, which they can no more concretely envisage than they can practically bring about. 'Is this it?' wonders the inner self, unable to pin down what the whole 'it' is, other than that it must consist in some supplement to what there undeniably is in front of it. Music, supremely among the arts, is capable of expressing desolate longing, the passive expectancy of a defeated hope whose defeat may not be final, and Adorno adduces Berg's opera *Wozzeck* (1922) as containing passages of unexampled pathos of this type. The pathos is redoubled by the fact that nothing about the testing to spiritual destruction that waiting comports ensures that it will be rewarded, notwithstanding the old lie that everything comes to him who waits. 'Idle waiting does not guarantee what we expect,' says Adorno, on a rare excursion into the first person; 'it reflects the condition measured by its denial. The less of life remains, the greater the temptation for our consciousness to take the sparse and abrupt living remnants for the phenomenal absolute.' And yet, precisely the form of the stubbornly rhetorical question, 'Is this all there is?', positively demands that the remnants not be the whole story. Only some intimation of the transcendent confers whatever life there is on present circumstances. If the line of thought begins to sound as though it may be veering towards a theodicy, however, the dialectical sting is impossible to miss. 'The transcendent is, and it is not,' he warns. Despair at privative existence expands to encompass the realm that was to have delivered us from it, exactly because it does not deliver us. To those sufficiently embroiled in worldly affairs, such metaphysical hope looks close to madness, and to those bereft of such productive engagement, it degenerates to empty solace. Should theology be inclined to talk its own promises up by encompassing the present course of the world as part of a mysterious divine plan, it relapses not into the moth-eaten dignity of paradox so much as 'outright blasphemy'.[4] And yet, simmering in dialectical tension with that observation, is the assertion of the previous meditation, 'Dying Today', that existential despair is the objective evidence that what it regrets the lack of must exist. If historical materialism teaches the subject that the metaphysical ideas, including those of revealed religion, have no concrete reality, a gesture that in itself becomes a metaphysical idea, then the subjective will that nonetheless goes on intuiting them must also become a source of despair to itself. 'The secret paralogism is that despair of the world, a despair that is true, based on facts, and is neither aesthetic Weltschmerz nor a wrong, reprehensible consciousness, guarantees to us that the hopelessly missed things exist, though existence at large has [since Auschwitz] become a universal guilt context'.[5]

The fifth meditation addresses the philosophical stance of nihilism, and opens by dismissing all maundering over the question of the meaning of life, to which the standard answer, repeated everywhere in our own day from self-help manuals to online memes, is some variation of the homily that life is whatever its owner makes of it – 'a sense that is "made" is already fictitious,'[6] says Adorno. This thought-form is obviously ideological, in the sense that its all-encompassing sweep is reduced to rubble every time real adversity stands in its way. Only fragments of the fulfilled life, whatever that might conceivably be, point the way to a life outside the present one. They shine out in retrospect from the better moments of the past, even if hope is only generated by what seems doomed for now. 'Only for the sake of the hopeless ones have we been given hope,' writes Benjamin at the close of his essay on Goethe's *Elective Affinities*,[7] a thought that stands in juxtaposition with Kafka's dictum that there is plentiful hope, though not for us. For the utterly hopeless, hope consists in a truthfulness that appears deferred into an indeterminate future, as in Beckett's world, but that for that very reason, is impossible to discount.

'Only A Parable', the tenth meditation, taking its title from Goethe's *Faust*, reflects on the degree to which religious hope depends on a level of literalness that sceptical secularism will not tolerate. The complicity of theology with rationalism transfers its arcana to the realm of the purely symbolic, the symbols of the Revelation, for example, standing for nothing but other symbols beyond them. Either one believes implicitly in the mysteries, which appears to return thinking consciousness to a primitive state, or they are merely symbols of the abstract, in which case faith is essentially empty. And yet, 'if the possibility, however feeble and distant, of redemption in existence is cut off altogether, the human spirit would become an illusion, and the finite, conditioned, merely existing subject would eventually be deified as carrier of the spirit'.[8] If there is to be a redemption, it has to partake of concrete materiality, not simply involve a vanishing of the individual spirit into the beyond. This, among other things, is what is wrong with the notion of spiritualism, with its phosphorescent apparitions and disembodied voices. An immortal realm of the insubstantial would hold its own concept in contempt, which is why a faith based on resurrection has a material side too. 'Christian dogmatics, in which the souls were conceived as awakening simultaneously with the resurrection of the flesh, was metaphysically more consistent – more enlightened, as it were – than speculative metaphysics, just as hope means a physical resurrection and feels defrauded of the best part by its spiritualisation'.[9] If the body is destined for nothing other than the pain and frustration of its present existence, in what sense indeed could it be redeemed by its wholesale conversion into the incorporeal? It would not have begun the full extent of its sensuous life before it was being abolished. It is in the interface between the material and spiritual, though, that truth must be sought. If the promises of religion were literally true, space probes might by now have sent back photographs of the outer walls of Heaven as they sailed past it, but truth will not be found in the reversion to myth, for all that the impulse to redemption in present conditions bears the stigmata of myth. In possibly the most acutely personal sentence of this entire late work, Adorno writes of the supremacy of truth among the metaphysical ideas in theological terms: 'It is why one who believes in God cannot believe in God, why the possibility represented by the divine name is maintained, rather, by him who does not believe'.[10] Demythologisation has demolished the old myths, but left behind only the residue of what merely, contingently, happens to be. This demythologisation is what in the later Hegel becomes the rationale of history, progressive self-realisation, and yet, as the *Dialectic of Enlightenment* had argued, demythologisation reverts to myth by devouring itself, and leaves the closed circuit of an empirical reality as the only human fate, the secularised myth of an ineluctable eternal present. The burden that must be carried by a thinking that tries to overturn the antinomy of mythical enlightenment is that it too must run the risk of falling into the snares of untruth, of contravening the ban on images by succumbing to false representations of hope. That it cannot avoid the attempt, though, is what absolves negative dialectics of the related charges of nihilism and pessimism.

What is clear is that, for Adorno, the categories of theology that a materialist philosophy thought to have discarded retain their usefulness, in however transfigured a form. As Christopher Craig Brittain puts it, 'Adorno argues that theological concepts like the messianic, the prohibition of images, and the idea of redemption are required to prevent actuality from foreclosing on alternative possibilities'.[11] Theology can perhaps assist for Adorno in the attempt by reason to resist absolutising itself into a system of rigid domination, while at the same time a self-reflecting reason will have critical things to say about traditional theology. There can be no leap into an alternative system of rationality, which would inevitably end in irrationality, and is anyway what enabled the catastrophic political systems of the twentieth century to gain ascendancy over human beings, but there still has to be a way of thinking that does not just conform to the closed systems of explicative totemic rationalism in which the fetishisation of science has resulted. The chorus of criticism of these positions, particularly with regard to the hopeful requirement Adorno places on the subject to negate its own transcendentally constitutive role, as in the Kantian conception of reason, and replace it with a subjective efficacy that disavows its own constituting and conceptualising agency, sees in them a double aporia: firstly, that negative dialectics is functionally self-contradictory, and secondly, that it lacks a normative foundation from which to build a workable alternative social vision. What these criticisms miss is that this is not a foundational philosophy, not a systematic methodology to which everything concrete could be referred back, but something more like an ethical call for thought to reflect precisely on its own unexamined foundations. The subject is no longer to be the source of truth, but to become, through its own self-objectification, a lightning-conductor for truth. It cannot free itself from the delusions of ideology by its own strength of will, but can be responsive to moments of genuine enlightenment in its relation with the objective. If the theological concepts are liberated from their implication in dogma, they are one of the ways in which a thinking subject can see beyond its immersion in present conditions. All the talk of normative foundations wishes to establish a positivistic ground on which the contemporary subject should stand, from which vantage it might judge the world around it, but this is precisely what sinks it when the world moves on. As Craig Brittain summarises it, 'Rational thinking points beyond itself, as is testified to by the fact that it cannot itself be grounded on a logical foundation, and finds itself dependent on an "irrational" decision in its favour, which must be continually nurtured by creative imagination if it is to avoid becoming a rigid and self-absorbed worldview that resists criticism. Adorno calls this recognition a "metaphysical experience".'[12] Adorno's contention is that because human suffering, and concepts such as freedom, point beyond themselves as long as they are not resolved or realised, then social theory must contain within it the implicit demand that the present world be transcended, not simply described in the phenomenological fashion. This is where metaphysical or theological concepts become useful.

Anybody attempting to map orthodox religious belief on to Adorno's negative dialectics will quickly come to grief. His thought is hostile to much of the repressive and triumphalist temper of institutional religion, and bitterly critical of the tenor in which some of its own reassurances to itself are couched: 'Of all the disgrace deservedly reaped by theology, the worst is the positive religions' howl of rejoicing at the unbelievers' despair. They have gradually come to intone their Te Deum wherever God is denied, because at least his name is mentioned'.[13] If religion would give up its credal dogmatism, as well as its occasionally fatuous ethical engagements with the ephemera of civil society, its status as the incarnation of an otherness that did not simply speak the language of the surrounding world, much as autonomous artworks refuse to do, might still empower those with whom the world would have its way to resist being recruited to its cause.

While the theological current seems an awkward enough fit with Adorno, the attempt to reconcile his work with contemporary themes in ethics is, paradoxically enough, still less likely to result in a workable alignment. Adorno remained interested in what was then more generally known as moral philosophy, as witness the 1963 lecture course, 'Problems of Moral Philosophy', which seems to have portended a book-length study that would have followed the *Aesthetic Theory*. It is true, as is well known, that Adorno exhorts post-war societies to a new categorical imperative, the obligation to ensure that what happened at Auschwitz should never be allowed to recur. This imperative would involve not simply the abolition of concentration camps, but the vigilant refusal of all habits of mind out of which the germ of Auschwitz thinking might propagate. These are ethical concerns writ large, and it is precisely their largeness that sets this stance apart from the micro-concerns of Kantian and post-Kantian ethics, as they have been extrapolated in the Atlantic academic traditions in particular. The contextualist and contractualist forms of justice, as conceived in the pragmatic legalistic tradition exemplified in the post-war era by the work of John Rawls, does nothing to

address the fundamental injustice on which all juridical structures are founded, that of the exchange principle. Justice is not an
autonomous principle of capitalist society, but functions differen-
tially among different classes and groups within society, determining not just what justice they objectively receive, but whether
they consider themselves likely subjects of justice in the first
place. The majoritarian totem, the arithmetical principle that
decides that as long as the majority is – or can be persuaded it is
– satisfied by the present dispensation, the weight of their
numbers should crush the life out of the claims of minorities, and
which has gradually undermined faith in parliamentary electoral
systems all over the western world, is not a progressive principle,
and justice is nothing if it does nothing to help the interests of
human beings to progress. There is a world of difference between
the hope for a true restitutive social justice, and the patient
setting out of ways in which the current system might ideally
function, should it ever begin to take an interest in ideal
functioning. Indeed, the question of whether justice can ever be a
mere matter of administrative distribution remains in doubt. A
more pressing challenge would involve formulating a process
that would stop judicial institutions from becoming reified structures of authority, and turn to what they could do to help
repressed subjects resist other forms of authority.

If there is nothing like a micro-ethics, with its thought experiments and Aesopian paradigms, in Adorno, neither is there
anything like a plan for living well. There is no right life amid the
wrong, as the adage from the *Minima Moralia* had taught, and no
indication on what are today seen as ethical guideposts for guilt-
free living. Instead, there is what *Negative Dialectics* calls a
context of universal guilt, in which the subjective reason that
might transcendentally decide ethical questions in the alienated
conditions of each individual's life is itself a product of alienation. To constitute himself as a person in the ethical sense, the
individual subject would have to be distinguished from his mere

existence, but not at the expense of his subsumption into an identity. Identities, in the sense intended today by identity politics, in which each interest group holds out for its own maximum advantage in unfavourable conditions, in the interest primarily of self-preservation, are what stop people from being individuals. Their individuality, indeed their very humanity, is to be found in their nonidentity with both social and political normativity. 'The subject is the lie,' Adorno writes, 'because for the sake of its own absolute rule it will deny its own objective definitions. Only he who would refrain from such lies – who would have used his own strength, which he owes to identity, to cast off the façade of identity – would truly be a subject'.[14] As long as people have yet to become themselves, they cannot draw on whatever substantiality would be necessary to allow them to fulfil their potential, or indeed to attain to the transcendence that would allow them to be fully cognisant ethical subjects. Anything else, meanwhile, is overlaid with what Adorno calls 'the oily tone of unbelieved theology'. Ethical philosophy in the present day is predicated on the idea that morality begins with individual persons as their own inalienable property, and as in the Kantian manner is universalisable to a general principle, but takes no account of the context in which it is instilled.

> Freedom, which would arise only in the organisation of a free society, is sought precisely where it is denied by the organi-sation of the existing society, in each individual, who certainly has need of it, but to whom it cannot, in the present condi-tions, be guaranteed. Reflection on society does not occur in ethical personalism, no more than reflection on the person itself. Once detached entirely from the universal, the person cannot constitute a universal either; the universal is therefore secretly founded on extant forms of rule.[15]

People who express outrage on social media at every careless word, real or imagined, directed against them and their like, by media presences whose every utterance is deliberately served up for public consumption, are under the impression that they are articulating their own personal opinions, at which they have freely arrived. What they are articulating, rather, is an identity, constituted out of conditions of heteronomy, in which a figuration of the pressure of the universal is, not so secretly, shouted out.

A reconsideration of Adorno's reconsideration of the culture industry need not detain us for long. The apparatus of mass deception diagnosed in the 1940s, in which Ernst Lubitsch and Arturo Toscanini participated as enthusiastically as Guy Lombardo and Duke Ellington, in phenomena that look positively innocent in the retrospect of the digital era, was only extending its sway in the midst of the 1960s counterculture that imagined it was subverting it. A theory of mass hypnosis, the adventures of which deserve a separate study of their own, is a durable legacy of the modern historico-philosophical era initiated by Marx and Engels' critique of ideology and the mesmerism of the commodity fetish. It proceeded through the account of social reification given by Lukács, through Adorno and Horkheimer's culture industry, through Marshall McLuhan's mass media messages that merge with the medium that expresses them, through Guy Debord's society of the spectacle to Jean Baudrillard's simulations and simulacra. In the present day, the documentary filmmaker Adam Curtis uses jumpcut and montage techniques in cyberspace to argue that cyberspace is hypnotising us into a state of unreality, precisely through the use of such techniques. What all these arguments have in common is not just that things are not as they seem, but that the way they seem has become how things are. There was a time when there were only two or three television channels, and each small town had one cinema. The radio played music you could listen to while you drove your car, its programmes interspersed with news bulletins and commercials. If buying paperback novels was an unconscionable expense, you could join the local library. There was a feeling that everything was run by some authority or some giant corporation, to which appeal was practically pointless, but which apparently did its best to keep people satisfied and entertained. In the age of social media and universal connectivity, a spurious anarcho-democracy has been birthed, which has replaced the old structure of an unresponsive corporation overseeing a global herd of consumers, the form appropriate to industrial society, with the chattering, disputing throng of the ancient *agora*, where opinions of every shade of vituperation and fatuity fill the air, and a multitude of goods is offered, while zero-hours workers, underpaid migrant labour and unpaid interns, the people once known as slaves, maintain the continuing viability of the entire racket. Habits of consumption are the greatest determinants of consciousness, now as ever, far more than political conceptions, for all that they originate from the most successful political conception in human history. Allegiances flare and intensify, wither and reignite, over commercial products, not excluding the celebrities whose market status is formally indistinguishable from that of cream doughnuts. A bourgeois liberalism that holds liberally expressed opinion in contempt observes that everybody is permanently ready to take offence, but fails to notice equally that a media system that thrives on clicks and likes and instant petitions is permanently ready to provoke it. When terrorists slaughter satirists for insulting what they revere, voices are raised in defence of the right to be offended, which has not existed in any democratic polity from Athens on, precisely because it would be predicated on an inalienable right to offend, and in the depravity of the response, the ethical principle of trampling over other people's sensitivities is more hyperbolically refuted than ethics could ever have foreseen. Culture, which once hoped to civilise a bruised world, and in Frankfurt theory was guilty of offering nothing better than kicking over the traces of its own failure, has discovered that it could do more after all, and now willingly participates in the bruising. The production of consciousness is managed at all levels by a culture that is even more crucial to the world economy than manufacturing and services ever were.

Notwithstanding the enormous insolence of its ubiquity, global culture harbours within it the same frail hope that flickered in the days of MGM musicals and dance-orchestras. Even if nobody other than the very elderly and those living in war-zones can escape it, people are not entirely incapable of seeing through it. Its own reckless need to go on expanding, like all capital markets, produces periodic implosions, while if it tries to maintain itself in a steady state, it risks becoming boring and thereby transparent. As the commercial entity that it is, it must keep on offering its consumers something, even though the profit principle dictates that it must inevitably also cheat the great majority of them of what it promises. Its most overt attempt at sidestepping that process is the mechanism of competitions, prize draws, lotteries, 'your chance to win', 'it could be you', in which the player must simultaneously compete against every other player, as in the employment rat-race, but also accept the virtually perfect inevitability of disappointment as a mathe-matical law of nature, for which the competition organisers can hardly be blamed. Recurrent disappointment is the antithetical obverse of what the culture industry claims to supply, and is the only fugitive chance there will ever be to awaken from it. If every losing ticket reminds its purchaser that he is one of culture's losers, while the bloodsuckers who sold it to him have always won again, it could also be the material evidence that he could cease to be their host. That this may seem about as likely for the time being as a spontaneous outbreak of autonomous reason amid the tide of delusion suggests that the theory of the culture industry was not so outlandish after all.

What frustrates so many commentators about Adorno's body of theory, in all disciplines, is that it appears to leave only the tiniest gaps for any light to shine through. A thought that refused to give up on the utopian moment, which sees that moment indeed in the continuities between thinking itself and the categories that a declining metaphysics threw overboard as it plummeted to the material earth, nonetheless appears to harbour so little hope for utopia. 'Without hope, there is no good,' he wrote in *Negative Dialectics*,[16] in a sentiment on which even traditional theology could stand, and without the redemptive illumination of a better state of things to guide it, the present nocturnal world would look as hopeless as both Sade and Schopenhauer saw it in their different ways. The question is: is there a utopia left for us? Is there, despite Kafka's avowal, any hope?

Over the course of the last century, on Adorno's construction of history, the impulse for change has migrated from the political to the social to the cultural, and ultimately to the personal level. At the dawn of the modernist age, great political movements convulsed the advanced world, and resulted in concrete revolutionary upheaval in the less advanced. Constitutional and absolute monarchies, larcenous empires and corrupt oligarchies, toppled under the impress of war and popular discontent, with radical political prescriptions for redistribution and extension of the franchise spurring the masses to concerted opposition. The coming of totalitarianism and more war, accompanied by the retrenchment of capitalist economics in the aftermath of its severest tests in the 1930s and 1940s, sucked the life out of the leftist parties and the trade union movements, which were left setting their sights no higher in the western world than the piecemeal amelioration of hegemonic conditions. By the 1960s, dissent had become purely social, a matter of alternative lifestyles lived in the midst, and to the periodic chagrin, of mainstream society. The Cold War put paid to whatever residual dignity the notion of Marxist politics still had in western orthodoxy, which only felt it needed to point to the grisly misery of life in the Eastern Bloc to justify its own comparative benevolence. At the same time, those for whom the appeal of wallowing in the ordure at Woodstock in a state of stoned contentment was next to indiscernible looked, as Adorno himself did, to cultural dissent in other forms. Referring to protest songs against the unbearable savagery of the Vietnam War, he declared on German television that the maudlin songs themselves were unbearable too, because they did nothing other than use the popular music genre that was a constitutive part of the entertainment industry to express their horror in a commercially consumable way. By contrast, the kinds of autonomous artworks that Adorno discussed in the *Aesthetic Theory* at least refused the language and techniques of entertainment, as a surer route to putting distance between themselves and the unbearable. In the period since his death, it is undoubtedly the case that even alternative currents in art have been absorbed into the machine of administered culture. Conceptual artists who imagine their work to be confrontational in nature find the doors of the old academies flung wide to them, and the attempts that their forebears made to short-circuit the economic imperatives of the art market have long since been surrendered to the chance to milk as much ready money from the system as professional footballers do. The trend that book publishing has brutally reflected in the most recent decade, that there is no longer any middle ground between bestsellers and books that virtually nobody reads because nobody has heard of them, is true of investment in the arts generally. Either creators generate an instant return, or they are dumped. Everything has its market value, and the market, which it is not given to anybody alive to control, decides its fate.

The individual human being is thus left as the final cell of resistance to the overwhelming current. In his state of isolation, at worst, he convinces himself that his fear of the collective forces that surround him is mere paranoia, an adaptation failure brought on by poor adjustment skills in early adulthood. This state then becomes paradoxically what unites him to the others in a doomed solidarity. Adorno analyses this tendency in a reflection on paranoia from the *Minima Moralia*: 'the bottomless solitude of the deluded has a tendency to collectivisation and so quotes the delusion into existence. This pathic mechanism harmonises with the social one prevalent today, whereby those socialised into desperate isolation hunger for community and flock together in cold mobs. So folly becomes an epidemic: insane sects grow with the same rhythm as big organisations'.[17] The intimation arises that what unites the human race, more firmly than the Internationale anyway, is not hope but the potent conviction of their impotence, that they are all adrift on the same doomed life raft, and exactly that shared feeling brings the hopelessness into concrete existence. The delusion is after all a delusion, as Adorno states, but it becomes reality when people see it as the bridge between them, which is how patently ludicrous sects such as Scientology come to recruit their members. Communities of the fearful and the deluded, above all the paranoid, provide the structures in which their members' wildest imaginings reinforce each other. At the rightward extremity of political prejudice, society's scapegoat groups, classifiable by identity, are held to blame for the general unhappiness, because they are undermining the economy or disrespecting the dominant culture, provoking explosive reactions that appear genuinely unaware of their own molecular affinity to fascism, while leftist paranoia retains its pathologically healthy conviction that everything is cynically calculated, not just the price-fixing of multinational corporations, but also the tiny moments of apparent kindness that individuals show the less fortunate, organising outings for the elderly, memorialising the war dead. Those united in these beliefs that the world is rotten to the core are simultaneously right, and also themselves part of the rottenness. Their own helplessness is rationalised into the wrong kind of solidarity, so that people are united only by the chimera of what defeats them, the mirage-like quality of which recalls the 'continuous dreams that agree perfectly with one another' that Leibniz described to a correspondent in 1712,[18] in the light of which only isolated monads, and not the substantial bonds between them, are real. In a society in which people came together of their own volition, free of delusion because freed from the imperative to self-preservation, the substantial bond would be paradoxically liberating, a social version of what Adorno means by using the power of concepts to rid thinking of the reifying force of conceptualisation.

The perils of being forced into monadic resistance at the purely personal level consist not just in the obvious psychosis of paranoid fear, but in the complex relations between such fear and objective empirical reality. Only time will tell, as the cliché has it, whether the perceived threat was illusory or the muted resonance of historical catastrophe. 'The points of communication are the overwhelming confirmations of persecution-fantasies which, mocking the invalid with being right, only plunge him deeper in them. The surface of life then at once closes together again, proving to him that things are not so bad and he is insane'.[19] Psychotherapy may help with removing the paralysing terrors that arise endogamously, but can do nothing at all to address actually existing terror, even where that terror is what has produced in the sufferer the craven state of being frightened of everything. The alternative to paranoia in the discontented may well be displacement activity, such as substance addiction, habitual drunkenness, overeating. These behaviours are dysfunc-tional in a double sense. Not only do they turn something pleasurable into nothing more than an instrumental means to elude displeasure, so that pleasure itself becomes parasitic on misery, but pleasure is thereby transformed into the negation of its own negation. Overeaters live under the tyrannous rubric that overeating is better than not eating at all, the imagined threat of which impels them to take as much as they can. These antagonisms are part and parcel of what, for Adorno, is the overriding contradiction at the heart of individuality as presently constituted, the problem we addressed in chapter 1. This is that the individual is a product of social forces, emerging in its most ideological form as the creation of the free-market economy. Even in the sense that only the individual can stand against the pressures of socialisation, he remains the product of exchange relations, the paradigm client of the consumer bazaar, made in its image as he was once made in the likeness of God. This has an unmistakable influence on his capacity for resistance, which is indissociable from private interest: 'What enables him to resist, that streak of independence in him, springs from monadological individual interest and its precipitate, character. The individual mirrors in his individuation the preordained social laws of exploitation, however mediated'.[20]

We might return then, by way of closing, to considering this dilemma once more, with a view to a possible resolution of it. The streak of bloody-minded independence that leads individuals to resist the power of assimilation, says Adorno, is vitiated by its nature as a product of the very exploitative society it wishes to resist. Its own instinct for primitive self-preservation is what lends the individual's struggle for survival under the pressure of social asphyxiation its many idiosyncratic forms. Adorno excoriates the kind of conservative cultural criticism, once the preserve in the British realm of the likes of Aldous Huxley, now degraded to opinion pieces in the conservative tabloids, that correctly sees the shallowness and bewitchment by materialistic society that prevail in individuals, but blames them for the dysfunctionality of that society. Society is not the aggregate of the pre-existing dispositions of individuals, according to Adorno, but rather they and their attitudes are the products of a reified social structure. Even while accusing human beings of being responsible for the parlous state of society, always of course compared to how it was the day before yesterday, conservative critics implicitly accept the way things are now as being non-negotiable. In its dynamic phase, the bourgeoisie was well aware of these continuities, but has wilfully forgotten them in its routing of socialist alternatives and its determination to blame the victims. The decline of individuality as a social category has probably been going on since earlier than that, though, and Adorno notes that the historian of classical culture Jakob Burckhardt traces it back to the decline of the Athenian *polis,* a time when, paradoxically, the cult of individualism was at its height. It is as though the waning of individual thought and inspiration had to be marked, as an extreme compensation reaction, by a turn to worshipping supposedly heroic individuals instead of gods. The democratic polity succumbed to dictatorial city-states, and was then consummated as an absolute political principle in the Roman imperium. The same trend was at work rolling through the valorisation in the Victorian era of pioneering individuals, strong men with big visions, into the fascism that supervened in the following century.

Once again, there is a crucial antinomy at work in the notion of individual freedom under present conditions. 'Within repressive society,' Adorno writes, 'the individual's emancipation not only benefits but damages him. Freedom from society robs him of the strength for freedom'.[21] Why? Because in freeing himself at the mental level from the machinations of social interests, he reduces himself to a mere cipher. His relations with others, even in the repressive society, are what constitute his reality, whereas his individuality is something like Leibniz's windowless monad, bereft of any relation to anything around it, with not even a pane of glass through which to view it. At the very moments when he thinks he is transcending social pressure, he is most willingly helping it transcend itself by letting it off the hook, by saying that it isn't after all entirely hegemonic over him.

Absolute individuality has its theological roots in the principle of personal salvation, that every soul, regardless of its blemishes, can be saved, but that principle only works, Adorno states, because it applies to the whole of humanity, not because it promises each individual that salvation is for him alone. When social relations were transformed into a mediating context of the exchange process of capitalism, the erosion of the individual was prepared in the neutralisation of particular personal interests that the abstract principle of like for like enshrined, and the convulsions of history only resuscitated him as the one megalomaniac who takes charge of everything. The principle of the strongest overcoming the rest has not, however, been superseded following the defeat of the dictatorships, but lives on both in the form of socioeconomic heteronomy itself, and in the continued impoverishment of the individual, who no longer even enjoys the residual privilege of being mediated within himself through his economic relations, but is purely the object on which the social structure operates.

Despite its dilapidation in the present age, the individual remains the only hope for setting limits to the coercive force of the social collectivity. Somehow a way must be found to preserve its traces of independence, without surrendering it to the nullification of being nothing more than an abstract principle, and without again raising the standard of acquisitive bourgeois selfishness on its ground. 'If today the trace of humanity seems to persist only in the individual in his decline,' says Adorno, 'it admonishes us to make an end of the fatality that individualises people, only to break them completely in their isolation. The saving principle is now preserved in its antithesis alone'.[22] That last sentence is a classic Adornian dialectical move. The saving principle, which refers jointly to the principle of self-preservation and to the Gospel text he has cited a few lines earlier in the theological reference – 'He that loses his life shall save it' – can only be realised by abandoning the competitive urge to survive at the expense of all others. No longer is the individual the crowning achievement of the bourgeois political economy, but is instead its battered remnant, the product not of the nurturing of every last man, woman and child, but of the dividing and ruling that makes the exploitative system run. Only by working against his own preservation can the individual hope to preserve his own true individuality. If not inspected too closely, this type of thought may be mistaken for a straightforward paradox, or something like the looking-glass logic Alice encounters in a world where, to arrive at the garden, you have to start walking away from it in the direction of the house. Rather, it embodies the tension of two poles of a proposition that are held in productive opposition to each other. These constructions frequently appear at the close of a section or aphorism, and are often couched in an implied call to action, or at the very least to a different thinking, giving the lie to the notion that Adorno's is not a hortatory philosophy. In fact, this is a language in which he is fluent: 'It is the sufferings of men that should be shared: the smallest step towards their pleasures is one towards the hardening of their pains'.[23] 'The cause of immediacy is now espoused only by the most circumspect reflection'.[24] 'Thought honours itself by defending what is damned as nihilism'.[25] 'The word that was to name truth against ideology comes to be the most untrue: the denial of ideality becomes the proclamation of an ideal sphere'.[26] '[The hermetic artwork] expresses meaning through its ascetic stance towards meaning'.[27] 'Only by sacrificing life did Benjamin become the spirit that lived by the idea of a way of life without victims'.[28]

Dialectical thinking, thinking against itself, has not, despite the intellectual celebrity status of Slavoj Zizek in the most recent generation, been a conspicuously popular methodology for a long time. Where the desperation of the times appears to call for unambiguous opposition to the temporal powers, its perpetually open-ended nature, its self-cancellings and allergic antipathy to any thought-form that looks to be on the verge of precipitating into an unexaminable cliché, has the nature of an impediment rather than a breakthrough. These were more or less the terms of the dispute over the relations between theory and praxis that erupted in the turbulence of the student dissent of the 1960s. A revolutionary moment, such as had precisely not arrived at that juncture, may indeed call for the fortress to be stormed while the chance presents itself, and the necessary thinking over what to do next then take its place the morning after. In the absence of revolutionary moments with which the western world has mostly lived since the wake of the Great War, thinking is more necessary than ever, and not just because there isn't anything else. Without thought, as Adorno tirelessly argued in his final years, whatever activity is staged is nothing more than pseudo-activity, symbolic protest for its own sake that is not, as is frailly hoped, better than nothing, but worse than nothing, because it comes to stand in for that genuine oppositional practice for which thought is duty-bound to remain vigilant. Despite the enthusiasms it generated among the liberal bourgeoisie, the Occupy movement was the distillate of a pure pseudo-activity that, once it had established itself as a public obstruction, discovered that it had nothing substantive to demand, other than the pitiful demand to be noticed. The terrible inarticulacy to which the increasingly restive and fractious disenfranchised are condemned is manifested as much in empty mimetic forms of protest as in detonations of vitriolic online rage, for which latter purpose the administered world at its most nefarious could very well have invented social media. What is missing is thought, but thought itself only has anything to offer if it results from the continuous application of its own principle, instead of being reached down off the peg second-hand. Complicated situations, it should go without saying, require complicated thought processes, which remain beyond the reach of countless millions of the citizens of a world that would like them to think everything is perfectly simple.

Register to vote and make your voice heard. If you've done nothing wrong, you have nothing to fear. If you're not with us, you're against us. Thinking against these diabolical nostrums is hard work in both senses. It demands skilful acuity, but is also exhausting. Dialectics is hard work, which is what, if nothing else, reveals theory to be not the antithesis of praxis, but part and parcel of it.

In the twelfth and final metaphysical meditation from the *Negative Dialectics*, Adorno argues that all thinking proceeds from a felt need. It does not have to be wishful thinking in the sense of trying to will something into existence by merely hoping for it, for all that hope must spring eternal. There is a compulsiveness to thought, the need to know why and what and how, which enlightenment conceived only under the sign of demythologisation, stripping away the unknowns by explanation, until the metaphysical, what could not be known, Kant's thing-in-itself, was not the transcendent kernel but the discardable husk. The mistake Kant made, Adorno claims, is that instead of letting the thing-in-itself stand as the irreducible core of what was heterogeneous to rational thought, it became the principle by which rational thought anthropomorphised everything to conform to itself. This is why the motor force of negative dialectics is not to establish something positive by negating the negations, but to preserve the negative element as what is not like thought itself. It does not, however, imagine itself to be applying its procedure transcendentally, in the Kantian style, but immanently. Dialectical consciousness of the world can only emerge from within the world itself, from which it endeavours to break out, its tiniest particles being the elements that elude classification under the overarching concepts of nondialectical identity thinking. 'The smallest intramundane traits would be of relevance to the absolute, for the micrological view cracks the shells of what, measured by the subsuming cover concept, is helplessly isolated and explodes its identity, the delusion that it is but a specimen'.[29]

Those shells, the integuments that enclose everything within their subsuming conceptual structures, are not cracked from the outside like walnuts, be it noted, but are splintered from within, as by the hatching out of young, but only if they are incubated by a non-identitarian thinking. There is a formal homology – more than that, a 'solidarity' – between the microscopic elements of thought that evade conceptualisation, and which only a dialectical process given to self-reflection can isolate, and the vestigial traces harboured within metaphysical experience when scientific materialism has finished stripping it.

After everybody's indignation at his distaste for popular music has been allowed its airplay, Adorno is chiefly criticised today for his assault on the instrumentality of reason. Ever since this critique was mounted by his former student and successor as director of the Institute for Social Research, Jürgen Habermas, in *The Philosophical Discourse of Modernity* (1985), it has gained in traction and persistence. Adorno, runs the argument, failed to appreciate the gains the Enlightenment made possible in subjecting ossified tradition to rational interrogation, and where it undeniably resulted in the ruinous domination of nature, as with the present ecological calamity, or in the domination of human souls by technology, which has led to their universal entrancement by digital devices, these are aberrant divagations in what is otherwise an overwhelmingly benevolent course of development. These criticisms unite the second and third generations of the Frankfurt School with Anglo-American pragmatism, analytical philosophy, and the attentive gaze of the late mutations of phenomenology, permanently agawp as they are at the kaleidoscope of media spectacles and cultural differences they see before them.

Habermas saw in the critique of instrumental rationality a performative contradiction, which essentially stated that you could hardly make a case for the triumph of destructive rationalism over the whole of society, unless there was at least a corner of it from which that argument could be put, and then you had to explain what it was that enabled those putting that argument to have escaped rationalism's spell. At the first level, the obvious riposte to this would be that the case applies to the great mass of society, but that not absolutely everybody is incapable of thinking against it. It remains the duty of those who do see through the delusion, whether they are tenured academics, TV documentary-makers or indigent freelancers, to speak against it. There are those who find this argument intolerable, as though being in the minority were always a condition of Olympian privilege, as opposed to what it more likely is, which is being taken for an axe-grinding fool. And then of course, what doesn't help to persuade Habermas and his many allies in the English-speaking academic milieu is that the rhetorical force of Adorno's work in particular is so often hostile to the nuance of exceptions. The spell is universal, everybody is deluded, the culture industry allows nobody to escape, enlightenment is totalitarian. This is what makes many readers uncomfortable about Adorno. Either he is exaggerating for oratorical effect, the precise habit he criticises in the right-wing ranters on American radio in the 1950s, or he knows perfectly well that what he is saying cannot formally be true. Which leads us back to the twist that he gives in the *Minima Moralia* to Hegel's postulate of the veracity of totality: 'the whole is the untrue'. What we should hear in this is not that everything on earth is a lie, or indeed that totalising statements such as 'everybody lives under a spell' are lies. Rather, it is the moment at which the all-consuming sweep of rational conceptuality, identitarian thinking, the wholly administered world, call it what we will, presumes to account for everything that it subsumes. As soon as anything is constituted as a whole by authority structures, or the iron regime of deductive logic, the very premises on which this panoptical gaze are predicated are false. At some micrological level, they are false. What does not fit has to be made to fit, and if it cannot be made to fit, it has to be presumed for the sake of argument to have been so made. When Adorno addresses the masses who live under the spell, what is untrue is not this statement as a logical proposition, but the constitution of the masses that the administration of the spell itself makes possible. Even those who can sometimes think outside the current structure of social conformity will find that they cannot do so all the time. The effort is too great, the rewards meagre, and the psychological side effects often highly damaging, but that state of affairs reflects more on that structure itself than it does on those to whom its siren song rings out not in seductive harmony but in monitory dissonance.

Principally, however, the argument that a critique of reason cannot be reasonable is a renunciation of dialectical thinking, which has possibly been the primary undertaking of the later Frankfurt generations. The notion that every thought-form that hopes to escape coagulation into ideology must produce from within itself its own refutation, the immanent movement that enables it to continue to animate living thought in a deadened world, is the motor of non-identitarian thinking. What the *Dialectic of Enlightenment* argued was that rationality, precipitating out of myth, retained within its structure enough of the explicative generality of mythology, that it reverted in itself to the status of myth. By the same token, a scientific-technological rationalism inflated to the level of a primitive belief system, to which all are expected to pledge their consent, will eventually generate from within a critical theory that punctures its hegemony. Berating it from outside will fail. It already knows the arguments against itself and anticipates every attack. If there is to be a post-technological humanity, in which technology would fulfil the promises it has always made, to liberate rather than enslave, and become the humane support of a non-antagonistic society instead of the functional context of mechanised social relations, it will only come about if human beings induce it to face its own contradictions. The antinomy lies not in the critique of reason, but in the extraordinary claim that reason has liberated humanity from its darker angels, except where it hasn't. In the celebrated etching by Goya from the satirical series *Los Caprichos*, the sleep of reason produces monsters, staring-eyed nocturnal birds of irrationality flapping around the artist slumped unconscious over his desk. The epigraph to the picture affirms that they need to be joined to his waking reason to produce the marvels of art. Just so does reason need to be conjoined to critical consciousness if it is not to become the raptor that preys on a slumbering humanity. 'Just as, under the primacy of the autonomous production process,' Adorno writes, 'the purpose of reason dwindles away until it sinks into the fetishism of itself and of external power, so reason itself is reduced to an instrument and assimilated to its functionaries, whose power of thought serves only the purpose of preventing thought'.[30] By contrast, knowledge, which is not to be pursued and captured like quarry, could rather be a condition in which humanity would come to full consciousness of itself, by surrendering to the internal laws of the objective.

'Always the same world,' sighed Walter Benjamin in the midst of one of his experiments with hashish, before adding the self-rallying qualifier, 'yet one has patience'.[31] Adorno's lifetime of theoretical work assuredly has that, but it also lights the way towards a possible liberation, in which a world that can only offer the ruthless demand for patience would pass away.

Bibliography

Works by Adorno

'The Actuality of Philosophy', trans. Benjamin Snow, in *Telos* 31, Spring 1977, pp 120–133

Aesthetic Theory, trans. Robert Hullot-Kentor, London and New York, 2013

Against Epistemology – A Metacritique: Studies in Husserl and the Phenomenological Antinomies, trans. Willis Domingo, Oxford, 1982

Alban Berg: Master of the Smallest Link, trans. Juliane Brand and Christopher Hailey, Cambridge, 1994

Beethoven: The Philosophy of Music, trans. Edmund Jephcott, Cambridge and Malden, MA, 2002

Can One Live After Auschwitz? A Philosophical Reader, ed. Rolf Tiedemann, Stanford, CA, 2003

Critical Models: Interventions and Catchwords, trans. Henry W. Pickford, New York, 1998

The Culture Industry: Selected Essays on Mass Culture, ed. JM Bernstein, London, 1991

Current of Music: Elements of a Radio Theory, ed. and trans. Robert Hullot-Kentor, Cambridge and Malden, MA, 2009

Essays on Music, ed. Richard Leppert, Berkeley, CA and London, 2002

Hegel: Three Studies, trans. Shierry Weber Nicholsen, Cambridge, MA and London, 1993

History and Freedom: Lectures 1964–1965, trans. Rodney Livingstone, Cambridge and Malden, MA, 2006

In Search of Wagner, trans. Rodney Livingstone, London, 2009

Introduction to Sociology (1968), trans. Edmund Jephcott, Cambridge and Malden, MA, 2000

Introduction to the Sociology of Music, trans. EB Ashton, New York, 1976

The Jargon of Authenticity, trans. Knut Tarnowski and Frederic Will, London, 1973

Kant's 'Critique of Pure Reason' (1959), trans. Rodney Livingstone, Cambridge and Malden, MA, 2001

Kierkegaard: Construction of the Aesthetic, trans. Robert Hullot-Kentor, Minneapolis, MN, 1989

Lectures on Negative Dialectics: Fragments of a Lecture Course 1965–1966, trans. Rodney Livingstone, Cambridge and Malden, MA, 2008

Mahler: A Musical Physiognomy, trans. Edmund Jephcott, Chicago, 1996

'Messages in a Bottle', trans. Edmund Jephcott, in *New Left Review* 200, July-August 1993, pp 5–14

Metaphysics: Concept and Problems (1965), trans. Edmund Jephcott, Cambridge and Malden, MA, 2001

Minima Moralia: Reflections from Damaged Life, trans. EFN Jephcott, London, 1974

Negative Dialectics, trans. EB Ashton, London, 1973

Night Music: Essays on Music 1928–1962, trans. Wieland Hoban, Kolkata, 2009

Notes to Literature, volume 1, trans. Shierry Weber Nicholsen, New York, 1992

Notes to Literature, volume 2, trans. Shierry Weber Nicholsen, New York, 1992

Philosophy of New Music, trans. Robert Hullot-Kentor, Minneapolis, MN, 2006

Prisms, trans. Samuel and Shierry Weber, Cambridge, MA, 1982

Problems of Moral Philosophy, trans. Rodney Livingstone, Cambridge and Malden, MA, 2001

Quasi Una Fantasia: Essays on Modern Music, trans. Rodney Livingstone, London and New York, 1992

Sound Figures, trans. Rodney Livingstone, Stanford, CA, 1999

The Stars Down to Earth, and other essays on the irrational in culture, ed. Stephen Crook, London and New York, 1994

'Theses on the Language of the Philosopher', trans. Samir Gandesha and Michael K. Palamarek, in *Adorno and the Need in Thinking: New Critical Essays*, eds. Donald A. Burke, Colin J. Campbell, Kathy Kiloh, Michael K. Palamarek and Jonathan Short, Toronto, 2007

Adorno and Walter Benjamin, *The Complete Correspondence 1928–1940*, trans. Nicholas Walker, Cambridge, 1999

Adorno and Hanns Eisler, *Composing for the Films*, London and New York, 1994

Adorno and Max Horkheimer, *Dialectic of Enlightenment*, trans. John Cumming, London, 1973

Adorno and Max Horkheimer, *Towards A New Manifesto*, trans. Rodney Livingstone, London and New York, 2011

Secondary sources

Adorno: Eine Bildmonographie, Frankfurt, 2003

Bauman, Zygmunt, *The Art of Life*, Cambridge, 2009

Benjamin, Walter, *On Hashish*, ed. and trans. Howard Eiland, Cambridge, MA, 2006

Benjamin, Walter, *The Work of Art in the Age of Its Technological Reproducibility, and Other Writings on Media*, eds. Michael W. Jennings, Brigid Doherty and Thomas Y. Levin, Cambridge, MA and London, 2008

Bernstein, JM, *Adorno: Disenchantment and Ethics*, Cambridge, 2001

Brittain, Christopher Craig, *Adorno and Theology*, London and New York, 2010

Buck-Morss, Susan, *The Origin of Negative Dialectics: Theodor W. Adorno, Walter Benjamin, and the Frankfurt Institute*, New York, 1979

Claussen, Detlev, *Theodor W. Adorno: One Last Genius*, trans. Rodney Livingstone, Cambridge, MA and London, 2010

Cook, Deborah, *The Culture Industry Revisited: Theodor W. Adorno on Mass Culture*, Lanham, MD, 1996

Critchley, Simon, *Very Little... Almost Nothing: Death, Philosophy, Literature*, London and New York, 1997

Cunningham, David and Nigel Mapp, *Adorno and Literature*, London and New York, 2008

Dews, Peter, *Logics of Disintegration: Post-Structuralist Thought and the Claims of Critical Theory*, London and New York, 1988

Douglas, Andrew J., *In the Spirit of Critique: Thinking Politically in the Dialectical Tradition*, Albany, NY, 2013

Eagleton, Terry, *The Ideology of the Aesthetic*, Oxford and Malden, MA, 1997

Foster, Roger, *Adorno: The Recovery of Experience*, Albany, NY, 2007

Freyenhagen, Fabian, *Adorno's Practical Philosophy: Living Less Wrongly*, Cambridge, 2015

Geuss, Raymond, *The Idea of a Critical Theory: Habermas and the Frankfurt School*, Cambridge, 1981

Gibson, Nigel and Andrew Rubin, eds. *Adorno: A Critical Reader*, Oxford and Malden, MA, 2002

Gordon, Peter E., *Adorno and Existence*, Cambridge, MA and London, 2016

Hammer, Espen, *Adorno and the Political*, Oxford and New York, 2006

Hammer, Espen, *Adorno's Modernism: Art, Experience, and Catastrophe*, Cambridge, 2015

Hegel, GWF, *Lectures on the Philosophy of History*, trans. John Sibree and Ruben Alvarado, Aalten, 2011

Helmling, Steven, *Adorno's Poetics of Critique*, London and New York, 2009

Hohendahl, Peter Uwe, *The Fleeting Promise of Art: Adorno's Aesthetic Theory Revisited*, New York, 2013

Hohendahl, Peter Uwe, *Prismatic Thought: Theodor W. Adorno*, Lincoln, NE, 1995

Holloway, John, Fernando Matamoros and Sergio Tischler, eds. *Negativity and Revolution: Adorno and Political Activism*,

London, 2009

Horkheimer, Max, *Eclipse of Reason*, London and New York, 2013

Huhn, Thomas, ed. *The Cambridge Companion to Adorno*, New York, 2004

Huhn, Tom and Lambert Zuidervaart, eds. *The Semblance of Subjectivity: Essays in Adorno's Aesthetic Theory*, Cambridge, MA and London, 1997

Hullot-Kentor, Robert, *Things Beyond Resemblance: Collected Essays on Theodor W. Adorno*, New York, 2006

Jäger, Lorenz, *Adorno: A Political Biography*, trans. Stewart Spencer, New Haven, CT and London, 2004

Jameson, Fredric, *Late Marxism: Adorno or The Persistence of the Dialectic*, London and New York, 1996

Jarvis, Simon, *Adorno: A Critical Introduction*, Cambridge and Malden, MA, 1998

Jay, Martin, *Adorno*, London, 1984

Jay, Martin, *The Dialectical Imagination: A History of the Frankfurt School and the Institute of Social Research, 1923–1950*, Berkeley, CA, 1996

Jay, Martin, *Marxism and Totality: The Adventures of a Concept from Lukács to Habermas*, Berkeley, CA, 1984

Jenemann, David, *Adorno in America*, Minneapolis, MN, 2007

Kant, Immanuel, *Critique of Pure Reason*, trans. Paul Guyer and Allen W. Wood, Cambridge, 1998

Lanning, Robert, *In the Hotel Abyss: An Hegelian-Marxist Critique of Adorno*, Chicago, 2014

Lee, Lisa Yun, *Dialectics of the Body: Corporeality in the Philosophy of TW Adorno*, New York and Abingdon, 2014

Leibniz, GW, *The Leibniz-Des Bosses Correspondence*, ed. and trans. Brandon C. Look and Donald Rutherford, New Haven, CT, 2007

Lukács, Georg, *The Theory of the Novel*, trans. Anna Bostock, Monmouth, 1971

Morgan, Alastair, *Adorno's Concept of Life*, London and New York,

2007

Müller-Doohm, Stefan, *Adorno: A Biography*, trans. Rodney Livingstone, Cambridge and Malden, MA, 2005

Nealon, Jeffrey T. and Caren Irr, eds. *Rethinking the Frankfurt School: Alternative Legacies of Cultural Critique*, Albany, NY, 2002

Neiman, Susan, *Evil in Modern Thought: An Alternative History of Philosophy*, Princeton, NJ and Woodstock, 2015

Noys, Benjamin, *Malign Velocities: Accelerationism and Capitalism*, Alresford, 2014

Noys, Benjamin, *The Persistence of the Negative: A Critique of Contemporary Continental Theory*, Edinburgh, 2012

O'Connor, Brian, *Adorno's Negative Dialectic: Philosophy and the Possibility of Critical Rationality*, Cambridge, MA, 2004

Paddison, Max, *Adorno, Modernism and Mass Culture: Essays on Critical Theory and Music*, London, 2004

Pensky, Max, ed. *The Actuality of Adorno: Critical Essays on Adorno and the Postmodern*, Albany, NY, 1997

Richter, Gerhard, ed. *Language Without Soil: Adorno and Late Philosophical Modernity*, New York, 2010

Rose, Gillian, *The Melancholy Science: An Introduction to the Thought of Theodor W. Adorno*, London and New York, 2014

Ross, Nathan, ed. *The Aesthetic Ground of Critical Theory: New Readings of Benjamin and Adorno*, Lanham, MD, 2015

Taubes, Jacob, *The Political Theology of Paul*, trans. Dana Hollander, eds. Aleida Assmann and Jan Assmann, Stanford, CA, 2004

Thomson, David, *The Big Screen: The Story of the Movies and What They Did To Us*, London, 2012

Wiggershaus, Rolf, *The Frankfurt School: Its History, Theory and Political Significance*, trans. Michael Robertson, Cambridge and Malden, MA, 2010

Witkin, Robert W., *Adorno on Music*, Abingdon and New York, 1998

Witkin, Robert W., *Adorno on Popular Culture*, Abingdon and New York, 2003

Zizek, Slavoj, *Absolute Recoil: Towards a New Foundation of Dialectical Materialism*, London and New York, 2014

Zuidervaart, Lambert, *Adorno's Aesthetic Theory: The Redemption of Illusion*, Cambridge, MA, 1993

Notes

Abbreviations:
DoE: *Dialectic of Enlightenment*
MM: *Minima Moralia*
ND: *Negative Dialectics*
NtL: *Notes to Literature*

Preface and Acknowledgements

1. School of Life, 'Sociology – Theodor Adorno', available at youtube.com/watch?v=4YGnPgtWhsw

Introduction: Nothing Innocuous Left

1. Cited in Stefan Müller-Doohm, *Adorno: A Biography*, trans. Rodney Livingstone, Cambridge and Malden, MA, 2005, p 32.

2. Adorno, *Erinnerung* [Recollection], in *Gesammelte Schriften in 20 Bänden*, ed. Rolf Tiedemann, assisted by Gretel Adorno, Susan Buck-Morss and Klaus Schulz, vol 20.1, Frankfurt, 1986, p 175, cited in Detlev Claussen, *Theodor W. Adorno: One Last Genius*, trans. Rodney Livingstone, Cambridge, MA and London, 2010, p 97.

3. Adorno, §41, 'Inside and outside', *Minima Moralia: Reflections from Damaged Life*, trans. EFN Jephcott, London, 1974, p 67.

4. Cited in Müller-Doohm, p 128.

5. Adorno, 'The Actuality of Philosophy', trans. Benjamin Snow, in *Telos* 31, Spring 1977, p 130.

6. Ibid, p 133.

7. Adorno, 'Cultural Criticism and Society', in *Prisms*, trans. Samuel and Shierry Weber, Cambridge, MA, 1982, p 34.

8. Cited in Müller-Doohm, p 480.

Chapter 1: Society and the Individual

1. ew.com/article/2014/02/17/creepy-tv-ads-can-now-target-individual-viewers, accessed 14 January 2016.
2. Theodor Adorno and Max Horkheimer, *Dialectic of Enlightenment*, trans. John Cumming, London, 1979, pp 11–12.
3. Ibid, p 9.
4. Ibid, p 17.
5. Adorno, §66, 'Mélange', in *Minima Moralia*, pp 102–103.
6. Ibid.
7. *DoE*, p 22.
8. Ibid.
9. Ibid, p 3.
10. Ibid, p 33.
11. Ibid.
12. Ibid, p 36.
13. Theodor Adorno, *Negative Dialectics*, trans. EB Ashton, London, 1973, p 311.
14. Ibid, p 312.
15. Ibid, p 313.
16. Ibid, p 343.
17. Ibid, p 344.
18. Ibid.
19. Ibid, p 284.
20. Theodor Adorno, 'Some Ideas on the Sociology of Music', in *Sound Figures*, trans. Rodney Livingstone, Stanford, CA, 1999, p 14.
21. Adorno, §66, 'Mélange', in *MM*, pp 102–103.
22. Ibid, p 103.
23. Ibid.
24. Ibid.
25. Ibid, §31, 'Cat out of the bag', p 51.
26. Ibid, §5, 'How nice of you, Doctor', p 26.
27. Ibid, §6, 'Antithesis', p 26.

28. Theodor Adorno, *The Jargon of Authenticity*, trans. Knut Tarnowski and Frederic Will, Evanston, IL, 1973, p 162.

29. *MM*, Dedication, pp 17–18.

30. Theodor Adorno, 'Messages in a Bottle', trans. Edmund Jephcott, I, 'Key people', in *New Left Review* 200, July-August 1993, p 6.

31. Ibid, VII, 'Come closer', p 9.

32. Ibid, p 10.

33. Nigel Gibson, 'Rethinking an Old Saw: Dialectical Negativity, Utopia, and *Negative Dialectic* in Adorno's Hegelian Marxism', in Nigel Gibson and Andrew Rubin, eds., *Adorno: A Critical Reader*, Malden, MA and Oxford, 2002, p 274.

34. Ibid, p 276.

35. Max Horkheimer, *Eclipse of Reason*, London and New York, 2013, p 108.

36. *MM*, §88, 'Simple Simon', p 135.

37. Ibid, p 136.

38. Ibid, p 135.

39. Ibid.

40. *Eclipse of Reason*, pp 99–100.

41. *MM*, §36, 'The Health unto Death', p 58.

42. Ibid, p 59.

43. Ibid, §19, 'Do not knock', p 40.

44. Zygmunt Bauman, *The Art of Life*, Cambridge, 2009, p 14.

45. *ND*, p 219.

46. Ibid.

47. Ibid.

48. Ibid, p 222.

49. Ibid.

50. Ibid, p 219, translation amended.

51. Ibid, p 223.

52. Alastair Morgan, *Adorno's Concept of Life*, London and New York, 2007, p 22, citing Adorno, 'Sociology and Psychology',

trans. Irving Wohlfarth, *New Left Review*, no 46, Nov-Dec 1967, pp 73–74, and no 47, Jan-Feb 1968, p 89.

53. Fabian Freyenhagen, *Adorno's Practical Philosophy: Living Less Wrongly*, Cambridge, 2015, p 238, citing Adorno, *History and Freedom*, trans. Rodney Livingstone, Cambridge, 2006, pp 151–152.

54. Cf. Benjamin Noys, *Malign Velocities: Accelerationism and Capitalism*, Alresford, 2014.

55. *MM*, §153, 'Finale', p 247.

56. Ibid.

57. Jacob Taubes, *The Political Theology of Paul*, trans. Dana Hollander, eds. Aleida Assmann and Jan Assmann, Stanford, CA, 2004, p 75.

58. *MM*, op cit.

59. Ibid, §152, 'Warning: not to be misused', p 246.

60. *Adorno's Concept of Life*, p 109.

61. *ND*, p xx.

62. *MM*, §50, 'Gaps', p 81.

Chapter 2: History, Philosophy, Politics

1. GWF Hegel, *Lectures on the Philosophy of History*, trans. John Sibree and Ruben Alvarado, Aalten, 2011, p 100.

2. Theodor W. Adorno, *Hegel: Three Studies*, trans. Shierry Weber Nicholsen, Cambridge, MA and London, 1993, p 82.

3. Adorno, *History and Freedom: Lectures 1964–1965*, ed. Rolf Tiedemann, trans. Rodney Livingstone, Cambridge and Malden, MA, 2006, pp 44–45.

4. Adorno, §97, 'Monad', in *MM*, pp 149–150.

5. Adorno, *ND*, pp 319–320, translation modified.

6. Paul Nadal, 'The Force of Reason: Development in Hegel's Philosophy of History', 2010, belate.wordpress.com/2010/09/11/hegel-philosophy-of-world-history/, accessed 7 July 2016.

7. Hegel, op cit, p 23.

8. Adorno, *ND*, p 328.

9. Ibid, p 337.

10. Karl Marx, Preface, *A Contribution to the Critique of Political Economy*, marxists.org/archive/marx/works/1859/critique-pol-economy/preface.htm, accessed 11 July 2016.

11. Adorno, *History and Freedom*, pp 170–171.

12. Adorno, 'Late Capitalism or Industrial Society?: The Fundamental Question of the Present Structure of Society', in *Can One Live After Auschwitz? A Philosophical Reader*, ed. Rolf Tiedemann, trans. Rodney Livingstone, Stanford, CA, 2003, p 117.

13. Ibid, p 124.

14. Adorno, 'Reflections on Class Theory', trans. Rodney Livingstone, in *Can One Live After Auschwitz?*, p 93.

15. Ibid, p 95.

16. Ibid.

17. Ibid, p 96.

18. Ibid, p 97.

19. Ibid, p 100.

20. Ibid, p 105.

21. Ibid, p 106.

22. Ibid, p 107.

23. Marx, *The Eighteenth Brumaire of Louis Bonaparte*, marxists.org/archive/marx/works/1852/18th-brumaire/ch01.htm, accessed 18 July 2016.

24. Adorno, 'Reflections on Class Theory', p 110.

25. Ibid.

26. Adorno, 'Late Capitalism or Industrial Society?', p 125.

27. Adorno and Horkheimer, *Dialectic of Enlightenment*, p 224.

28. Ibid.

29. Slavoj Zizek, *Absolute Recoil: Towards a New Foundation of Dialectical Materialism*, London and New York, 2014, p 35.

30. Ibid.

31. Adorno, 'Why Still Philosophy?', in *Critical Models:*

Interventions and Catchwords, trans. Henry W. Pickford, New York, 1998, p 14.

32. Ibid.
33. Adorno, 'Marginalia to Theory and Praxis', in *Critical Models*, p 267.
34. Ibid, p 277.
35. Adorno, *ND*, p 367.
36. Ibid.
37. Ibid, p 368.
38. Adorno, §71, 'Pseudomenos', in *MM*, p 108.
39. Ibid, pp 108–109.
40. Adorno, *ND*, p 363.
41. Ibid.
42. Adorno, *Aesthetic Theory*, trans Robert Hullot-Kentor, London and New York, 2015, pp 464–465.
43. Georg Lukács, *The Theory of the Novel*, trans. Anna Bostock, London, 2006, p 22.
44. Adorno, *ND*, pp 146–147.
45. Robert Lanning, *In the Hotel Abyss: An Hegelian-Marxist Critique of Adorno*, Chicago, 2014, p 203.
46. Adorno, *ND*, p 147.
47. Ibid.
48. Lanning, op cit, p 197.
49. Ibid, pp 197–198.
50. Adorno, *ND*, p 147.
51. Gibson, 'Rethinking an Old Saw', pp 270–271.
52. Ibid, p 266.
53. Adorno, *ND*, p 374.
54. Ibid, p 375.
55. Peter Uwe Hohendahl, *Prismatic Thought: Theodor W. Adorno*, Lincoln, NE, 1995, p 17.
56. Adorno, 'Resignation', in *Critical Models*, p 290.
57. Ibid, p 291.
58. Ibid, p 293.

59. Ibid.

60. Susan Neiman, *Evil in Modern Thought: An Alternative History of Philosophy*, Princeton, NJ, 2015, p 308.

61. Adorno, *ND*, p 398.

62. Ibid.

63. Neiman, p 308.

64. Adorno, *ND*, p 398.

65. Terry Eagleton, *The Ideology of the Aesthetic*, Oxford, 1997, p 358.

66. Adorno, 'Cultural Criticism and Society', in *Prisms*, p 34.

67. Adorno, *ND*, p 362.

68. Robert Musil, *The Confusions of Young Törless*, trans. Shaun Whiteside, London, 2001, pp 130–131.

69. 'One of two things is usually lacking in the so-called Philosophy of Art: either philosophy or art.' 'Critical Fragments', §12, in *Friedrich Schlegel's* Lucinde *and the Fragments*, trans. Peter Firchow, Minneapolis, MN, 1971, p 144.

70. Adorno, §78, 'Over the hills', in *MM*, pp 121–122.

Chapter 3: Metamorphosis of the Dialectic

1. Karl Marx, Afterword to the Second German Edition, *Capital*, 1873, marxists.org/archive/marx/works/1867-c1/p3.htm#3b, accessed 4 August 2016.

2. Adorno, *Hegel: Three Studies*, pp 9–10.

3. Ibid, p 13.

4. Ibid, p 18.

5. Ibid, p 24.

6. Ibid, p 37.

7. Ibid.

8. Ibid.

9. Ibid, p xxxvi.

10. Immanuel Kant, *Critique of Pure Reason*, Preface to the Second Edition, trans. Paul Guyer and Allen W. Wood, Cambridge,

1998, p 110.

11. Adorno, *ND*, p xx.
12. Ibid.
13. Ibid, p 11.
14. Ibid, p 12.
15. Ibid, pp 17–18.
16. Ibid, p 20.
17. Ibid, pp 27–28.
18. Ibid, p xix.
19. Ibid, p 406.
20. Ibid.
21. Ibid, pp 352, 353.
22. Ibid, p 109.
23. Ibid.
24. Ibid, pp 7–8.
25. Adorno, §29, 'Dwarf fruit', in *MM*, p 50.
26. Adorno, *ND*, p 363.
27. Ibid, p 9.
28. Adorno and Horkheimer, *DoE*, p 243, translation modified.
29. Adorno, §152, 'Warning: not to be misused', in *MM*, p 245.
30. Ibid, pp 246–247.
31. Ibid, p 247.
32. Andrew J. Douglas, *In the Spirit of Critique: Thinking Politically in the Dialectical Tradition*, New York, 2013, p 79.
33. Adorno, *ND*, p 141.
34. Ibid, pp 142–143.
35. Mauro Bozzetti, 'Hegel on Trial: Adorno's Critique of Philosophical Systems', in Gibson and Rubin, eds., *Adorno: A Critical Reader*, pp 307–308.
36. Ibid, p 309.
37. Simon Jarvis, *Adorno: A Critical Introduction*, Cambridge and Malden, MA, 1998, p 182.
38. Adorno, *ND*, p 26.
39. Jarvis, p 253.

40. Roger Foster, *Adorno: The Recovery of Experience*, Albany, NY, 2007, p 193, emphases original.
41. Steven Helmling, *Adorno's Poetics of Critique*, London and New York, 2009, p 126.
42. Alastair Morgan, *Adorno's Concept of Life*, London and New York, 2007, p 136.
43. Fabian Freyenhagen, *Adorno's Practical Philosophy: Living Less Wrongly*, Cambridge, 2015, p 13.
44. Ibid, p 14.
45. Adorno, 'Notes on Philosophical Thinking', in *Critical Models: Interventions and Catchwords*, p 131.
46. Ibid, p 128.
47. Ibid.

Chapter 4: Aesthetics and the Promise of Happiness

1. Adorno, *AT*, p 242.
2. Ibid, p 259.
3. Ibid, p 308.
4. Ibid, p 40.
5. Ibid, p 425.
6. Ibid, p 280.
7. Ibid, p 371.
8. Ibid, p 326.
9. Ibid, p 308.
10. Ibid, p 131.
11. Ibid, pp 39–40.
12. Peter Uwe Hohendahl, *The Fleeting Promise of Art: Adorno's Aesthetic Theory Revisited*, New York, 2013, p 22.
13. Adorno, *AT*, p 160.
14. Hohendahl, p 98.
15. Adorno, *AT*, p 50.
16. Ibid, p 73.
17. Hohendahl, p 125.
18. Adorno, *AT*, p 394.

19. Ibid, p 185.

20. Ibid, pp 409–410, translation modified.

21. Ibid, p 410.

22. Adorno and Horkheimer, *DoE*, p 121.

23. Ibid, p 153.

24. Ibid.

25. Ibid, p 221.

26. Adorno, 'The Schema of Mass Culture', in JM Bernstein, ed., *The Culture Industry: Selected Essays on Mass Culture*, London, 1991, p 53.

27. Ibid, p 55.

28. Ibid, p 77.

29. Ibid.

30. Ibid, p 78.

31. Ibid.

32. Ibid, p 83.

33. 'Resignation', in Bernstein, op cit, p 175.

34. 'Culture and Administration', in Bernstein, op cit, p 109.

35. 'Culture Industry Reconsidered', in Bernstein, op cit, p 89.

36. Ibid.

37. Ibid, p 91.

38. David Thomson, *The Big Screen: The Story of the Movies and What They Did To Us*, London, 2012, p 445.

39. Ibid, p 447.

40. 'Culture Industry Reconsidered', p 92.

41. Adorno-Benjamin, *The Complete Correspondence 1928–1940*, p 130.

42. Ibid.

43. Ibid, p 129.

44. Ibid, pp 132–133.

45. Walter Benjamin, 'The Work of Art in the Age of Its Technological Reproducibility: Second Version', trans. Edmund Jephcott and Harry Zohn, in *The Work of Art in the Age of Its Technological Reproducibility, and Other Writings on*

Media, eds. Michael W. Jennings, Brigid Doherty and Thomas Y. Levin, Cambridge, MA and London, 2008, pp 50, 51.

46. Adorno, 'On Popular Music', in *Essays on Music*, ed. Richard Leppert, Los Angeles, 2002, p 468.

47. Deborah Cook, *The Culture Industry Revisited: Theodor W. Adorno on Mass Culture*, Lanham, MD, 1996, p 68.

48. Adorno and Horkheimer, *DoE*, p 161.

49. Cook, p 74.

50. Lisa Yun Lee, *Dialectics of the Body: Corporeality in the Philosophy of TW Adorno*, New York, 2014, p 38.

51. Adorno and Horkheimer, *DoE*, p 144.

52. Espen Hammer, *Adorno's Modernism: Art, Experience, and Catastrophe*, Cambridge, 2015, pp 97–98.

53. Adorno and Horkheimer, *DoE*, pp 140–141.

54. Hammer, p 142.

55. Simon Critchley, *Very Little... Almost Nothing: Death, Philosophy, Literature*, London and New York, 1997, p 159.

56. Samuel Beckett, *Endgame: A Play in One Act*, at samuel-beckett.net/endgame.html, accessed 5 October 2016.

57. Adorno-Benjamin, *The Complete Correspondence 1928–1940*, p 130.

58. Adorno and Horkheimer, *DoE*, p 144.

59. Ronald V. Bettig, 'The Frankfurt School and the Political Economy of Communications', in *Rethinking the Frankfurt School: Alternative Legacies of Cultural Critique*, Albany, NY, 2002, p 90.

60. Adorno, *AT*, pp 164–165.

61. Müller-Doohm, p 467.

62. Adorno, *AT*, p 242.

63. Ibid, p 319.

64. Ibid.

65. Ibid.

66. Adorno, 'On the Fetish-Character in Music and the Regression of Listening', in *Essays on Music*, ed. Richard

Leppert, Berkeley, CA, 2002, p 314.

67. Adorno, 'Night Music', in *Night Music: Essays on Music 1928–1962*, ed. Rolf Tiedemann, trans. Wieland Hoban, Kolkata, 2009, p 82.

68. Adorno, 'Beethoven's Late Style', in *Night Music*, p 11.

69. Ibid, p 15.

70. Ibid, pp 17, 18.

71. Ibid, p 18.

72. Adorno, *Alban Berg: Master of the Smallest Link*, Cambridge, 1994, p 5.

73. Joseph Weiss, 'The Composer as Producer', in *The Aesthetic Ground of Critical Theory: New Readings of Benjamin and Adorno*, ed. Nathan Ross, Lanham, MD, 2015, p 116.

74. Adorno, *AT*, p 151.

75. Adorno, *Philosophy of New Music*, trans. Robert Hullot-Kentor, Minneapolis, MN, 2006, p 127.

76. Adorno, 'Farewell to Jazz', trans. Susan H. Gillespie, in *Essays on Music*, p 496.

77. Adorno, 'On Jazz', trans. Jamie Owen Daniel and Richard Leppert, in *Essays on Music*, p 483.

78. Adorno, 'Perennial Fashion – Jazz', in *Prisms*, p 131.

79. Max Paddison, *Adorno, Modernism and Mass Culture: Essays on Critical Theory and Music*, London, 2004, p 96.

80. Lanning, p 99.

81. Ibid, p 100.

82. Douglas Kellner, 'Theodor W. Adorno and the Dialectics of Mass Culture', in Gibson and Rubin, *Adorno: A Critical Reader*, p 91.

83. Aratta, 'Ton Guka', available at youtube.com/watch?v=q xQp4DeFxHU, accessed 14 October 2016.

84. Adorno, *Prisms*, pp 126–127.

85. Adorno, 'Theses on the Language of the Philosopher', trans. Samir Gandesha and Michael K. Palamarek, in *Adorno and the Need in Thinking: New Critical Essays*, eds. Donald A. Burke,

Colin J. Campbell, Kathy Kiloh, Michael K. Palamarek and Jonathan Short, Toronto, 2007, pp 35–36.

86. Ibid, p 36.

87. Adorno, 'The Essay as Form', in *Notes to Literature I*, trans. Shierry Weber Nicholsen, New York, 1991, p 10.

88. 'Punctuation Marks', in *NtL I*, p 95.

89. Georg Lukács, 'Healthy or Sick Art?', in *Writer and Critic and Other Essays*, trans. Arthur Kahn, New York, 1971, p 103.

90. Lukács, *The Theory of the Novel*, p 38.

91. Ibid, p 104.

92. Ibid, p 152.

93. Adorno, 'Notes on Kafka', in *Prisms*, p 261.

94. Ibid, p 268.

95. Martin Ryle and Kate Soper, 'Adorno's Critical Presence: Cultural Theory and Literary Value', in *Adorno and Literature*, eds. David Cunningham and Nigel Mapp, London and New York, 2008, p 29.

96. David Cunningham, 'After Adorno: The Narrator of the Contemporary European Novel', in *Adorno and Literature*, pp 191–192.

97. Adorno, 'The Position of the Narrator in the Contemporary Novel', in *NtL I*, p 30.

98. Ibid, p 33.

99. Adorno, *The Jargon of Authenticity*, p 24.

100. Cunningham, op cit, p 198.

101. Adorno, 'Trying to Understand *Endgame*', in *NtL I*, p 274.

102. Beckett, *Endgame*, op cit.

Chapter 5: Cracking the Shells: Adorno in the Present Day

1. Adorno, 'Reason and Revelation', in *Critical Models*, p 140.

2. Ibid, p 142.

3. Adorno, *ND*, p 375.

4. Ibid.

5. Ibid, p 372.
6. Ibid, p 376.
7. Walter Benjamin, 'Goethe's *Elective Affinities*', in *Walter Benjamin: Selected Writings, volume 1: 1913–1926*, eds. Marcus Bullock and Michael W. Jennings, Cambridge, MA, 1996, p 356.
8. Ibid, p 400.
9. Ibid, p 401, translation modified.
10. Ibid, pp 401–402.
11. Christopher Craig Brittain, *Adorno and Theology*, London and New York, 2010, p 46.
12. Ibid, pp 80–81.
13. Adorno, *ND*, p 372.
14. Ibid, p 277.
15. Ibid, p 276, translation modified.
16. Ibid.
17. Adorno, §103, 'Boy from the heath', in *MM*, p 163.
18. GW Leibniz, *The Leibniz-Des Bosses Correspondence*, eds. and trans. Brandon C. Look and Donald Rutherford, New Haven, CT, 2007, p 227.
19. Adorno, *MM*, op cit, p 164.
20. Adorno, §97, 'Monad', in *MM*, p 148.
21. Ibid, p 149.
22. Ibid, p 150.
23. §5, 'How nice of you, Doctor', in *MM*, p 26.
24. §116, 'Just hear, how bad he was', in *MM*, p 182.
25. Adorno, *ND*, p 381.
26. Ibid, p 200.
27. 'Presuppositions', in *Notes to Literature II*, trans. Shierry Weber Nicholsen, New York, 1991, p 108.
28. 'Benjamin the Letter Writer', in *NtL II*, p 239.
29. Adorno, *ND*, p 408.
30. Adorno, §79, 'Intellectus sacrificium intellectus', in *MM*, p 123.

31. Walter Benjamin, 'Protocols of Drug Experiments §12', in *On Hashish*, ed. and trans. Howard Eiland, Cambridge, MA, 2006, p 100.

Zero Books
CULTURE, SOCIETY & POLITICS

Contemporary culture has eliminated the concept and public figure of the intellectual. A cretinous anti-intellectualism presides, cheer-led by hacks in the pay of multinational corporations who reassure their bored readers that there is no need to rouse themselves from their stupor. Zer0 Books knows that another kind of discourse - intellectual without being academic, popular without being populist - is not only possible: it is already flourishing. Zer0 is convinced that in the unthinking, blandly consensual culture in which we live, critical and engaged theoretical reflection is more important than ever before.

If you have enjoyed this book, why not tell other readers by posting a review on your preferred book site. Recent bestsellers from Zero Books are:

In the Dust of This Planet
Horror of Philosophy vol. 1
Eugene Thacker
In the first of a series of three books on the Horror of Philosophy, *In the Dust of This Planet* offers the genre of horror as a way of thinking about the unthinkable.
Paperback: 978-1-84694-676-9 ebook: 978-1-78099-010-1

Capitalist Realism
Is there no alternative?
Mark Fisher
An analysis of the ways in which capitalism has presented itself as the only realistic political-economic system.
Paperback: 978-1-84694-317-1 ebook: 978-1-78099-734-6

Rebel Rebel
Chris O'Leary
David Bowie: every single song. Everything you want to know, everything you didn't know.
Paperback: 978-1-78099-244-0 ebook: 978-1-78099-713-1

Cartographies of the Absolute
Alberto Toscano, Jeff Kinkle
An aesthetics of the economy for the twenty-first century.
Paperback: 978-1-78099-275-4 ebook: 978-1-78279-973-3

Malign Velocities
Accelerationism and Capitalism
Benjamin Noys
Longlisted for the Bread and Roses Prize 2015, *Malign Velocities* argues against the need for speed, tracking acceleration as the symptom of the ongoing crises of capitalism.
Paperback: 978-1-78279-300-7 ebook: 978-1-78279-299-4

Meat Market
Female flesh under Capitalism
Laurie Penny
A feminist dissection of women's bodies as the fleshy fulcrum of capitalist cannibalism, whereby women are both consumers and consumed.
Paperback: 978-1-84694-521-2 ebook: 978-1-84694-782-7

Poor but Sexy
Culture Clashes in Europe East and West
Agata Pyzik
How the East stayed East and the West stayed West.
Paperback: 978-1-78099-394-2 ebook: 978-1-78099-395-9

Romeo and Juliet in Palestine
Teaching Under Occupation
Tom Sperlinger
Life in the West Bank, the nature of pedagogy and the role of a
university under occupation.
Paperback: 978-1-78279-637-4 ebook: 978-1-78279-636-7

Sweetening the Pill
or How We Got Hooked on Hormonal Birth Control
Holly Grigg-Spall
Has contraception liberated or oppressed women? *Sweetening
the Pill* breaks the silence on the dark side of hormonal
contraception.
Paperback: 978-1-78099-607-3 ebook: 978-1-78099-608-0

Why Are We The Good Guys?
Reclaiming Your Mind from the Delusions of Propaganda
David Cromwell
A provocative challenge to the standard ideology that Western
power is a benevolent force in the world.
Paperback: 978-1-78099-365-2 ebook: 978-1-78099-366-9

Readers of ebooks can buy or view any of these bestsellers by
clicking on the live link in the title. Most titles are published in
paperback and as an ebook. Paperbacks are available in traditional
bookshops. Both print and ebook formats are available online.

Find more titles and sign up to our readers' newsletter at
http://www.johnhuntpublishing.com/culture-and-politics
Follow us on Facebook at https://www.facebook.com/ZeroBooks
and Twitter at https://twitter.com/Zer0Books